PASTORAL CARE AND SOCIAL CONFLICT

Charles V. Gerkin

PASTORAL CARE AND SOCIAL CONFLICT

Pamela D. Couture
and
Rodney J. Hunter,
—— Editors ——

ABINGDON PRESS
Nashville

PASTORAL CARE AND SOCIAL CONFLICT

This book is printed on acid-free recycled paper.

Library of Congress Cataloging-in-Publication Data

Pastoral care and social conflict : essays in honor of Charles V. Gerkin / Pamela D. Couture
and Rodney J. Hunter, editors.
  p.   cm.
  Includes bibliographical references and index.
  ISBN 0-687-30267-6 (Pbk. : alk. paper)
  1. Pastoral counseling. 2. Social ethics. 3. Minorities—Pastoral counseling of. 4. Church
work with minorities. I. Gerkin, Charles V., 1922– . II. Couture, Pamela D., 1951–.
III. Hunter, Rodney J.
BV4012.2.P279 1995
253.5—dc20   94-36291
                                                                              CIP

Scripture quotations, except for brief paraphrases or unless otherwise noted, are from the New
Revised Standard Version Bible, Copyright 1989 by the Division of Christian Education of the
National Council of the Churches of Christ in the USA. Used by Permission.

95 96 97 98 99 00 01 02 03 04—10 9 8 7 6 5 4 3 2 1

MANUFACTURED IN THE UNITED STATES OF AMERICA

CONTENTS

CHARLES V. GERKIN

Pamela D. Couture and Rodney J. Hunter

These essays honor the pastoral work of Charles V. Gerkin. By "pastoral work," Gerkin's own term, we mean his pastoral vocation as it was expressed in his practice in chaplaincy, counseling, institutional leadership, and academic scholarship.

In his writing Gerkin, drawing upon the Gadamerian hermeneutical method, aimed toward a "fusion of horizons" of the Christian story and human story. While he valued the individual conversations of chaplaincy and pastoral counseling, he also challenged pastoral care to consider the congregational, social institutional, and cultural aspects of its work.

"Chuck" Gerkin's insistence on these aspects of pastoral theological method may grow from the fusion of his personal story with his Christian vocation. On rare occasions, Chuck speaks of his own formation under the influence of his father, a United Methodist clergyperson in Kansas, who carried on the family tradition of standing against racism. He recalls how, as a young child, he watched the flames of the cross of the Ku Klux Klan burning in the front yard of their parsonage. The scare tactics failed; rather, the flames tempered within the child's heart a sense of determination and strength to prevail against the evils of racism.

Perhaps the most vocationally formative step in Gerkin's career, formative in terms of his impact on the social world around him, was his move from Kansas to Atlanta to create the chaplaincy department of Grady Memorial Hospital. Chuck was already a veteran of the early clinical pastoral movement, having studied and served with Anton Boisen at Elgin State Hospital. Grady, however, moved him from the world of the private pastoral conversation into public institutional ministry.

Grady Memorial Hospital, the large public hospital in Atlanta, was also a teaching hospital associated with Emory University. Nicknamed "the

Gradies," Grady was an entirely segregated institution, with duplicate housing and services for its white and black patients. Even though substantial pressure for the integration of Grady came from the civil rights movement and federal civil rights legislation, the Grady administration stood by its segregationist policies. When the chief administrator died and Gerkin, as head chaplain, conducted his memorial service, Gerkin also stood his ground and refused to conduct two formal services, one for whites and one for blacks. Rather, by maintaining the integrity of the worship setting, he presided over the first integrated event at the Gradies. The service was informally structured, allowing persons to come and go, but all persons worshiped together.

Chuck went on to develop one of the nation's premier clinical pastoral education programs at Grady. His achievement there so impressed then Dean of Candler School of Theology, James Laney, that he recruited Gerkin to join the Candler faculty in order to establish a new kind of program in "contextual education." Laney wanted Gerkin to apply the action-reflection methods of clinical pastoral education to the teaching of general ministry and the formation of pastoral identity within the regular theological curriculum. The program Gerkin established at Candler is distinctive among programs in supervised ministry. It places students in secular social service institutions, within which they can experience human suffering firsthand and reflect on the role of ministry. It involves both site supervisors and regular faculty (in "classical" as well as "practical" fields) in reflection seminars. Gerkin's experience at Grady provided the insight that students preparing for pastoral ministry need to conceive of their ministries in the broader social world. He also became convinced that the academic faculty needed to be involved in the supervisory process in a substantive way so that the program would be integrated significantly into the curriculum and into the life of the school.

Chuck's other monumental institutional achievement was his visionary and formative role in creating the Georgia Association for Pastoral Care in 1957. Drawing on the resources of Atlanta's psychiatric and religious communities including its three seminaries and the Emory University School of Medicine, Chuck pulled together an organization dedicated to promoting the highest quality of pastoral care and counseling in response to the full range of human suffering and need, with special emphasis on social problems, interprofessional relationships, and institutional processes. Eventually GAPC grew into one of the nation's leading pastoral care institutions, sponsoring institutional chaplaincies and clinical pastoral education programs in the Atlanta area and a large program for training specialized pastoral counselors. As its first executive director, Chuck gave GAPC early visionary leadership and executive skill, bringing together a deep sense of value of clinical wisdom for the church's ministry, of the integral relation of pastoral care and counseling to social and institutional issues, and of the need for the pastoral care field to be in close, creative relation to theological education.

Yet Chuck never lost touch with his pastoral heart. Through his more than twenty years on the Candler faculty, Chuck maintained a continuous ministry of pastoral counseling and was widely sought by colleagues and others as a wise, understanding—and often disturbingly insightful!—pastor. An early member of the American Association of Pastoral Counselors, Chuck also served as president of the Association of Clinical Pastoral Education and consulted frequently and widely with colleagues in clinical pastoral education and pastoral counseling.

We can find, then, in Gerkin's life the impetus for concepts which became distinctive in his writing. Drawing upon the work of critical theory and of Erich Fromm in particular, Chuck was concerned with criticism of social institutions as they perpetuated injustice. He looked, as did others in the immediate post–World War II era, toward psychotherapeutic counseling as a practice that could liberate people from a moralistic and institutionally constricted society.

He retrieved the concept of the living human document from Anton Boisen, and developed out of that insight a sophisticated new understanding of pastoral counseling as a retelling of the human story in ways that expand social horizons and liberate persons from oppressive forms of consciousness and destructive patterns of interpersonal relationship. Finally, one finds his reflection on his experience in institutions in the concept of "changing the common sense of the community" in *Prophetic Pastoral Care.*

Through his counseling and educational work Gerkin was also an exemplary pioneer of what is today called the "reflective practitioner," following the course earlier charted by Boisen. Like Boisen, Gerkin believed passionately that careful listening and depth reflection on the "living human documents" of pastoral experience could yield profound and stimulating insights of a theological order. Such insights can both guide pastoral practice and enhance the church's understanding of its faith. In his first book, *Crisis Experience In Modern Life* (Abingdon, 1979),

Chuck plumbs the depth of the meaning of crisis in multidimensional detail—psychological, social, historical, and theological—and emerges with a rich concept of pastoral care method and a reconstructed understanding of the meaning of divine providence in the midst of life's most anguishing moments. His later books, especially *The Living Human Document: Revisioning Pastoral Counseling in a Hermeneutical Mode* (Abingdon Press, 1984), carry his pastoral theological work—his commitment to learning theology and ministry from the *practice* of ministry—into a new and original dimension. Working carefully with the hermeneutical theories of Hans-Georg Gadamer, Paul Ricoeur, and others, Gerkin creates a powerful new form of pastoral care and counseling in which the telling of one's story and the creation and re-creation of meanings in dialogue with the sacred stories of the faith become the focus of pastoral concern. Yet even in this "revisioned" conception of the pastoral task, Gerkin's lifetime commitment to relate personal ministries to social and institutional dynamics, and to critique society from the perspective of pastoral care, shines through, as evident in his most recent book, *Prophetic Pastoral Practice* (Abingdon Press, 1991).

The essays in this book represent an attempt to continue and advance Gerkin's legacy of pastoral theological scholarship. Like him, we have sought to develop pastoral care and counseling in critical dialogue with its social environment and to deepen its self-understanding sociologically and theologically as well as psychologically. Our focus is social conflict— the work of pastoral care and counseling within the distinctively pressing features of our time. These include the emergence of economic, ethnic, political, racial, and gender tensions as defining characteristics of contemporary social and personal experience. Such tensions pervade every pastoral relationship and personal need today, and often form the explicit agenda for our pastoral ministries. Thus it seems uniquely appropriate, in honoring Charles Gerkin at his retirement from Emory University's Candler School of Theology, that we pursue the social themes and concerns to which his professional career was devoted and to which he made such a distinguished lifetime contribution.

INTRODUCTION

Pamela D. Couture

Pastoral care and counseling of the twentieth century was born in social change. At the turn of the century, Americans were becoming increasingly interested in psychology as a way to interpret human life. Early architects of the pastoral care and counseling movement rose to meet the challenge offered by psychology to church and theology. The way that church and theology responded to psychological culture was deeply influenced by social conflict and by conflict with the movement itself.

The "first serious effort to transform the cure of souls in light of the new psychology and theology" began, according to historian Brooks Holifield, in 1905 with the Emmanuel Movement (Holifield, 1983, 201). Following the lead of Emmanuel Church, Boston, participants in the Emmanuel Movement wedded the social reform efforts of the social gospel and the new psychology, ministering among those who had been physically or mentally diseased by the effects of poverty. Psychology and social reform, however, were not for the poor alone, other practitioners discovered. Middle-class persons came in great numbers to the lectures of Drs. Richard Cabot and James Jackson Putnam on the general psychological treatment of nervous and emotional disorders. Finally, the Reverend Anton Boisen's own experience of the way in which doctors dismissed the spiritual aspects of his own mental breakdown brought pastoral care into the world of the pathologies of specific mental diseases.

Within a few years conflict developed among the early practitioners of psychotherapy over formative questions: Who should treat the distress of the soul? Physicians? Ministers? Among those physicians and ministers who looked to both theology and psychology, whose approach was best: those who sought to minister to the poor and reform society? those who

11

wanted to educate the middle classes? those who thought that the critically mentally ill illumined spiritual aspects of the human condition? Eventually, the movement embodied adherents to all three positions, although the latter two predominated.

International conflict accelerated the dominance of psychology in American culture. World War I brought the first psychological testing of soldiers; during World War II the armed services employed psychologists and psychiatrists in great numbers. After World War II, the uses of psychiatry in wartime were applied to the productivity of industry during peace.

While war and the economy contributed to the American culture's dependence on psychology, theology contributed its impetus from a different angle of vision. During World War I antiwar sentiments emerged. Critics of the war culture, including the theological realists Richard and Reinhold Niebuhr and Paul Tillich, began to doubt that society could be reformed through social institutions. Instead, psychological insight into the behavior of individuals could serve as the conduit of reform. Tillich, in particular, would become the theologian of the post–World War II pastoral care and counseling movement (Holifield, 1983).

During the early postwar period, the movement's particular ideology of social reform oriented the minister toward a therapeutic model of helping parishioners create change, first through individuals and later through families. As it took that turn, pastoral care and counseling seemed worlds apart from the apparent, dominant social conflicts of the time: life with the nuclear threat, the rise of the cold war, superpower hegemony, and the advance in technology through the space race. Behind the facade of this seeming progress, the power of another kind of social conflict was building: the civil rights movement, then the women's liberation movement, and later the gay pride movement. Individuals within the pastoral care and counseling movement cared deeply about various of these issues and participated in their movements.

Even so, the momentum of the dominant culture pushed against these efforts. As pastoral care and counseling became a mature movement with its own pedagogy, multiplicity of therapeutic theories, organizations, and accrediting bodies for its practitioners, the people in care and counseling whose identities were deeply formed by liberation movements struggled to keep one side of their efforts in social reform and one side in the need of the movement to legitimate itself according to the demands of technological society. These demands created within the movement a bifurcation of pastoral theology from social ethics, increasing specialization of pastoral counselors, a focus on individuals and families almost to the exclusion of groups and communities, and a loss of connections with local congregations.

Social and professional conflict created conflict in the core identities of many persons in the pastoral care and counseling movement. In the present culture, so unlike that of the early part of the century, did the therapeutic paradigm help or hinder the movement's social agenda? Persons in pastoral care and counseling who cared deeply about individuals and families *and* about social reform wanted to offer alternatives within and beyond the therapeutic paradigm to a movement which was becoming increasingly truncated.

Today many persons hope for experiments in care and counseling that will be creative and diverse in response to the challenges of class, gender, race, sexual orientation, ecclesiologies, and other issues. They seek new and deeper ways of describing the culture, communities, society, and world of which families and individuals are a part. They have offered a ministry of presence to suffering persons in the pastoral counselor's office and pastor's or professor's study, and they think that the insights gained from these experiences have much to offer to theology and social policy as it is created in the present era.

This book offers a forum for a variety of voices in the pastoral care and counseling movement who articulate such concerns. Some authors have thought about discrete issues related to pastoral care and social conflict; others are comprehensive in their theory building. Not all agree with one another about particular answers to specific questions. Their voices represent the presence of many others, however, who do agree that the core identity of the movement of pastoral care and counseling— with its twin emphases on persons *and* society as they inform theology— remains intact.

In part 1 the authors review the context of pastoral care as we find it today: the tradition that developed, the values that tradition attempted to convey, and the way it has been shaped by secular economic forces. In part 2 the authors talk concretely about various social issues—abortion, aging, parenting, race, politics, sexuality—and their interface with care and counseling. In part 3 the authors talk about the ways in which the practice of pastoral care is being transformed in the congregation, hospital, and clinic. Taken together, the authors offer a new image of pastoral care as it met, meets, and will meet the challenges of society and culture.

PART I
TRADITION AND CONTEXT

CHAPTER 1

The Therapeutic Tradition of Pastoral Care and Counseling

Rodney J. Hunter

The purpose of this chapter is to sketch the contours of what this book broadly refers to as the "therapeutic tradition" of pastoral care and counseling. It is the editors' premise that there is an identifiable tradition of pastoral theory and practice which merits this name because of its fundamental commitment to healing or "therapeutics" as its master metaphor and operative principle. This tradition is relatively coherent and specific, can be readily identified among its variations, and stands in relatively clear distinction from the pastoral care and counseling of earlier modernity and often from Christian ministry today in traditions other than liberal Protestantism.

Historically and institutionally, the therapeutic tradition of pastoral care is rooted in the religion and health movement, the religious education movement, and the academic interest in psychology of religion that developed around the turn of the twentieth century. By the 1930s these movements were beginning to be embodied in chaplaincies and training programs in health care settings, and eventually in professional associations. These professional associations and their programs of clinical pastoral education, and the style of general ministry associated with them, have been long established in "mainline" Protestant seminaries where they have profoundly influenced the theory and practice of Protestant ministry in North America.

What follows is an attempt to state the general principles and methods that mark the "therapeutic" approach to pastoral care and counseling, and to identify its principal unresolved issues. It is these principles, methods, and issues that subsequent chapters in this book evaluate. The guiding question in these chapters is whether, in what ways, and to what extent these principles and methods are likely to be relevant, effective, and appropriate in coming years as social differences and conflicts become more pronounced and more determinative of pastoral needs and problems.

THE THERAPEUTIC IDEAL

The term "therapeutic," whose Greek root means "to attend or to treat," points to the central, controlling metaphor of this tradition, that of "attending" or "presence" in illness and suffering with the intent and hope of healing. Pastoral care and counseling are conceived as a healing art, and the field as a whole has taken health and healing as its primary metaphors for personal caring ministry.

The metaphor of healing is not new in pastoral care. Healing imagery as a metaphor for ministry has its roots in the Bible, principally in the healing ministry of Jesus. The primary biblical and historical metaphor for pastoral care is the shepherd, but there is a long tradition in the history of the church in which salvation is understood as a kind of cure for sickness, Christ as the Great Physician, and the pastor as a physician of the soul. What is new in our time is the centrality and the controlling power this concept has acquired. It may therefore be instructive to identify its principal features.

The Human Condition

The therapeutic ideal tends to view the human "fault" or "predicament" as integral with distorted or limited psychosocial capacities. In the therapeutic perspective the distortions of human life are believed to be largely of contingent historical and social origin, accessible to human effort and intelligence; thus human beings are capable of participating in significant ways with God in saving and restoring human life at its deepest ("spiritual") levels of struggle and distortion. Such commitments are cautiously optimistic concerning human powers and possibilities, compared with the exclusive emphasis on sin, the bondage of the will, and dependency on divine grace that has characterized much of the

Western religious tradition. In this respect the therapeutic tradition stands in the stream of Protestant theological liberalism more than that of orthodox Lutheran and Calvinist theology. (See chapter 2 for a more complete discussion of this heritage.)

Behind this optimism lies an emphasis on God's immanent relation to the world. The divine role in the process of healing and salvation is believed to occur primarily (or even exclusively) through historical processes—rather than by supernatural means. Ministry is therefore viewed as a kind of partnership with the divine for bringing about wholeness. It is free to focus on psychosocial processes and to utilize the social sciences and therapeutic arts of the culture.

Yet the therapeutic tradition has generally resisted a simplistic Pelagian emphasis on human powers and possibilities. Instead, it has maintained, in paradoxical tension with its optimism, a strong awareness of the existential "caughtness" of human life—the limits of human power to redeem and the need to live in grace amid the awesome mystery of tragedy and inexplicable suffering. This has been evident from the time of Anton Boisen's struggles with mental illness, through the marriage of the field with Freudian psychologies and existentialist theologies in the fifties and sixties. In this strand of the tradition, human suffering and need are not problems to be solved by good clinical skill and theory alone. They are also, at a deep level, "predicaments" to be "suffered through" in faith and trust—problems whose core meaning ultimately exceeds human understanding and therapeutic amelioration. Indeed, Charles Gerkin defines the "crisis situation" as a "boundary situation in which the fundamental contradiction between human aspirations and finite possibilities becomes visible" (Gerkin, 1979, p. 32; see also "Human Condition/Human Predicament," in R. Hunter, 1990).

Healing and Salvation

In the therapeutic tradition salvation is "wholistic" in concept, though this term is not always used. Wholism is a comprehensive category denoting total human well-being, including physical, psychological, social, cultural, and spiritual aspects. The human being is a psychophysical whole, and salvation refers to the restoration and transformation of the full human being in his or her relationships; it thus encompasses the entire range of health and welfare needs. This includes what goes on *between* persons as well as what happens *within* them; personal and family relationships are integral to salvation; the soul is profoundly social.

19

Ministry rooted in a wholistic understanding of salvation attempts to address human needs in their totality from a perspective of faith, and is not confined to problems explicitly defined as religious or moral. It is also able to draw freely on natural healing forces of the soul and of society, and on the wisdom of secular healing arts and sciences. Thus a high level of cooperation becomes possible between ministry and medicine, psychiatry, psychology, social work, and other helping professions.

These convictions are today so well established in the liberal churches that it is difficult to appreciate how profound a revolution they represent in the history of Christianity. A sharp distinction between body and soul, and a narrow concentration on the soul and moral behavior, defined much of the church's pastoral ministry through the centuries and was not significantly challenged until the latter part of the nineteenth century in the religion and health movement, from which the clinical pastoral education (and later the pastoral counseling) movements emerged. In these developments the integration of physical health into the concerns of religion was fully accomplished. As a result, health care concerns, including psychological and psychiatric disorders, became integral to the work of pastoral care and counseling, and theologians like Paul Tillich, David Roberts, and Daniel Day Williams initiated systematic theological study of religion-health relationships and their implications for ministry.

But the wholistic definition of salvation has also had internal tensions and limitations. Although the concept of wholistic salvation easily included family and personal relationships, it did not incorporate political and economic dimensions into its theory and practice of care. Its tendency was to focus on psychological and social psychological dimensions of wholeness with only lip service paid to cultural, economic, and political aspects of human problems and the practical actions appropriate to addressing them.

This was not always the case, however. Many of the pioneers of the clinical pastoral education and pastoral counseling movements—in the twenties, thirties, and forties—were keenly concerned about social questions and viewed the pastoral care movement as a direct response to the alienations and conflicts of modern industrial society. Anton Boisen, for instance, was very sociologically minded (cf. his *Religion in Crisis and Custom,* 1955), and one of his principal successors, Seward Hiltner, was heavily influenced by Erich Fromm and the Frankfurt School of social theory, which sought to combine Marxist and Freudian perspectives.

Fromm also exerted a formative influence on Charles Gerkin. And recently, among younger pastoral theologians influenced by feminist and liberation theologies, a strong cultural, political, and economic interest has returned to the field, especially regarding gender and race. Thus, while therapeutic pastoral care and counseling on the whole has failed to integrate political, economic, and cultural features fully into its theory and practice, the question of what constitutes a true "wholism" has never been entirely absent and has emerged with new force in recent years.

The Secular and the Sacred

The therapeutic tradition has always been, and continues to be, inherently religious in character despite secular features. This thesis cannot be fully expounded here, but its truth can be seen when the principal contours of the field are contrasted with the general backdrop of secular therapeutic culture in America. The tradition's deep commitment to moral integrity and to a sense of life's mystery and deeper meanings is not only distinctive but is to a significant degree countercultural. This is evident in comparison with medicine, psychiatry, psychotherapy, and social work, fields that typically espouse more exclusively scientific and technological models of care, prize "value neutrality," and generally avoid engagement with philosophical, ethical, and religious questions.

At the same time the therapeutic tradition stands in a complex, critical, and perhaps dialectical relation to institutional religion. It has already been noted that the clinical tradition does not typically draw a sharp line between sacred and secular, and is inclined to find religious depths of meaning in nonreligious, mundane, or secular forms of experience (especially existential boundaries and crises). This tendency has led to a wholesale, often uncritical incorporation of secular theories of personality and therapy into pastoral care and counseling, a development that some view with alarm as representing a loss, or threatened loss, of religious identity and integrity.

But it is important to note that the therapeutic pastoral tradition from its earliest days represented a creative and courageous attempt to carry a comprehensive, religiously conceived therapeutic ministry beyond church walls into the health care institutions of industrial society (general and mental hospitals). Working in secular, bureaucratic, scientifically rational environments, pastors attempted to bring an incarnate,

21

wholistic word of salvation. It was perhaps inevitable that heavy pressure to legitimate themselves professionally vis-à-vis physicians and other health care professionals should build under such circumstances.

But institutionally based pastoral care and counseling did not simply submit to the secularizing pressures of the ruling class. By becoming an identified part of the "health care team," the therapeutically oriented chaplain was also in a position to represent an implicit (and sometimes explicit) "humanistic" or "personalistic" critique of scientific medicine and its cognate disciplines from within the establishment, and to advocate for the "person of the patient" in the midst of often dehumanizing health care practices and procedures. Moreover, it was precisely the "secular" quality of the pastoral tradition that enabled it to be prophetic. Therapeutically trained pastors refused to confine their ministries to explicitly "religious" problems and they carried no bag of religious techniques like their medical counterparts; they lived in the margins of their institutions. But this social location enabled them to make a countercultural witness to human values amid the culture of scientific technocracy, and, by implication, to represent a radical questioning presence concerning the limits of the rational-technical values of the institution itself.

The sacred-secular tension in this field is also complex in its relation to the churches. Some have viewed the secularizing of clinically oriented pastoral care and counseling as evidence of disaffection with the traditional congregation and its religious life. No doubt this has been true in some instances. But when viewed in light of the fundamentally religious character of the tradition, it must equally be said that the therapeutic movement represents a prophetic word to and for the churches as well as a defection from them, and thus a kind of reform movement within the religious establishment. As countless trainees in clinical pastoral programs will attest, the depth of human relationship that they have experienced and struggled to develop in their training groups has set a challenging standard for human relationships and community. These experiences often make the fellowship, worship, and spirituality of traditional congregations seem pale by comparison. The hunger of the human heart for significant love, care, and honest truthfulness requires effort, courage, and struggle. The therapeutic pastoral tradition represents, in this respect, a powerful vision and methodology of religious community closely integrated with ideals of service, and it calls the churches to develop comparable forms of moral and religious life.

THERAPEUTIC PRACTICE

The general outlook just identified as the therapeutic ideal finds practical expression in a certain style of pastoral care and counseling broadly defined by the following features.

Health and Well-being as the Goal of Care

Therapeutically oriented pastoral caregivers are generally as much concerned about enhancing the underlying functional capacity, well-being, or "health" of the persons and families seeking their care as they are about solving the immediate practical problems that constitute the "presenting issues" (e.g. family and marriage difficulties, alcoholism, grief).

From the perspective of Christian ethics, this represents a slant in the direction of "character ethics" or the "ethics of virtue" over the ethics of decision and action. This is not to say that the pastoral therapeutic orientation is unconcerned with questions of right action, but only to say that it has shown greater concern for nurturing those qualities of personhood and interpersonal relationship (like emotional honesty, nondefensiveness, and the ability to love and work without undue conflict) that make responsible moral life possible.

The concern for character ethics has seldom been identified by that language in the pastoral tradition, but it has been present in the language of "personhood" and in wholistic conceptions of health and "wellness," which include elements of moral character (Poling, 1984). It is often also expressed as a preference for the values of "being" over those of "doing." And it appears in the tradition's preference for the language and questions of theology over those of ethics (as in "pastoral theology," "the theology of pastoral care," and "personality and theology"). Since the mid-seventies, however, Don Browning has argued for more explicit ethical reflection in the field, and feminist, black, and liberation theologies and the family systems approach have pressed the case for pastoral advocacy, systemic intervention, and for focusing on questions of behavior, power, exploitation, and justice as well as traditional concerns for character and the subjective dimension of interpersonal relationships.

Phenomenological Stance, Empathic Listening, and Positive Regard

Carl Rogers' classic concept of unconditional positive regard still expresses a cardinal feature of the therapeutic tradition's method of care despite its current disinclination to employ Rogers' specific terminology or therapeutic theories. This principle, along with that of empathic listening, points to the importance of simple, warm, caring presence as crucial in any healing relationship, and to the priority given to relating to persons in the immediacy and concreteness of their existence, with respect for their unique way of experiencing their situation, as distinguished from focusing principally on ideological or institutional agendas that pastors may otherwise bring with them. One's first impulse in the therapeutic tradition is not to speak but to listen, not to exercise authority but to be simply and immediately present.

Therapeutic pastors listen to persons tell their own stories as they have experienced them, empathically, as if from within their "internal frame of reference" (Rogers, 1951). This means not stereotyping them in terms of a casuistry of problems, and not assuming too quickly that one understands what is going on or what needs to be done. Thus, the pastor's comments are typically couched in terms of what he or she "perceives," not what the reality putatively "is." (For example, "I experience you as angry," not "You are angry.") The language of perception expresses a recognition that human realities are subjective and that care must honor and elicit the experience of those cared for through empathic dialogue.

The therapeutic tradition's distinctive relation to ethics appears in this connection. Pastoral care and counseling involve an essentially nonjudgmental stance, an easing up (or "bracketing") of moral judgments in order to create a gracious, trusting environment of personal space within which healing can occur. Ministry's historical tendency to give priority (and often vigorous expression) to moral evaluation, correction, and guidance, and to offer an explicitly theological definition of or solution to problems, is subordinated to the aim of allowing a healing process to occur, which encourages moral responsibility and character. It is also widely held (and supported by empirical research) that a relationship of empathy or "unconditional positive regard" (Rogers, 1951), made popular in the fifties in the Tillichian language of "acceptance," is among the "therapeutic conditions" deemed crucial for establishing a process of healing and growth.

It would be misleading, however, to suggest that the principle of acceptance or nonjudgmental presence excludes the exercise of moral judgment (what the older tradition called pastoral "discipline"). It is more accurate to say that the therapeutic tradition has developed its own style of discipline, a style most commonly referred to as "confrontation."

What is distinctive and perhaps novel in this approach is the degree to which therapeutic confrontation enlists the responsibility and capacities of persons to critique themselves rather than requiring persons to submit to judgments passed on them by authority figures (pastors). Typically, in the therapeutic approach, the caregiver raises open-ended questions or invites persons to look at themselves and their actions reflectively from some angle of vision that implies a questioning of meanings or motives. This may or may not involve direct value questions or didactic input from the pastor. But the pastor's contributions are timed and expressed in ways that seek to maximize the counselee's ability to take responsibility for himself or herself as a moral agent, thus reducing dependency on "outside" authorities or institutions. Although this approach may appear to lack rigor compared with more traditional, authoritarian methods, in fact, when done artfully, it can evoke deep self-examination and trans-formative moral power.

A key feature of therapeutic confrontation is avoiding punitive attitudes and expressions. It is assumed that one can be critical or self-critical without being moralistic or condemning. The aim is not to instill guilt or impose punishment, or to correct behavior by repressively imposing new patterns of behavior, but to grow and change in one's "personhood" and interpersonal relations—to develop greater capacity for responsibility and moral life. Faults and deficiencies are problems to be understood, explored, "accepted," and modified. Acceptance does not mean moral approval; it means support for the person, and an encouragement to recognize and take responsibility for one's shortcomings and for that which one is seeking to become.

Therapeutic confrontation is a powerful and significant moral practice whether or not the language of ethics is used. But it does not achieve all of ministry's traditional aims of authoritative moral critique, reform, and guidance. The therapeutic approach gives prominence to the individual's self-perception and evaluation, but it generally gives priority to enhancing moral capacities and the exercise of moral judgment over obedience to moral rules or the pursuit of moral goals. This tendency has given rise to charges of ethical egoism and individualism against the therapeutic pastoral tradition, and has evoked corrective proposals (Browning, 1976, 1983). The issue is far from clear or settled. But it seems likely that compassionate understanding and the providing of nonjudgmental "space" for personal reflection will continue to be definitive features of therapeutic pastoral care and counseling, however much they may be supplemented in the future with other methods and principles.

Care as Conversation, Dialogue, and Process

The therapeutic tradition has emphasized conversational methods of care and counseling almost to the exclusion of the other traditional forms of religious care such as sacrament, sermon, prayer, and penitential practices. The therapeutic orientation tends to regard the conversational "counseling model" as normative for all forms of pastoral care, and it typically regards less structured forms of care in congregational settings as scaled down forms of counseling. In its conversational approach, the therapeutic method seeks to bring hidden or unseen aspects of a situation into view and to articulate them openly. Verbalizing not only helps to identify therapeutically useful insights, it also draws persons out of depressive or destructive isolation.

The conversational style engenders a mode of care that gives prominence to exploration and the gradual emergence of solutions, insights, personal growth, and the transformation of perspective through a dialogical process (Howe, 1963). Dialogue and process are thus key themes, suggesting a mode of involvement in which the caregiver works cooperatively and interactively with persons or families, evoking and drawing out natural healing tendencies instead of imposing authoritative solutions. Specific ideas and insights may be introduced by the pastor as resources, but such "resourcing" is provided mainly in relation to the readiness of persons to appropriate and utilize it effectively. Except in situations such as those involving perpetrators of violence and abuse, where therapeutic confrontation, limit setting, or the exercise of public or ecclesial authority may claim priority, one generally "goes with the flow."

This approach stands in contrast to traditional forms of pastoral practice that have centered on authoritative guidance or ritualized resources provided by the pastor and have thus entailed an underlying emphasis on discipline, control, and submission to authority. At the same time, in recent years, a renewed appreciation has developed for the pastoral use of prayer, ritual, scripture, and the "Christian story" in ways that are expressive of—or in constructive tension with—therapeutic principles. Charles Gerkin's attempt to "revision pastoral counseling in a hermeneutical mode," and the work of Donald Capps, William B. Oglesby, Jr., Elaine Ramshaw, Ralph Underwood, and others represent significant moves in this direction.

Personal Nature of Care and the Issue of Pastoral Identity

"Only persons cure persons" and "truth is personal" have become cliches in the tradition, but such epigrams point to the importance it places on the pastoral caregiver's personal relationship with those seeking help, on being able to form therapeutic relationships, and on the role of personal relationship in communicating the "inner meaning of the gospel" (Wise, 1989 [1966]). Neither abstract ideas (psychological or theological), nor the symbolism of pastoral office, nor the traditional means of grace (Word and Sacrament) have magical power to change or save human life. Religious symbols and rituals need to be integrated existentially into the personhood and personal relationships of the pastor. By the same token, however, psychological techniques possess no magical power to function therapeutically; if not well integrated into the identity and personality of the caring person, they can in fact work antitherapeutically.

Thus, the clinical tradition affirms the importance for pastoral caregivers of developing a theological, subjectively coherent, personally integrated, "comfortable" sense of themselves as pastors. Pastoral identity means that the pastor has found a way to unite the formal meanings of the pastoral office with her or his uniquely personal dynamics and life history, so that the energy and strength of that coherence can be made available when caring pastorally for others. At the same time, the therapeutic tradition recognizes an internal tension between the pastor's personality and the symbolic power of the pastoral role. Although the tradition has rejected the temptation to attribute supernatural or quasi-magical powers to religious symbolism, it has always valued the way in which the pastor's identity as "representative Christian person" can function as a quiet, subliminal reminder of the depths of mystery in which human life exists and of the healing presence and power of God in the midst of life's tribulations. The symbolism of the office is therefore valued psychologically both for its power to identify the religious character of the caring ministry and as a reminder of the limits of psychological theories and techniques.

The problematic aspects of pastoral identity arise chiefly in relation to lay religious caregiving, the significance of ordination, and the meaning of the term "pastoral." While the issue is clearly most pressing for Roman Catholic women, who are forbidden ordination by the church, the question finds expression throughout the pastoral care movement. Lay caregiving movements have sprung up in churches, and pastoral counseling has emerged as a specialized psychotherapeutic profession largely independent of ecclesiastical structures.

The issue of ordination and the meaning of "pastoral" are likely to be unresolved problems for some time. But the therapeutic pastoral tradition continues to think of them in subjective terms rather than in terms of formal institutional status. To be "pastoral" in the subjective sense means that one exhibits the qualities valued by the therapeutic tradition. In this sense one can be "pastoral" without being "a pastor" (i.e. ordained). It remains for the field to determine what importance to attach to ordination in its emphasis on pastoral identity.

Professional Accountability

The therapeutic tradition has emphasized the importance of professionalism and accountability in caregivers, over against folk traditions of care, intuitive, "seat of the pants" approaches, and gimmicky eclecticism. It has also emphasized a professional understanding of ordained ministry in theological education generally. While the precise meaning of professionalism continues to be debated, in general, in this field, it has referred to a cluster of values having to do with articulating and critiquing, with peers and supervisors, how one relates to others, how one performs ministry, and "who one is" in the practice of ministry. One must be able to articulate reasons ("theory"), look critically in depth at what one does and why one does it, and be able to articulate these discoveries in a community of professional practitioners. Disclosure of this kind entails a degree of personal self-revelation since one's personhood and one's practice cannot be entirely separated; professional accountability is also to a significant degree personal accountability. Moreover, being able to care responsibly for others requires a willingness to be examined by one's peers and teachers ("supervisors"), to study actual data from one's ministry (as distinguished from one's beliefs, hopes, and illusions about it). It also requires struggling with one's own hidden motivations, limits, and blind spots, receiving care for one's own needs and deficiencies, and being willing to participate in a community of mutual supervision and consultation (Feilding, 1966; Steere, 1989).

This standard implies a more profound understanding of professionalism than does its relatively superficial counterpart in popular American culture, where "the professional" is defined minimally as one who possesses technical expertise offered within a remunerative, contractual structure through a regulated guild. As an ideal for all aspects of ordained ministry, it also stands in contrast to parish ministry, which is normally practiced without accountability structures of comparable depth, detail, and collegial encounter.

There is a more problematic aspect to the tradition's commitment to professionalism and accountability, however. This has to do less with its rich, complex subjective criteria than with its objective, institutional dimensions. In the specialized pastoral counseling movement, the field has evolved into a virtually autonomous therapeutic profession modeled on psychiatric and psychotherapeutic practice. Though much of this specialized movement is formally linked with the churches, and most pastoral counselors view themselves as ministers, the operative day-to-day reference group for specialized pastoral counselors is not parish ministry but the secular therapeutic professions. Institutional links with the churches are often distant and sometimes nonexistent (as in the "private practice of pastoral psychotherapy"), at least in terms of economic and regulatory aspects.

Opinions differ widely concerning these developments. Some regard pastoral psychotherapy as a bold new extension of the church's ministry beyond its institutional walls, a prophetic witness to the true meaning of persons and personal care in an alienated society (Patton, 1983). Others view the situation as an escape from religious tradition and community, a new therapeutic culture of secularism thinly disguised as religion, supplanting the old religious values and eroding the communal and institutional character of American religion by further institutionalizing the culture's rampant individualism (Rieff, 1968 [1966]). Either way, these questions point to fundamental, unresolved identity issues in the therapeutic tradition.

Clear and Appropriate Loci of Responsibility

Clinically oriented pastors establish and maintain appropriate forms of self-differentiation, encouraging those in their care to take as much responsibility for themselves as possible, and not taking undue responsibility for them. This may seem unremarkable, but it needs to be viewed against the background of a tradition that often encouraged parishioner dependency on clergy as a means of maintaining the authority of the church and the religious culture, or out of sentimental misunderstandings of love and care.

Given the deeply personal character of caregiving in this tradition, it is not surprising that attention should be given to setting appropriate limits to personal involvement both for the sake of maintaining pastoral integrity and for the sake of the therapeutic process itself. Within the tradition this need is often dealt with by "managing transference and countertransference" (in psychoanalytic terms). But regardless of theoretical perspective, clinically oriented pastors are trained to "use" their own subjective qualities of personality in therapeutically useful ways—and to understand the therapeutically necessary limits of self-involvement. One must be "in" the relationship but not entirely "of" it.

A hallmark of the clinically trained pastor is the ability to maintain pastoral warmth, sensitivity, empathic understanding, clinical insight, and significant relationship in the midst of temptations to "take things personally," or to become defensive, controlling, and judgmental, or to inject oneself personally and inappropriately into the situation at hand. The stance of "nonanxious presence" does not mean that the pastor may not in fact feel anxious in some care and counseling situations, and it does not imply lack of concern, feeling, or care. It only means that clinically educated pastors are able to listen honestly to their own emotional reactions to others as a guide to deeper understanding and more effective care. At times they are even able to use these reactions as a source of deeper insight into the mysteries of human suffering and perhaps, into the presence—and absence—of God.

SUMMARY

Therapeutic pastoral care and counseling is defined by its fundamental commitment to the concept of healing. This involves a wholistic understanding of salvation, the human condition, and the relation between the sacred and the secular. It also involves a distinctive style of pastoral practice whose defining features include: an orientation to health and well-being as the goal of care, a phenomenological, empathic mode of pastoral relationship, a conversational style of caregiving that accents its personal qualities and the pastor's subjective sense of pastoral identity, an intimate, psychological form of professional accountability to peers in ministry, and a concern for keeping responsibility appropriately and clearly distinguished between pastor and parishioner or counselee.

Though its roots reach deep into our religious and cultural history, pastoral care and counseling thus understood and practiced is a distinctively twentieth-century religious phenomenon. It is a product of its time, caught within yet seeking to minister to the difficult life issues facing contemporary persons and families in our complex, rapidly changing, conflict-ridden society. The truth and value of its traditional therapeutic convictions for these new social realities are the questions that the remaining chapters in this volume seek to clarify. In what ways is this tradition an adequate practical expression of the Christian faith for our time? In what ways, if any, does it need to change?

CHAPTER 2

The Therapeutic Tradition's Theological and Ethical Commitments Viewed Through Its Pedagogical Practices: A Tradition in Transition

Rodney J. Hunter and John Patton

The modern pastoral care and counseling movement is a tradition in transition. Beyond sixty years of age and still in its early stages in some respects, the movement today is being powerfully challenged and changed by issues of social conflict, those identified and explored in this book. Our concern in this chapter is to identify in broad historical terms the generating theological tradition out of which modern pastoral care was formed, to explore some of the principles that formed the movement into an identifiable tradition as revealed in its educational programs and traditions, and to suggest the emerging form of the pastoral care and counseling tradition at century's end.

THE GENERATING AND SUSTAINING TRADITION: PROTESTANT LIBERALISM AND PIETISM

The early clinical pastoral pioneers—Boisen, Cabot, Dunbar, Dicks, Hiltner, Johnson, Guiles, and others—despite differences in style and temperament, were in fact all heirs to, and representatives of, a single, broad theological tradition, that of liberalism in Protestant theology, which stretches from Schleiermacher to Boston personalism and the empirical theology of the Chicago school (Holifield, 1983; Kemp, 1947; Strunk, 1973). Common to this tradition were certain convictions that were to prove crucial in the emergence of modern pastoral care and counseling. These included: an emphasis on the universal saving work of God and God's active immanence in the world, hope concerning the possibility of redeeming the world within the course of history, a positive role assigned to human capacities and culture (including science) exercised in cooperation with divine saving activity, and a theological epistemology giving significant place to religious experience and advocating openness to the new truths of science. With few exceptions, these theological ideas are assumed in the greater part of the literature and practice of the pastoral care movement from Boisen through the seventies.

But the pastoral care movement was also deeply influenced by pietism. Originating in the seventeenth century as a reaction against Protestant formality and rationalism, and given new life through the later Methodist and holiness movements, pietism is an understanding of Christian life and the church that assigns high importance to the personal experience of God and the intimate sharing and strengthening of spiritual life through common prayer and devotion. The early clinical pastoral education movement largely sloughed off pietism's religious features—its emphasis on personal relationship with God through devotional practices—but retained its experiential and emotional emphasis in religion and its cultivation of intimate forms of community.

The pastoral care and counseling movement brought these two strands of theological tradition together through the new therapeutic psychologies. This was the family of psychological theories and therapies stemming from William James and the psychoanalytic movement that were concerned with broad questions of human personality, its pathological conflicts and distortions, and its restorative possibilities. Drawing upon William James' descriptions of the struggle of the soul and its quest for integration, and from the controversial new theories of psychoanalysis, therapeutic psychology captured the imaginations and energies of the pastoral movement's "founding fathers" (and a few unsung mothers). What they saw in these psychological developments was a way of giving contemporary, effective expression to the old liberal and pietistic ideals in modern society. Pietism emphasized the experiencing of faith and of human community; the therapeutic psychologies showed the depths of experience that are possible when one ventures (in Boisen's words) to "explore the inner world" of the "living human document." Theological liberalism affirmed the powers of human reason to work with God in bringing about a better world; therapeutic psychology provided a map and a set of psychological techniques for getting there— or at least for ameliorating the soul's sufferings en route.

This distinctive turn in the tradition can be seen more clearly in terms of the effects of two particular forms of therapeutic psychology on pietistic liberalism. On the one hand was the psychology and psychotherapeutic method of Carl Rogers, which made a strong impact on the pastoral care movement. Rogers' optimistic understanding of the helping relationship and the person being helped clearly reflected the progressive, optimistic stance of the Protestant liberalism from which Rogers himself had come. More important, Rogerian psychology represented a democratization of counseling and psychotherapy that extended therapeutic praxis beyond the doctor-patient relationship to include counselors from a wide variety of backgrounds and professions. Rogerian psychology became in effect the psychology of the nonpsychologist. Rogers was also instrumental in opening the counseling room to the tape recorder; in the true spirit of liberalism, what had been mysterious now became operational and available for study. Moreover, Rogers' emphasis on intimacy and trust in the counseling relationship— "unconditional positive regard"—sounded all the old themes of the pietist tradition in a fresh new key.

Psychoanalysis, on the other hand, brought a contrasting emphasis on the depth and complexity of human pain and conflict. Psychoanalysis was, in effect, a kind of neoorthodoxy in pastoral care, reminding psychological liberalism of the intractable conflicts and pathological tendencies of the soul, which tended to get lost or muted in the more optimistic Rogerian approach. Moreover, suspicion of unconscious motives and conflicts was inherent in psychoanalysis; no experience or behavior, sinful or righteous, was ever quite what it appeared to be on the surface. These insights undermined pietistic liberalism's confidence in the power of conscious persuasion to heal the soul, and brought about a shift to more indirect, evocative, and dialogical styles of "working with people."

Thus the insights of Rogerian and psychoanalytic theories psychologized, reshaped, and turned pietistic liberalism in new directions. Ultimately, it was this form of the liberal tradition that came down to contemporary mainline churches, profoundly influencing their styles of ministry, corporate life, understandings of faith, and moral practices.

THE OPERATIONAL TRADITION OF THERAPEUTIC CARE AND COUNSELING

It is one thing to identify a movement's theological sources, and something else to identify what it did with those sources, how they were forged into a distinctive theological tradition. How, specifically, has pastoral care and counseling combined its liberal pietist heritage with the therapeutic psychologies? What have been the distinctive and guiding theological convictions in this combination of traditions?

The pastoral care movement has primarily been concerned with pastoral practice, a fact that has led some to the mistaken conclusion that it was indifferent or hostile to theology. But an examination of its central practices, its "operational tradition," will show that the movement has in fact been deeply committed to a broad but identifiable and coherent faith and value stance throughout its history. By "operational tradition" we mean the beliefs and values that are implicit in its distinctive operations, its characteristic patterns of action or "praxis."

To bring these embedded convictions into the open, we have chosen to focus on the movement's educational practices. This is partly because we know pastoral care education firsthand through many years of teaching and supervision, but also because educational methods and principles usually express a movement's essential meaning and value commitments. Many could be identified, but five of the most important are these:

1. Priority of the Person and the Pastoral Relationship of the Caregiver over the Formal Content of Its Religious Message. Priority has most often been given to examining personal meanings, motives, and relationships rather than communicating religious meanings. Questions about how and when to talk directly about faith are not completely ignored in clinical pastoral supervision and instruction. But clinical supervisors have generally regarded issues involving the formal message of faith and how best to talk about it as matters to focus upon *after* consideration is given to personal identity, styles of interpersonal relationship, and the unresolved problems that students may have in those areas (Oates, 1953; Wise, 1989 [1966]). The importance of this is evident, negatively, when one considers the potential for distorting the message of faith that exists with a pastor's unresolved problems of personality or personal relationships. The positive point is the importance of representing the affirmations of faith "incarnationally," so that (for example) something of the love of God is in fact experienced in the love of the pastoral caregiving act itself.

However, this emphasis on the person and the pastoral relationship over the formal content of the religious message has also often tended to produce, not a mutual enriching, but an unfortunate opposition between person and message, with the message sometimes devalued in order to give priority to personhood and relationship.

Today the sharp distinction between the "person" of the student and the "message" of faith, which characterized several decades of clinical pastoral education, is being softened. There is a growing awareness that one's life history can be viewed not only psychologically but also as a story of faith, and that unresolved psychological issues like identity and conflicted relationships can also be regarded as incomplete life stories or faith journeys. Moreover, the religious meanings entwined within these personal narratives can be regarded as important in their own right without being explained away psychologically. Hermeneutical theories of pastoral care and counseling directly express this new understanding and reflect the rising interest in the theological importance of narrative and metaphor in theology (Capps, 1984; Fowler, 1986; Gerkin, 1984). What continues, however, is the field's commitment to the centrality of the student in the educational and supervisory process—the priority of dealing with the student's life issues as the crucial context for theological and professional development, over abstract discussions of theology and pastoral method.

2. Priority of What Human Beings Have in Common over Ways in Which They Differ from One Another. In the early psychology of religion and clinical pastoral movements, the accent (following William James) fell on discerning individual differences—the "varieties"—of religious experience and pastoral need. For most of its subsequent history, however, the pastoral field and its related therapeutic psychologies accented the idea of a "common core" of experience, and assumed that psychological and pastoral knowledge is equally applicable to either gender and to all races and classes of persons. This principle expressed a deep and important moral conviction: What is most truly and profoundly human, hence of religious and pastoral concern, is that which is universal, transcending differences of race, class, and culture.

The assumption of a common human "core" was, in its own way, morally inspired, a noble attempt to value human beings equally and unreservedly and to escape the demeaning and divisive uses made of race, sex, class, and ethnic differences. But it involved a curious irony. It tended to assign secondary importance to social and cultural forms as such, to view them as secondary features to be set aside rather than as essential components of human existence. To say that "it doesn't really matter" whether one is man or woman, black or white, Protestant or Catholic seems commendable as a moral rejection of racial, sexual, or religious prejudice. But it also tacitly devalues those particular ways of being human, and may conceal tendencies to equate the "core" with one's own cultural, racial, and gender identity and to regard other identities as secondary—and second rate.

Recently this set of assumptions has been undergoing a correction (Augsburger, 1986; Glaz and Moessner, 1991; Graham, 1992; Wimberly, 1991). Differences of gender, race, social class, generation, and ethnicity now receive considerable didactic and supervisory attention in many educational programs, and often constitute the principal focus of case analysis and pastoral response. In this newer view, what is most profoundly true, real, and relevant to religious ministry may not be what is most general or universal among human beings but what is most particular, indigenous, and different. Moreover, this perspective explicitly recognizes the power of institutions and traditions to shape personhood at its deepest levels.

3. Priority of Personal Needs over Institutional Needs. The clinical pastoral movement has emphasized the difference between the personal needs of individuals and the needs and agendas of institutions (including the church) of which individuals are a part, which make claims of belief, conduct, time, energy, and money on them. Both individual and institutional needs are important and must be tended to, but modern pastoral care and counseling has sought, on principle, to avoid confusing them. In situations of intense personal need, institutional agendas often appropriately need to be subordinated to personal needs. Institutional agendas can be relevant in caring for individual needs and problems, but they can also be asserted in ways that ignore or do violence to personal needs in given situations.

The secular institutional setting in which most pastoral care and counseling education has occurred has enabled it to focus almost exclusively on matters of personhood and relationship through its singular attention to one role function of ministry (pastoral care) with relatively little attention to those functions that more directly represent collective, institutional claims and agendas, such as administration, finance, liturgy, preaching, and education. This arrangement has given clinical pastoral education great intensity and power, allowing students to make mistakes and to develop their own caring capacities experientially. But it has also given students relatively few opportunities to integrate care and counseling with ministry's role responsibilities that more explicitly represent institutional claims on individuals. Moreover, the emotional power of clinical programs may induce some students to believe that personal care and counseling constitutes the most authentic expression of ministry, and it may foster a narrowly pietistic view of the "true church" as a community of intimate interpersonal relations free of issues of power, authority, organizational needs, and authoritative rituals and traditions.

4. Priority of the Ordinary Experience and Language over Religious Experience and Language. The modern pastoral care movement has affirmed the appropriateness of pastoral involvement in virtually every kind of problem, religious or secular, that involves human beings in personal ways. CPE and pastoral counseling students are encouraged to discover deep meaning in the most ordinary and seemingly insignificant human experiences. All of life thus becomes potentially sacred, and seemingly secular experiences can acquire profound religious meaning. This conviction contrasts with those of earlier periods in which pastors and parishioners were assumed, by and large, to engage each other properly only on matters of faith and morals, or on problems like illness and mental disorders perceived strictly from a moral or religious perspective.

This theme in clinical pastoral care and counseling may be viewed as a continuing expression of the Protestant understanding of vocation in which secular work is valued equally with ordained ministry or religious vocation. It testifies to the encompassing grace of God for all of life and liberates faith and ministry from religious and clerical ghettos. But when the dividing line between sacred and secular is minimal and ambiguous, everything may be sacred—or nothing—and faith issues can easily be deferred or not dealt with at all (Pruyser, 1976). The traditional ritual actions of pastoral care—prayer, sacrament, the reading of scripture— may decline in importance and frequency, and the fusing of the sacred-secular distinction may end up not liberating the pastor so much as confusing his or her symbolic identity and sense of purpose.

5. Priority of the Student's Evaluation and Appropriation of the Religious

Tradition over the Tradition's Institutional and Traditional Authority. Pastoral formation is conceived as the integration of person and tradition. It is achieved when there is a psychological integration of the religious tradition and the person of the pastor that is evident in the way the student practices ministry. Thus, for example, pastors who have a quarrel with their tradition's official theology are required to deal with their questions openly and either change themselves or their understanding of the tradition (or both). The emphasis on integrating person and tradition in clinical pastoral education represents a powerful enhancement of ministry, liberating it from narrow or conflicted theological thinking and stereotyped role performance, and investing it with a deep sense of personal appropriation and authority. It does not—as is sometimes maintained—inevitably substitute a psychotherapeutic orientation for the student's theology or theory of ministry.

However, the process of personal integration does tend implicitly to subordinate the authority of religious tradition to the student's personal evaluation and appropriation. One is expected to take the tradition seriously—but not submissively. In recent years, under the impact of feminism and other forms of radical tradition criticism, this emphasis has become even more marked. The older clinical tradition assumed a consensus concerning the value of the tradition and "which tradition" was of value, leaving to the student the problem of coming to terms with it. Recent opinion questions the normativity of the dominant tradition itself and challenges its authority in the name of ethical principles or the claims of other, suppressed religious expressions of it (e.g., related to black or feminine experience).

Such "tradition criticism" in pastoral education enlivens the student's awareness of the importance of tradition and presses for a greater critical seriousness in relating to it; it also stimulates creativity in the attempt to form new, superior versions of the received tradition. At the same time it can elevate the authority of individual judgment and experience above all tradition and institutional authority, relieving the student of the important integrative task of coming to terms with the formative power of any established, authoritative tradition.

THE EMERGING TRADITION AND ITS FUTURE

Under the impact of contextual and social concerns, pastoral care and counseling's operational theological tradition is now at a point where—

to use Charles Gerkin's image—the field is beginning to "widen its horizons." We see four such points, each with promising beginnings and as yet unfulfilled hopes.

1. Care for Systems and Communities as Well as for Individuals. The operating tradition of modern pastoral care has focused primarily on the care and counseling of individuals, though an understanding of organizations and systems, of group dynamics and leadership, and the transferability of clinical learning to corporate contexts has been a part of most CPE for many years. Early CPE sought to develop the relationship between the small interpersonal group and the larger ecclesial and secular systems of which that group is a part, and Seward Hiltner (1958) made a theoretical beginning in this direction with his "organizing perspective." Recently, however, systems thinking is coming forward as a prominent feature of the field. Edwin Friedman (1985) and Larry Graham (1992), among others, have used family therapy theory and practice to assist pastors in dealing with ecclesial, social, political, and economic systems. A recent practical expression of the systems orientation is the emerging emphasis on enabling lay caregiving in the faith community (Patton, 1993). These new directions not only broaden participation in caregiving; they reorient the pastor from being the "official" caregiver to facilitating and guiding the caregiving of a community. And they may indicate a shift in the field's underlying assumptions about the church—its ecclesiology—from an individualistic-interpersonal model to a more organic-institutional one.

However, there is a further aspect of social systemic process that the field has only begun to engage seriously, having to do with the power and authority that larger systems normally exercise over smaller ones. All groups and organizations make claims on their participants that eventually come into tension with individual needs, wishes, and rights. Thus to care for systems means that the community's claims must at times be supported and asserted over the claims and wishes of individuals. Striking pastoral examples of the need for asserting the priority of larger systems can be seen in situations of family violence and clergy sex abuse, when a need clearly exists for firm discipline as a context for therapeutic care and counsel. The field needs to devise practical means for asserting and adjudicating such conflicts constructively, not merely punitively, and needs to create more sophisticated understandings of how individual welfare is intimately connected to the systemic and institutional welfare of groups and communities. The moral language of commitment, loyalty, responsibility, obligation, and devotion, long neglected in pastoral care, also needs to be critically reappropriated as part of this task.

2. *Concern for Theory and Principle as Well as for Practice and Function.* Early in the modern tradition the dominant pedagogical concern of the field was to break away from theory-bound educational methods of the seminary classroom. This often led to an unfortunate opposition between theory and practice in the field. In the emerging pastoral care and counseling tradition today, theory and practice, however, are growing closer; there has been a turn back toward defining and developing the theoretical base of the pastoral care movement. The *Dictionary of Pastoral Care and Counseling* (1990), for instance, has been important in making a claim about what is and what is not included in the field and how that theoretical base might be organized. Don Browning's work in practical theology and ethics also has drawn theory and practice closer together through his argument that practical thinking is at the heart of all thinking and that theoretical and technical thinking are abstractions from it (Browning, 1991). Hermeneutical theory in the work of Winquist, Gerkin, and Capps, and the concern with methods of pastoral theological reflection in the work of the Whiteheads (1980), Poling and Miller (1985), Kinast (1993), Patton (1993), and others, further express this growing rapprochement. Moreover, while for many years clinical supervisors have asked for theological reflection on case studies and verbatims, recently it has become an important emphasis.

Nonetheless the field as a whole still needs to move from these promising beginnings into sustained theological reflection. Can pastoral theology contribute, for example—beyond its concern to develop "theologies of pastoral care"—to theological anthropology, soteriology, and ecclesiology? Can it also develop distinctively pastoral theologies of faith, hope, and love—or sexuality, power, and death?

3. *Contextual Particularities as Well as Broad Visions of What Is Essentially Human.* As pastoral care and counseling has become an international movement, both professors and practitioners have discovered the extent to which clinical education in care and counseling is culturally bound (Augsburger, 1986; Hall, 1989; Kleinman, 1988). But how many contextual grids need to be taken into account in order to do responsible pastoral care and pastoral care education? We are perhaps most aware of gender, race, and power as contextual issues, but an important part of the development of clinical skill in the pastoral care of the future will be determining criteria (including theological criteria) for judging con-

textual relevance. What aspects of culture are theologically critical in the theory, pedagogy, and practice of pastoral care and counseling, and *why*?

4. Further Extension of the Clinical Method into Congregations. Increasingly, the training of laity in clinical methods (like the popular Stephen Ministry program) has led to an increased openness in congregations to understanding themselves as "teaching parishes," a trend that will continue to grow. But how will the use of congregations for training in pastoral care change the content and style of clinical education and its internal "operative theology"? The congregational context is likely to have a deep impact on the educational method, opening new possibilities (e.g., the analysis of congregational systems and cultures) and limiting or eliminating others (e.g., the intense and continuous exposure to crisis of hospital-based CPE programs). Clearly, gains and losses are both involved. But fundamental, and ultimately theological, questions emerge: What do we basically expect the clinical method to accomplish? What constitutes its essential, nonnegotiable core? What should be the "essence" of pastoral care and counseling?

CONCLUSION

Will the emerging field give the old liberal and pietist traditions yet another "spin" comparable to the one given them by the therapeutic psychologies sixty years ago? Will the four emerging directions we have identified—the emphasis on systems, theory construction, cultural particularity, and congregational settings—turn pastoral care and counseling away from the dominance of psychology toward the more dominant use of social and cultural perspectives?

Such a redirection would clearly entail a change in the field's underlying theology, such as a renewed consideration of divine transcendence and the authority of traditions and institutions to claim and shape individual experience. It would also call for an emphasis on "doing" or "praxis" over "experience," and on enacting faith in community. The new theology is therefore also likely to have important points of contact with liberation theology (Chopp and Parker, 1990; Graham, 1992). Obviously, it cannot be said at this time how far such developments may go. But clearly a great ferment is occurring in the pastoral care field that involves its deepest historical convictions and value commitments.

Undoubtedly this ferment reflects the social and cultural struggles of the larger church and society. In particular, there seems to be a general need in our time for more viable and cohesive social structures (families, communities, churches, institutions) capable of tempering and managing social conflict and violence in humane and gracious ways. The moral challenge in this situation is whether attempts to rebuild social order and authority will be achieved by combining and balancing a gracious concern for individuals with concern for the necessary and appropriate needs of collectivities, or, negatively, by coercive and repressive means. Pastoral care's roots in pietistic liberalism and the therapeutic psychologies, if expanded and reoriented as suggested here, may provide a small but gracious leavening of our social loaf, softening harsh authoritarianism of the left and right and tempering our culture's excessive individualism. It may thereby open new possibilities for human beings to flourish as individuals in just and loving communities.

CHAPTER 3

The Future of Pastoral Care and Counseling and the God of the Market

Pamela D. Couture and Richard Hester

Pastoral care in all its forms is the priests' real instrument of power, particularly over the workaday world, and it influences the conduct of life most powerfully when religion has achieved an ethical character.
(Max Weber, Sociology of Religion, *75)*

As we prepare for the twenty-first century, psychological questions are giving way to economic ones. Once economic language belonged only to the economists and a few wealthy families, but now ordinary men and women discuss the economy on the airwaves, in popular magazines, and around the kitchen table. Some individuals still believe that the economy is the narrow gate of opportunity through which a game of entrepreneurship should be played, risked, won, and lost. Many others, however, experience the economy as if it were an arbitrary boss who wields his power regardless of his effect on others. Ordinary people are increasingly vocal about their awareness that the economy influences all of us.

Chaplains and counselors once discovered that they relied on psychologies which were laden with questionable theological assumptions. We will argue that theological beliefs are embedded in economic thought and practice. If that is true, how might pastoral care and counseling develop a critical perspective on these assumptions? And how might pastoral care and counseling maintain and practice its theological vision?

THE ROLE OF PASTORAL CARE IN TWENTIETH-CENTURY CULTURE

Although the biological sciences ruled with authority in the late 1800s, psychology came to dominate American culture early in the twentieth century. As our civil religion, psychology's assumptions are woven into the very fabric of our commonly held beliefs. Its texts and rituals are easily accessible on television, in the news media, and in books. Basic beliefs about personal self-esteem and families of origin are often better known to church people than the stories of scripture. Psychology's spokespersons are legitimate conversation partners in most social institutions (Rieff, 1968; Bellah, 1985; Tillich, 1984).

Max Weber's observation about the power of pastoral care proved prophetic for the twentieth century. The tradition of clinical pastoral education, and then of pastoral counseling, contributed to and was shaped by psychology's rise to power. Since psychology offered creative new ways of exploring what had traditionally been theological and philosophical questions, the fathers and mothers of clinical pastoral education had the foresight to plumb this new psychology for its benefits to religion.

Chaplaincy and early explorations into psychology grew in an atmosphere of continued hope for progress and change through social institutions. Two world wars, however, took a heavy toll on ideas of human progress. In the wake of this disillusionment, a philosophical and cultural turn to the individual occurred. This turn was expressed in a growing interest in psychology and psychotherapy that focused on the intrapsychic world of the individual. When the fathers of pastoral counseling began to explore how psychology might become a new frontier in theological education, church ministry, and institutional ministries, they became innovators in seminaries, hospitals, and social agencies.

Chaplaincy and pastoral counseling established themselves in a cultural and economic climate which fostered state expansion of social institutions, such as public hospitals, prisons, and the military. Chaplains and the clinical pastoral education (CPE) students they supervised became professional allies of the clinical staff of hospitals. As institutional

45

support for chaplains grew, chaplains were able to care for indigent persons beyond the reach of local churches.

Pastoral counselors proliferated as people increasingly believed in "therapy" as a practice which not only cured illnesses but also enriched personal and spiritual growth. This belief grew in a robust national economy. Free-standing centers could support themselves through middle-class church contributions and client fees. These centers were hard pressed, however, to fulfill the ethical mandate of ministry, which called upon them to provide pastoral counseling for all, regardless of the client's ability to pay.

Subsequent to these origins, practitioners of pastoral care and counseling fought their way from the margins of culture, society, and religion toward their centers. In the process, pastoral care and counseling became increasingly legitimate as a participant in the medical hospital, the local community, the state, and the economy. It did so primarily by demonstrating its competence in the field of medical psychotherapy.

THE SACRED CANOPY OF MEDICINE

Early experiments in pastoral care and chaplaincy began in medical hospitals. One of the principal pioneers of clinical pastoral education was a medical practitioner, the other a mental patient. Richard Cabot, medical director at Harvard Medical School, sought a more wholistic approach to healing than the developing scientific medical model allowed. Anton Boisen, a patient at Elgin State Hospital, wanted to convince the medical community that spiritual as well as psychological forces were moving in his mental illness and healing. Chaplains won acceptance in the medical setting by demonstrating their competence in scientific clinical assessment and treatment.

Pastoral counseling emerged from chaplaincy as a distinct example of the scientific approach to what had previously been called "the care of souls." As such, pastoral counseling demonstrated competence in a medical model of therapy. This model is characterized by the following features, derived from psychology and psychoanalytic theory: a therapeutic contract between the client and the therapist that involves the payment of a fee for therapeutic time; a secure setting in which the privacy of the client is ensured; a therapist who is identified as "a trained, socially sanctioned healer," that is, one who has the credentials that certify his or her training and competence to do therapy; a structured sequence of scheduled, time-limited contacts in which the therapist "tries to relieve a sufferer's distress by facilitating certain changes in his feelings, attitudes, and behavior, through the performance of certain activities" (Frank, 165).

This model moved chaplains and counselors away from the sacred canopy of the congregation. In adopting this model, chaplains and pastoral counselors risked the "plausibility structure" that originally gave them legitimacy as a ministry of the church. Peter Berger points out that "religious traditions . . . require specific communities for their continuing plausibility" (Berger, 46). When separated from the ecclesial community, a religious tradition or practice loses its "plausibility" as a distinctly religious expression. As chaplaincy and pastoral counseling sought recognition under the sacred canopy of medical psychotherapy, its plausibility as a distinctly theological enterprise eroded.

SEPARATION OF PASTORAL CARE FROM THE WORSHIPING COMMUNITY

In the four decades after the end of World War II, training in pastoral care and counseling helped prepare ministers for more effective parish work. Many competent persons, however, who had advanced training in pastoral care and counseling moved away from the local church. In this relocation, pastoral care and counseling had an unexpected encounter with economics.

Before the emergence of psychologically and psychiatrically informed pastoral care and counseling, the arts of pastoral care and counseling were practiced by the parish minister who, in this country, was always dependent on the congregation for support. This economic contract between the minister, the congregation, and the larger church structure was negotiated and maintained, therefore, as a part of the congregation's life of word and sacrament, of teaching and service. Although care was often superficial or moralistic, doing pastoral care and counseling in the congregation provided a framework for a theologically informed vision of reality and a transforming experience of word and sacrament for pastor and counselee, particularly in the experience of worship.

As pastoral care and counseling split off from the congregation, some chaplains and pastoral counselors developed a different structure of accountability and an alternate vision of reality. This relocation offered parishioners a private place, a pure environment which could facilitate their healing. Furthermore, souls beyond the reach of congregations could be cared for. Removing severe human struggle from congregational life, however, meant that congregations less often had to grapple with the intense pain of their neighbors. As a result, the congregation's theological vision of humanity may have been distorted. Likewise, pastoral care and counseling practitioners tended to confuse their psychological and theological visions. As pastoral care and counseling became less connected to the support of the local congregation, it became more vulnerable to the economic organization which was developing in hospital medicine and medical psychotherapy.

THE ECONOMIC INFLUENCE OF THE MEDICAL MODEL

As pastoral care and counseling sought legitimacy in medical institutions and in the practice of therapy outside the church, it became further covered by the sacred canopy of medicine. During this time medicine evolved from an art distinguished by a discerning relationship between doctor and patient into a product of the health care industry sold and consumed according to the industry's economic assumptions. As these economic constraints increasingly controlled the practice of medicine, they also shaped the practice of pastoral care and counseling.

In our society, economic assumptions have been transmuted into theological ones. The laws of a market economy have become ultimate governing principles, akin to a theological creed. Douglas Meeks, in *God the Economist: The Doctrine of God and Political Economy,* characterizes this creed. The economic market is self-regulating and seeks a natural economic equilibrium. Natural laws governing this equilibrium can be discovered in society; they cannot be developed by human beings. The market reconciles self-interest with rational order and overcomes despotism. Market laws can best regulate human passions. Distribution of income, allocation of resources, and economic growth can be brought about by market laws without coercion. Human behavior is controlled by the market without domination or exploitation (Meeks, 51).

The economic creed suggests that people deliberately and freely pursue their self-interest in the market. The outcome of these decisions cannot be predicted, because market forces are automatic, unconscious, mechanistic, and unintended. The market becomes the mysterious, transcendent, numinous other. As such, the market transcends the state, the church, and the family as the ultimate source of authority.

Those persons who hold strictly to this economic creed contend that altruistic behavior toward persons in need inhibits the economic processes that will eventually benefit the most people. The common good, they argue, will not be achieved by allowing our perceptions of the needs of others to govern economic decisions. One should not try to meet needs directly but rather follow the abstract laws of the market. The largest number of people will benefit from the laws of the market if all people follow the principle of self-interest, act truthfully in social transactions, keep their promises, and respect the property of others.

The proponents of this market creed also view with concern theological beliefs that call for care of the poor, because these beliefs lead one to act contrary to market laws. Actions based on such beliefs risk upsetting delicate market processes, leading to social consequences so adverse as to negate the benefit of any theologically driven intervention on behalf of the poor.

CARE, COUNSELING, AND THE ECONOMIC CREED

Presently, the economic creed threatens to exact subtle but ultimate loyalty from pastoral care and counseling, just as the scientific creed once did. Economic legitimacy promotes the survival of specialized pastoral care and counseling; religious legitimacy may lead to its demise. Furthermore, economic law mandates profitable practice; religious law expects practitioners to minister regardless of financial gain.

When religious practitioners in private hospitals and centers negotiate with their administrators and boards, they frequently face a mindset shaped by economic interests. Formerly, practitioners in private hospitals had to legitimate themselves to the powerful medical profession; now they must convince economic powerbrokers of their right to exist. Administrators who govern the budgets of large institutions and the fund-raising boards of private centers may more easily understand the economic creed than the guiding principles of good pastoral care and counseling.

Pastoral counselors in many counseling centers, like medical psychotherapists, are often directly dependent upon fees from clients for their livelihood. The pastoral counselor experiences the ebb and flow of referrals, the client's ability to pay, and third-party payments. Because society seems determined by economic laws, the pastoral counselor must become an entrepreneur who follows the creed of the market. Successful pastoral counselors must be competent at marketing and selling their services to the public by means of appropriate advertising, effective public relations, building a network of relationships that can serve as a referral base, attracting and keeping clients who can afford to pay the fees necessary to provide an adequate income, being prudent business-persons, and securing available state credentials as therapists. As pastoral counseling tries to compete for legitimacy, funding, and clients in a world of licensing, insurance reimbursement, and litigation, it finds itself further from the sacred canopy of the church and inside that of the medical industry and state regulation.

ECONOMIC OR RELIGIOUS LEGITIMACY?

The sacred canopy of medical industry and state regulation has proved to be a risky shelter for chaplains and pastoral counselors, largely because pastoral counselors and chaplains exist on the margin between church and state. As states cut their budgets, public chaplains have become expendable. "How many sermons can they preach anyway?" one public official was heard to comment about the chaplains who were dismissed in the Georgia budget reductions. Likewise, in a society beset with out-of-control medical costs, pastoral counselors are rarely considered legitimate providers. Insurance companies fail to recognize that religious credentialing processes, such as those required by the American Association of Pastoral Counselors, produce a legitimate type of therapeutic specialist. Even so, as religious practitioners pastoral counselors have generally resisted involving themselves in political processes such as lobbying for state recognition.

Even though the economic creed exerts its influence on them, chaplaincy and pastoral counseling will remain on the margin of the sacred canopy of the medical industry as long as they are rooted in religion. This marginality may act as a thorn in the side of a chaplain or counselor, a reminder of religious values and identity in an otherwise economically structured world. Or it may so threaten the survival of the chaplain or counselor that it leaves him or her more willing to blindly adopt the economic creed as ultimate. It may also offer a chaplain or counselor the opportunity and the freedom to create enclaves of care which are not fully controlled either by the status quo of the church or that of the medical industry.

THE MARKET VIEW OF GOD

The creativity of the twentieth-century movement of pastoral care and counseling developed because it risked dealing with the god of psychology. After immersing itself in the wisdom of psychology, pastoral care and counseling began to gain some critical distance as the religious dimensions of the psychologies were uncovered and as human science itself was criticized as being less value-neutral than it once appeared (Browning, 1987). Now it finds itself increasingly enmeshed in an economic world view that makes claims that are as ultimate as those psychology once made.

According to Meeks, orthodox economics has no place for a view of God or a transcendent realm, yet it speaks of a level of reality beyond what can be empirically explored. It points to hidden forces that control the market mechanism.

> These "forces" are like the *deus absconditus*. They are known somewhat in the way the God of the cosmological and teleological proofs was known, that is, by argument from effects in the drives and institutions of the business world to their presumed cause. . . . Neoclassical economists speak of these forces as religious people speak of the numinous, for these mostly unexamined premises entail a "transcendent" destination of capital not of its own making. Though they must be held on faith, economists are sure of the allegiances of thought and action required by these God concepts. These forces or structures or laws reside, unalterably, in human nature. (Meeks, 65)

Economic orthodoxy holds that the market is free of God. The working of the market, however, depends on conceptions once applied to God but now viewed as immutable characteristics of the human being. The attributes given human beings in this process are drawn from God concepts that have been used to reinforce patterns of social domination. The image of God in market "theology" justifies the limitless power that human beings derive from the process of accumulation in a market society. Describing this process, Meeks identifies three God-economy correlations.

1. God as all powerful. In precapitalist economies God is viewed as an all-powerful being. Classical theology defined God as infinite, immutable, indivisible, immortal, independent, and self-sufficient. This God had

51

no needs and was incapable of suffering. These are attributes of domination that can be found at the heart of many economic theories. "God as absolute 'owner of the world' is a theological key to Western politics down to the seventeenth century and in a hidden way remains a key to economics in our time" (Meeks, 67). These dominative attributes of God have been used to defend slavery, patriarchy, and racial oppression.

2. *Elimination of God in the market revolution.* In order to have a market economy, the all-powerful God had to be eliminated, and the attributes once applied to God were ascribed to human nature. These attributes have entered into an anthropology in which some human beings are justifiably allowed to gain power in their market activity. The "invisible forces" of the market are, in fact, the needs and drives of human nature (Meeks, 69-70).

3. *The God who is beyond economics.* The God who is against all forms of domination and who suffers with those who have no power stands over against the "theologies" that underlie the market economy. This God is expressed in the church's doctrine of the trinity. This God is not the patron of those who succeed in accumulating wealth but is the friend of the dispossessed (Meeks, 71-72).

Twentieth-century pastoral care has generally rejected the all-powerful, remote god in favor of an image of a God who is intimately present with the sufferer. Care and counseling understands God as radically immanent, accepting, and graceful. While concentrating on the notion that God is present in humanity, however, it is an easy step across a chasm to the belief that God *is* humanity. We begin to lose sight of the God who has been central to pastoral care and counseling—God with humanity. Above all, we fail to recognize the God who stands over against, in judgment of humanity. All three God images are necessary if pastoral care and counseling is to be a friend of the dispossessed.

CARE AND THE DISPOSSESSED

Economic orthodoxy deems those who cannot pay to be less worthy of service than those who can, because the poor have not justified themselves within the terms of the economic laws. Pastoral care and counseling, as it moves toward economic orthodoxy, is forced to practice the economic creed of caring for those who can pay and ignoring those who cannot. A pastoral counselor who is required to live by economic law but whose identity is rooted in pastoral practice is thrown into a conflict between two opposing world views.

As we seek to keep our balance while the ground of our practice rumbles under our feet, we learn ways in which our house was built on rock or sand. The rock: We know how to be good at middle-class, growth-oriented pastoral care; we know how to counsel people in extreme life crises; we know how to care for the hospitalized and their families and legitimate ourselves with the hospital staff, if not with the bureaucrats. The sand: We never were very good at caring for the poor, the person of color, the person in extreme life crises who couldn't afford specialized counseling, the out-patient or the person quickly released from the hospital, and we have rarely attempted to articulate the interaction between the people for whom we care and the political, economic, and social conditions in which they live. We are very good at middle-class care in a middle-class economy, but as economic orthodoxy threatens and the middle-class shrinks, we face a choice: Care for fewer people, those who still fall within our established systems, or create practices that help us respond to increasing numbers of people who are otherwise likely to fall through the widening cracks.

How can we extend God's care to the most vulnerable in our midst, to those who cannot pay as well as to those who can? Chaplains have traditionally answered this question by using their institutional support to care for all persons regardless of economic status. Now we wonder whether the poor will have chaplains at all. Pastoral counselors have devised a series of responses to this problem. Some individual counselors in private practice designate a percentage of their time to clients who can pay only a little. Some well-established centers corporately underwrite satellites, which could not otherwise maintain economic self-sufficiency, or provide counseling subsidies from endowment or other sources. Some counselors participate in a pastoral counseling social concerns network, which brings larger social questions into dialogue with pastoral counseling.

These practices are creative and laudable. They also risk becoming additions to the pastoral counselor's central responsibility, fee-for-service counseling, without necessarily providing the range of support services the counselor needs when working with those who cannot pay. Present economic realities make additions to pastoral counseling a recipe for burn-out. The pastoral counselor who too long contemplates both the realities of increasingly strict economic structuring of the practice and the prophetic call of ministry to the poor may begin to feel great sympathy with the cubism of Picasso: the image of a self increasingly fragmented under forces which threaten to pull it apart.

TRANSCENDING THE GOD OF ECONOMICS

The God revealed in the prophetic tradition of the Judeo-Christian faith is a God of reversal. This God brings the powerful down and lifts up the powerless. Jesus revealed this God to be one who turns accepted economics on its head. This God becomes known in situations of suffering and oppression. Is it far-fetched to believe that this God can equip us to participate in the reversal of our social captivity to the economic creed? In counseling rooms and beside hospital beds we offer a message of trust, hope, and acceptance for those who experience betrayal, despair, and rejection. These reversals, however, are too often limited to intrapsychic, interpersonal, and familial conditions. We rarely try to understand these reversals in the larger institutional context of the church, hospital, or counseling center, much less in the society at large.

While pastoral caregivers and counselors do live in an economically structured world and must contend with economic circumstances, they cannot derive the mission and ministry of pastoral care and counseling from the god of economics. Pastoral care and counseling can still contend that God, not the gods of psychology or economics, deserves ultimate loyalty. If pastoral care and counseling is confident in this witness, its practitioners can respond to the interplay of theology, psychology, and economics in a variety of ways.

Some practitioners may minister at the margins of institutions, subverting and challenging economic forces.

Some practitioners may experiment with a closer relationship with congregations.

Some practitioners may become more actively involved in political participation, offering insights from pastoral care and counseling when society is being reorganized.

Some practitioners may experiment with state systems of care such as public health, taking particular heed of systems that are conduits of care to the underserved.

As did the fathers and mothers of pastoral care and counseling, might we remember our God as we become creative experimenters in a changing time?

PART II
SELECTED ISSUES

CHAPTER 4

Single Parents and Poverty:
A Challenge to Pastoral Theological
Method

Pamela D. Couture

Single parents and their children, we know, are particularly vulnerable to poverty. But there is no consensus in public policy or
religious thinking as to how this vulnerability is to be understood
or responded to. Indeed, a sharp debate has arisen both in the church
and in society having direct impact on pastoral theory and practice. In
this debate, the logic we employ to think about single parents and their
children is determined by the pastoral theological methods we choose.
In what follows, I will suggest that the debate over the vulnerability of
single parents and their children to poverty is far from value-free. Rather,
it is governed by unstated assumptions that constitute "faith worlds" for
two competing logics that are likely to structure the debate for years to
come. Because this debate is about faith in the guise of social science,
pastoral theologians will need to make several methodological choices
in assessing the theories and perspectives involved. In addition, pastoral
theology may help to mediate between these assumptive worlds. It offers
a language that appreciates the human condition of single parents and
their children and, therefore, may be useful in creating strategies for
their care.

SINGLE PARENTING: THE TERMS OF THE DEBATE

Increasing poverty among women and children was one of the tragic stories of the 1980s. Books and articles that told that story described how poverty among women and children of lower classes was increasing in poor communities. This problem became compounded by poverty among women and children in middle and upper classes as the divorce rate rose. The strategy to reduce the poverty of women and children in lower-class communities, according to many analysts of poverty such as William Julius Wilson, was identical to the strategy to reduce the poverty of men in those communities: Create jobs for men and women in communities hard hit by the decline of manufacturing, the flight of the middle class from the cities, and general economic decline (Wilson, 1987). The strategy to reduce the poverty of women and children in middle-class and upper-middle-class communities, according to analysts of divorce, lay in finding more equitable terms of divorce regarding housing, child support, and other assets of marriage. When the discussion entered church and theology, women of color took white feminists to task for emphasizing the problems of divorce in a way that obscured the economic decline of historically poor communities, especially African American communities in the inner city.

In *Blessed Are the Poor? Women's Poverty, Family Policy, and Practical Theology* (Couture, 1991*a*), I addressed this debate with three goals in mind. I wanted to show that if we reread the classic theological sources for references to poor women and children, we would discover that theological reflection on the poverty of women and children had actually changed the structure of theological thought. I also wanted to render explicit many theological assumptions that are hidden in public policy, and I wanted to clarify the theological grounds for the kind of social interdependence which, if we believed in it, would warrant such social supports for single parents and for all families. Finally, I wanted to help pastors and laity to understand single parents as subjects, rather than as objects of ministry.

In the few years since the publication of *Blessed Are the Poor?* the terms of the debate about single parenting have shifted significantly. The central focus is no longer poverty but family structure. On the far right, a few argue for the mother-homemaker, father-breadwinner model, but even the religious right recognizes the endurance of a variety of family forms. On the far left, few voices would now anticipate that the family will be absorbed into communal structures. Groups discussed in my book, while often represented as the extreme left, now regard family structure as one factor among many that determine a child's happiness. They demonstrate possibilities and pitfalls in different family structures (Coontz, 1992; Edelman, 1987; Kahn and Kamerman, 1975; Sidel, 1990; Stacey, 1991). A new, increasingly politically powerful point of view argues that single parenting is largely responsible for changes in the social and economic well-being of children. (Gallston, 1991; Popenoe, 1988; B. Whitehead, 1993). For this group, the best anti-poverty program is an intact nuclear family.

Researchers and commentators from both groups genuinely seek good outcomes for children and even have policy agendas that overlap. Yet their disagreement is emotional and nearly irreconcilable. By analyzing their assumptions regarding social science, individualism and parenting, public policy, rhetoric, and gender, we can account for the tenor of the debate by characterizing the two positions as two "faith worlds" to which the adherents gravitate out of a sense of generic trust. (Fowler, 1986). By rendering explicit the underlying assumptions of these "faith worlds," I hope to clarify some of the methodological choices pastoral theologians can make.

THE "TRUTHS" OF SOCIAL SCIENCE

Pastoral care in the second half of the twentieth century has depended on the insights of psychology to help describe the human condition, and it has rarely been required to justify the use of this social science over against others. As theoreticians of pastoral care make increasing use of sociological analysis, they will need to choose the social science methods that best illumine the subject they are studying. In the debate over single parenting, the two sides are divided by different epistemologies, or ways of determining truth, which are hidden in alternate sociological methods.

The new analysis places faith in knowledge gained by large-scale statistics and aggregate sociological trends. In one of the most articulate summaries of the new position, Barbara Defoe Whitehead begins with a litany of woes of the problems of children of single parents:

> Children in families disrupted by divorce and out-of-wedlock birth do worse than children in intact families on several measures of well-being. Children in single-parent families are six times as likely to be poor. They are also likely to stay poor longer. Twenty-two percent of children in one-parent families

will experience poverty during childhood for seven years or more, as compared with only two percent of children in two-parent families. A 1988 survey by the National Center for Health Statistics found that children in single-parent families are two to three times as likely as children in two-parent families to have emotional and behavioral problems. They are also more likely to drop out of high school, to get pregnant as teenagers, to abuse drugs, and to be in trouble with the law. Compared with children in intact families, children from disrupted families are at a much higher risk for physical or sexual abuse. (B. Whitehead, 1993, 47)

These conclusions are taken from large-scale statistics, controlled only for family structure. To challenge the truth of these trends on the basis of individual cases commits the fallacy of the "clinical veto," according to David Blankenhorn of the Institute for American Values, and creates dangerously misleading impressions. In my experience, when researchers who most trust aggregate trends do ethnographic studies, the subjects of study are likely to be determined by prior conclusions based on large-scale trends. For example, when aggregate statistics predetermine that two-parent families are better than single-parent families, researchers are likely to study couple-headed families of any family structure while single parents are left out of the sample.

In contrast, commentators who begin with a case-study approach to studying families, who infer aggregate trends from case studies, or who control for a series of variables in quantitative studies, invariably draw different conclusions from those of the other group. For example, Judith Stacey, in her ethnographic study of two families, demonstrates the possibility of a far greater continuum between the problems of "intact nuclear families" and female-headed households (Stacey, 1990) than the other analysis would uncover. Ruth Sidel, who uses widescale interviewing to test quantitative and qualitative trends, shares her concerns for young women who expect to parent and work on their own, but she suggests many ways to help them achieve their expectations (Sidel, 1990). David Ellwood, who uses less ethnography but controls aggregate statistics for more variables, challenges the notion of the intact family as an anti-poverty program on the basis that two-parent families working at or around minimum wage continue to remain below the poverty line (Ellwood, 1988).

The Search Institute, a Lutheran-based "non-profit organization dedicated to promoting the positive development of children and youth through scientific research, evaluation, consulting, and the development of practical resources," presents perhaps the best comparison to the

Whitehead model. The Search Institute relies heavily on aggregate statistics modified less by case studies than by multiple variables. In a study of 47,000 sixth, seventh, and eighth graders, researchers at the Search Institute concluded that in twenty categories of at-risk behavior (such as frequent alcohol use, binge drinking, daily cigarette use, illicit drug use, sexual activity, depression, suicide, theft, vandalism, school absenteeism, and riding with a drunk driver), children from single-parent homes are more at risk than children from two-parent homes. However, Search researchers also studied the assets of children who thrive in single-parent families over against "non-thrivers." "Thrivers" exhibit one or none of the at-risk behaviors; "non-thrivers" report five or more. Thrivers live in social environments where the assets such as family and school support, supervision, involvement in extracurricular activities, values that exhibit concern for self and others, and social skills, overcome the problems of family structure. Although Search Institute publications begin with a litany of woes similar to Whitehead's, they report substantially different conclusions, as indicated by their headline: "Growing Up in a Single-Parent Family Increases Risks but Doesn't Seal Destiny" (Benson and Roehlkepartain, June 1993).

INDIVIDUALISM AND PARENTING

Individualism is a long-term trend in which the values of freedom and maximizing one's self-interest have been promoted through democracy and capitalism. Early tracts that laid the grounds for democracy and free enterprise as far back as Locke and Rousseau cited the freedom to divorce as a sign of a truly free society. The 1970s saw men and women exercising this freedom in unprecedented numbers, especially as the psychologies of self-expression and personal growth took hold in popular culture. However, while commentators in both assumptive worlds rely on the forces of individualism to explain changes in family structure, they emphasize different aspects of the trend and, as a result, hold different views of the human parent.

Commentators for the new analysis contend that the culture of individualism values personal growth unmediated by other interests, and that families of divorce and out-of-wedlock children have imbibed this ethos. "Married partners are more likely to look to how well marriage serves their individual interests rather than how it increases the likelihood of successful outcomes for children," adherents to this position argue. Since

61

their social scientific epistemology has already led them to believe that children flourish only in two-parent families, they suggest that parents who divorce or bear children out of wedlock are willing to sacrifice their childrens' happiness to their own. Occasional single parents are heroes, but most single parents are guided by their own needs first. While parents in intact families are considered committed and self-sacrificing, parents who divorce or bear children out of wedlock are self-serving.

Commentators who take a more positive position toward single parents do look to the growth of individualism, as buttressed by women's increased self-esteem and economic freedom, as having created changes in family life (Stacey, 1990). They maintain, however, that these are positive aspects of larger trends toward more democratic family styles. Their primary assumption is not that parents are self-serving but that advanced capitalism, from which individualistic premises have been derived, has had a questionable effect on family life. Parents in intact families and single-parent families are united by a common theme: Life in families is marked by struggle. So-called intact families may in fact be subject to substantial turmoil; divorce usually culminates a long period of trying to make a marriage work; and out-of-wedlock parenting often reflects the parents' loss of hope for other possibilities for future achievements. The particular struggle of single parents includes their desire for achievement, including their ambition to support and care for their children. Their potential for realizing this ambition is bounded by minimal job opportunities for some and family-unfriendly workplace conditions for others. In this assumptive world, it is not individual parents who sacrifice children so much as a society whose priorities are determined by power politics.

THE ROLE OF FAMILY POLICY

Both positions urge a heightened role for public policy regarding the family; in fact, they agree on many of the same policy proposals. Both groups support laws requiring the identification of both parents by social security number when children are born, enforcing child support awards in divorce and paternity settlements, creating children's allowances, providing tax credits for families, and improving job opportunities. Their disagreements, however, are based on different philosophies of the role public policy should play in family life.

In the new analysis, the assumption that single parents are self-actualizing individualists leads to the conclusion that family policy should primarily write the script of the cultural values that the United States should promote. The value in this case is the intact family, and public policy should promote this ideal by creating greater institutional supports for marriage and by stigmatizing deviance from the ideal by coercing the behavior of those who do not comply. Therefore, adherents support policy proposals which make divorce more difficult for parents with children, reintroduce fault into divorce proceedings, and offer bonuses to welfare mothers who marry. They attempt to counter the individualism of divorce through such measures as the "Supervow," an agreement supposedly more binding than the marriage covenant. These policy proposals are aimed at deterring divorce and are based on the assumption that divorce could be avoided if parents were less oriented toward their own self-realization needs. These proposals also assume that family life for children will be happier if parents do not divorce, even if the quality of an unhappy marriage is not improved.

Adherents to this view will argue their particular emphasis in family policy on the basis that the family has lost many of its historical functions—the family is no longer the economic, educational, medical center it once was. This reduction in family functions has made families more fragile. Government interventions into family life that support single parents weaken the nuclear family. Therefore, while adherents will argue that government should not intervene in families by taking over family functions such as child care, they in effect argue that government should intervene in families to determine family structure. The underlying logic assumes that married parents make competent family decisions, but single parents, because of their individualistic tendencies, do not.

In contrast, the assumption that parents in intact, binuclear, and single-parent families are struggling leads the other commentators to the view that public policy and government is a way of taking shared responsibility for those who are most in need, regardless of whether they conform to certain cultural ideals of family life. A Children's Defense Fund poster, for example, shows the painting of the signing of the Declaration of Independence with the caption, "These fathers have failed to pay their child support." Adherents to this view assume that there is little wisdom in coercing people into particular family structures but that society does have a stake in being sure that persons and families are cared for. Government coercion is appropriate in family life in order to ensure that those with more assets provide for those with less and to ensure the absence of extreme conflict and violence in all families. The intrinsic complications of divorce and single parenting are themselves adequate deterrents to those who would divorce unneedfully. This group is particularly concerned that single parenting not be restigmatized, as it considers the stereotype of the "broken family" itself to be harmful for children.

Part of the struggle for all families is the fact that family functions have changed so dramatically. True, families no longer educate their children at home, but few people would eliminate teachers and doctors in order to return education and health care to parents. Rather, all parents face the difficulty of making decisions about ways to care for the education or the health of their children. Family life is changed, not weakened, by sharing "family functions" with social systems. In fact, family life is made more complex by the change in the number of social institutions that intersect with family life. This position assumes that government, as a way of sharing responsibility, should ensure that poor, single parents have access to the same support institutions as persons in more affluent families.

THE ROLE OF RHETORIC

Both sides of this debate believe in the power of words. Some persons believe that we socially construct our world by the words we use; others carry the point even farther, arguing that the meanings we attach to our experiences create not only our social worlds but our very selves (Kegan, 1982).

In the new analysis, the rhetoric takes on an apocalyptic edge, with single parenting representing that which is evil and married parenting representing that which is good. Single parenting threatens our national security and the very foundations of Western civilization. It is responsible for the evils of contemporary society—crime, poverty, low levels of education, domestic violence (Whitehead, 71, 77). The new rhetoric is actually directed toward reinforcing the behavior of married parents rather than blaming single parents, just as religious rhetoric about election was aimed at the elect not the damned. Those who use apocalyptic rhetoric seem to assume that the family can be saved in the beginning—while parents are still married and rational—if the married public can be scared into believing that single parenting would irreversibly harm their children. Since no words of substance are offered toward those who are already single parents, one is left with the sense that they have already passed through the apocalypse into irredeemable doom.

The analysis that views all parents, but especially single parents, as struggling and needing social support leads to a rhetoric which attempts to be prophetic toward society and pastoral toward families. In both its public and its private forms this rhetoric is marked by empathy. Empathy, as I am using it here, is not "unconditional positive regard," unmediated by reality; rather, it is the ability to find, in public or private, the words which so fully appreciate the reality of another that heart-to-heart contact is made. For instance, "prophetic preaching, at its best, begins in an experience of empathy between the preacher and the congregation—an expression of the way that we are human beings together. Together, we discover something illumining about the human situation when we examine our lives and actions, remembering that they are under the watchful eye of God. The true prophet brings us into a deepened relationship with one another and with God" (Couture, "Teaching," 1991*b*). Empathic rhetoric, in private or in public, attempts to capture the complexities of a situation, as, for example, in this statement by Peter Benson and Eugene Roehlkepartain of the Search Institute:

> If we could wave a magic wand, we would guarantee that every child had two responsible, caring, and committed parents. But given that this won't happen, our challenge is to discover ways to maximize the number of strong, two-parent families while also supporting all families—including single-parent families—in their efforts to raise healthy children. . . . Categorical statements about two-parent families being good and single-parent families being bad overstate the case. True, two-parent families have the edge. Being a single parent is tough work, and it is not optimal for children. But with special effort—and with the support of individuals, communities, and institutions around them—single-parent families can be supportive, healthy families in which young people will thrive. (Benson and Roehlkepartain, 1993)

In contrast to the apocalyptic rhetoric, which pits single parents against married parents in its attempt to reach married parents, this rhetoric is aimed toward single parents and those who want to understand their plight. This rhetoric is pastoral and prophetic toward single parents because it describes a fuller vision of their reality, their struggles, and their attempts to transform their circumstances. This rhetoric offers a way of constructing the world so that single parents, with adequate support, can provide environments within which children can flourish.

DOES THE PROBLEM OF GENDER EXPLAIN THE DIFFERENCE IN THE FAITH WORLDS?

I have sketched two "faith worlds" to which commentators on the family seem to gravitate. In one world, children of single parents do poorly for being in a single-parent family. They are in this situation because their parents put their own happiness before that of the children. This situation might have been avoided if government had enacted policies to deter divorce and out-of-wedlock childbearing or if parents had heeded the warnings of the social scientists. In the other world, most children of single parents may have a more difficult time than most children of two-parent families, but factors within the family, in addition to support institutions within the community, can compensate for the factor of family structure. All parents are having difficulty raising children in this complex world, but single parents may have a more difficult time since they generally have fewer assets. Therefore, they deserve the support of government and the general public.

What if we remove the generic term "parents" and substitute "mothers" and "fathers" in these statements? Although both arguments tend to use generic terms, the first faith world may really be talking about fathers while the second faith world may be talking about mothers.

The first faith world, having heeded the data on "deadbeat dads" in the 1980s, may really believe that *fathers* are the individualists who are seeking their self-interest. They fear two consequences of this trend: that fathers will genuinely abdicate their responsibilities for their sons and daughters, and that mothers will decide that fathers are more trouble than they're worth. Men, becoming detached from the family, will become increasingly unruly, and women, as matriarchs, will become inordinately powerful and further deter the possibility of positive male psychosocial development. Since the goal of this world is to gain a firm place for men within the nuclear family, little attention is paid to the complex ways in which men contribute as single parents to binuclear families.

Furthermore, if this faith world recognized that female-headed single-parent families or lesbian parenting couples could be "good enough" families, they would also need to acknowledge that healthy sons and daughters might actually be raised without men. Individual cases of women who raise children successfully without men must be considered token heroes, not the norm. Because the solution to family dissolution is oriented toward men, its proponents simply have little to say about the continuing struggles of women.

The second faith world is concerned that women will continue to carry the burdens not only for "deadbeat dads" but also for a "deadbeat society." In this world, couple-headed families have many family styles, some of which create parental absence which may be as significant or more significant than that of a single-parent family. Couple-headed families may be destructive rather than constructive, even when such aberrations as extreme physical abuse are not present. Overall, the second faith world believes that *mothers* are the struggling parents. They celebrate intact, happy families parented by women and men. They fear, however, that efforts which rely on intact family structures to remove the burdens of mothers will make it more difficult for women to leave unjust or abusive family situations and will ease the pressure on society to take collective responsibility for its women and children. In a world in which intact families are considered the only normative situation for raising sons and daughters, single mothers and their dependents will remain invisible and will "fall through the cracks." The goal of this faith world is to create an adequate enough safety net to allow single parents to raise their children without undue strain. A "universalized" safety net, which provides benefits to families regardless of family structure, would support original, binuclear, and single-parent families. This analysis is less concerned about women in general than it is about mothers as they are responsible for children.

Both kinds of analysis are replete with statistics documenting the quantities of father absence but rarely offer nuanced descriptions of the qualities of post-divorce or out-of-wedlock fathering. The voluntary contributions of single-parent fathers are too irregular to guarantee the security of single-parent mothers or to make a case for the attachment of fathers to the family. Therefore, neither faith world has a way of fully appreciating the constructive efforts of many men to sustain their connections with their children, even as single, noncustodial parents.

PASTORAL THEOLOGICAL METHOD AND FAMILIES

I have described the faith worlds, or trusted systems of assumptions, underlying two social-scientific positions on the family. Each category of assumptions raises a methodological question for the pastoral theologian. Which form of social science is authoritative for describing the subject? How does the anthropology implicit within the social science correlate with anthropologies suggested by the Christian tradition? What philosophy of public policy is more consistent with the love command-ment? How does the rhetoric of social science call upon the rhetoric of religious traditions, and how might religious traditions criticize how that rhetoric is employed? How might hidden agendas regarding gender (or race, class, geography, and so forth) be deconstructed so that pastoral theology might make suggestions for human flourishing?

Without proper theological language, the "faith worlds" of social science fall short of appreciating the ambiguities of family life. Theologi-cal language points toward a spirituality in family life which may be realized or may only be glimpsed. The absence of spirituality in family life creates a deep void. The kind of language one must call upon to express this spirituality pushes beyond the descriptions of social science to point toward the ambiguity of the family.

The faith worlds of social science, in contrast, lead us to believe that our family life is clearly within our control. The new analysis believes that we can will happy families into being; but even social science that recognizes the contingencies which influence family structure cannot capture the sense of grace and abundance that marks those persons and families who can live with the loss of control which is intrinsic in family life. Family life is marked by birth, death, loss, and life-stage transitions, all of which lie more or less beyond the control of one or more adults. From a theological perspective, loss of control does not mean the absence of responsibility for those things we can change. Rather, respon-sibility, as H. Richard Niebuhr suggests, involves a discriminating judg-ment of what is good, right, and fitting in concrete situations (Niebuhr, 1978). This understanding of responsibility would counsel us to incor-porate those aspects of family life we can change with those aspects of family life beyond our influence.

When the faith worlds of social science lead us to believe that we can control family life, they lead us into distorted understandings of human brokenness. The new analysis suggests that human brokenness should not exist; when brokenness occurs, no grace is available to help people move into new forms of wholeness. Likewise, the analysis that wishes to encourage persons in a variety of family structures may be reluctant to fully represent the tragedies of family life. Christians, however, face genuine brokenness—tragic, unmediated alienation—as it is repre-sented each year in Holy Week. Christian tradition testifies to God's power to offer human beings acceptance and forgiveness with which to continue their lives, regardless of the way they fall short of their family ideals.

Love, if it is mentioned at all in the world of social science, becomes almost exclusively an exercise of the will. In fact, "work" has become the dominant psychological metaphor for marriage and parenting in the last two decades. But marriage and parenting cannot live by work alone. In Christian spirituality, human will is counterbalanced by delight. Delight, as expressed by Mary in the Magnificat, transcends the troubles of family structure. Despite a pregnancy for which she could have been stoned to death, Mary sings

> My soul magnifies the Lord
> and my spirit rejoices in God my Savior.
> (Luke 1:46-47)

Love in the Christian tradition, according to Roberta Bondi, "has to do with delight in God and other people even at its hardest. . . . Delight in love is the gift of God, God loving in us. It is not something we can grit our teeth and do, nor is it a possession that, once we have it, makes us good and acceptable" (Bondi, 1987, 22). Delight invites us to enjoy the other person and to be enjoyed in return, to revel in one another, causing us creatively to transcend ourselves, to become more than we thought we were.

The spiritual aspects of the family intersect with the spirituality of the Christian community. The new analysis rarely speaks of the relationship of families to communities; the former analysis does speak of the breakdown of community networks and institutions, which have traditionally supported families. The language of Christian spirituality moves beyond institutions to suggest that persons are considered to be so in need of communion with God and one another that "the spirit of adoption" transcends structures of family, community, or state. In the spirit of adoption, familylike concern is expressed toward persons who are not biological or legal kin. According to Janet Melnyk, the motif of extra-biological or extra-legal kinship was so strong in the Hebrew scriptures that the spirit of adoption became a primary metaphor for community relations despite the fact that adoption was rarely practiced (Melnyk, 1993). The theme reappears in the work of Protestant theologians such as John Wesley. The spirituality of adoption suggests that the spiritual qualities of the family may transcend biological and legal kinship.

Furthermore, communal spirituality offers support and comfort when biological family structures break down. Paul wrote to the Corinthians to help them mediate the conflicts which arose between the claims of the family and the claim of God (1 Corinthians 7). Paul suggests several scenarios for maintaining marital relations when a conflict over spirituality occurs, but he also admits that irreconcilable situations do occur. In such cases, Paul suggests that believers let go of biological and legal ties, for "it is to peace that God has called you" (1 Cor. 7:15 NRSV).*

The qualities of human joy, despair, responsibility, brokenness, acceptance, forgiveness, and delight, taken together, bring us into an attitude of humility toward family life which social science cannot quantify or even qualify. Our families of choice and the families we have been given are capable of both more and less than we would have thought. How many parents have said that it was a good thing that they didn't know what they were getting into when they became parents? How many divorced parents have the paradoxical sense that the marriage was wrong from the beginning but that the children produced within the marriage are their greatest concern and gift? How often is an out-of-wedlock child, like Jesus, a continual source of joy to a parent? How many married parents, who have thought they gave their children all they could, have mourned the death, loss, or waywardness of their children? When we imagine ourselves into the age of our death, and reflect honestly on our lives—our aspirations, our successes, and our failures; losses despite our best efforts, and gains where we could not anticipate them; ways that we have inflicted hurt on those we love and times that we surprised ourselves by being prepared to offer forgiveness, acceptance, generosity, and hospitality—humility will have the last word. Spiritual reflections on the family might allow us to bring humility into our living, as well as our dying.

---

*I thank Carl H. Holladay for providing this insight.

CHAPTER 5

Children, Mothers, and Fathers in the Postmodern Family

Don Browning

Throughout the period in which pastoral care has been in dialogue with the modern psychologies, there has been a tension between empathy and moral guidance. We have generally felt the need to empathize with people needing the church's care. We have also, however, increasingly tried to inquire into and in some way uphold the church's ethical standards, no matter how difficult it may be to know them with certainty. The relation of ethics to pastoral care has been the subject of a friendly dialogue between Charles Gerkin and me for more than a decade. I use this occasion to further that conversation.

The relation of empathy and care has been concretely and vividly raised by sociologist Judith Stacey's recent book, *Brave New Families: Stories of Domestic Upheaval in Late Twentieth-Century America* (1991). Stacey's book asks how the church's care should respond to the growing trend toward matrifocal families throughout Western industrial societies. Her book is a study of two women and their families—their early marriages to workaholic husbands, their divorces and separations, their troubled children, and their slide to the edge of poverty. At the end of the story, these two women, Pam and Dotty, are the effective heads of matrifocal families. Although Pam is remarried to Al, a working-class and fundamentalist recovering alcoholic, she is the center of a diffuse family network, which entails some shared parenting with her former husband and his mistress, who now live next door to Pam. Dotty, whose semi-estranged husband has died, now lives with her daughter, Kristina, and her children. Together they are raising the children of Dotty's other daughter, who has recently died. These women, mother and daughter, live together raising their children and grandchildren by themselves.

Stacey, a social scientist and leading feminist theorist, does not hide her empathy for these women. She is correct, I believe, in celebrating their humanity and heroism and that of their families. But Stacey goes beyond this; she moves from empathy to full approval, indeed a stance of normative legitimation. She joins thinkers as diverse as Barbara Ehrenreich and Judge Richard Posner in seeing these new matrifocal families as both inevitable and worthy of emulation (Stacey, 1990, 251-78; cf. Ehrenreich, 1983; Posner, 1992). She sees Pam and Dotty as ushering into social reality, and eventually into the middle classes, what Andrew Cherlin calls "the feminization of kinship" (Stacey, 1990, 268). It is clear that, in spite of the difficulties of these new matrifocal families, Stacey believes that they are the wave of the future and represent an improvement over the traditional or modern family forms, forms that dominated the early marriages of Pam and Dotty. Stacey's book raises the age-old question: Where is the line between empathy and idealization?

Stacey presents us with a forced choice between the traditional family with its bread-winning father and domestic child-rearing mother and the new fatherless, matrifocal network she finds in the families of Pam and Dotty. But there may be a third perspective that would extend empathy, offer practical help, rally social and economic resources on their behalf, but define the moral context differently from these two extremes. It is my view that a proper reading of the Judeo-Christian tradition will help establish this third perspective—a perspective that has, on the whole, tried to balance the good of children with a covenant of equal regard between husband and wife, father and mother.*

---

*Dan Quayle helped establish the lines of debate during the 1992 presidential election. Those who agree on the limited point of the importance of the two-parent family, but not on the larger political agenda, were David Blankenhorn of the Institute for American Values, William Galston of the University of Maryland and the Progressive Policy Institute and advisor to Democratic presidential candidates including William Clinton, and the manifesto of the journal called *The Responsive Community*. A strong policy statement on behalf of the two-parent family can be found in the final report of the National Commission on Children titled *Beyond Rhetoric* (1991). They write, "Children do best when they have the personal involvement and material support of a father and a mother and when both parents fulfill their responsibility to be loving providers" (p. xix). This statement is noteworthy since it differs from more diffuse endorsements of various

For some years I have insisted that care and counseling, both secular and religious, are never neutral, that they always proceed in some moral context, and that within the church they achieve their norms through a correlational dialogue between its classics and various voices from its surrounding culture. I propose to take this general point of view into the present family debate that James Davison Hunter in his celebrated *Culture Wars* claims is dividing orthodox and conservatives in contemporary religious faiths and denominations (1991, 43).

On the whole, the orthodox position has tried to give a Christian defense of the modern, industrial, bourgeois family—the breadwinner husband and domestic wife. These groups do not understand that this particular family form was the product of the radical differentiation between home and paid work that emerged with the industrial revolution. This organization of the family, most historians and sociologists agree, is not the divinely sanctioned family form of the New Testament. Mainline churches have, on the whole, been silent on these divisive tensions, probably because they are themselves embedded in the same individualistic cultural trends that have been the principal causes of family fragmentation in the wider culture (D'Antonio and Aldous, 1983, 81-98, 113-40).

DESCRIPTIVE THEOLOGY
AND THE SITUATION OF FAMILIES

Before outlining this third position, I will offer a brief description of the situation of children, mothers, and fathers in American society today.

Description is never easy and is always embedded in certain normative commitments or preunderstandings (as Gadamer calls them), no matter how strenuous our attempts to gain distance and objectivity (Gadamer, 1982). I have my precommitments on issues pertaining to children and families that I will develop now and then test later in this essay. They

---

family forms in several earlier national commission statements. On the other hand, Betty Friedan, in an exchange with Blankenhorn, made a strong statement on the dangers of stigmatizing alternative families by elevating the importance of the two-parent, mother-father partnership. Joan Beck contributed to the debate by pointing out that men may need to be integrated into families even more than mothers and children need husbands and fathers. She writes, "Children need the civilizing, role-modeling influences of an on-the-scene father. But men also benefit and prosper from the civilizing, mutually nurturing effects of family life. Statistics show they are healthier, live longer, and are much less likely to be homeless or adrift in old age." See her "Maintaining the Father Connection," *Chicago Tribune* (June 18, 1992).

come from the synthesis of New Testament Christianity and Aristotelian philosophy found in the thought of Thomas Aquinas. In these sources one finds a vision of the family that sees it as a relative good needed for the raising of children and the mutual benefit and enrichment of parents as they proceed with that task. It is a relative good because the family must be subject to the rule of the Kingdom of God and finally measured by its contribution to the realization of that Kingdom. In this tradition, Aristotle was joined with interpretations of both Old and New Testaments to give strong, although not idolatrous, support to the importance of men and women becoming one flesh for the purpose of raising highly dependent human infants who would themselves develop into servants of the Kingdom of God. Historical research is now making it clear that Christian family theory is not a product, in any simple way, of the New Testament. It is a synthesis of New Testament and Aristotelian teaching that was achieved in Thomism and from there, with some amendments, in the Protestant Reformation (cf. Witte, 1988).

Aquinas followed Aristotle in basing his theory of the family in part on empirical observations about the long period of nurture and education required by the highly dependent human infant. Aquinas argued that this condition requires "certain and definite parents," by which he meant a "man and a definite woman" committed over time to the nurture and education of their children (Aquinas, 1948). The background of Thomas's position is best understood if traced to Aristotle's rejection of Plato's belief that the children of philosopher kings should be raised by the state rather than by their own parents (Plato, 1968, bk. 5). Such a social arrangement would extend, Plato believed, the philosopher kings' sympathy and identification with all children since they would have no way of knowing which specific child was theirs (Plato, 1968, bk. 5:462c).

Aristotle objected. He believed that sympathy spreads outward from particular, embodied, and special family relations. What is everyone's responsibility easily becomes, according to Aristotle, no one's responsibility (McKeon, 1941, bk. 2:1261b, 30). Empathy and a sense of social solidarity, for Aristotle, are generalized outward from particular investments in our own progeny to identification with the wider community. Aristotle was not saying that local communities and the state should not support families. Nor was he making a plea for family autonomy and isolation. He was simply arguing that we acknowledge the generally higher level of investment that most natural parents have in their children and what this does to provide these children with a base upon which to make later identifications with the wider community.

In spite of Jesus' seeming antipathy to the family in Matthew 10, most of modern Christianity has followed Aquinas's Aristotelian interpretation of such texts. In a section of the *Summa* titled "Of the Order of Charity," Aquinas argues for our special obligations to our own children and other close kin. In commenting on Jesus' alleged antagonism to the family, Aquinas writes, "We are commanded to hate, in our kindred, not their kinship, but only the fact of their being an obstacle between us and God" (Aquinas, 1917). We must remember that Aquinas saw these parental obligations falling on the shoulders of men as well as women, although perhaps not as equally as we would insist on today (Aquinas, 1948).

I will use this classical strand of Christian history to give heuristic guidance to my interpretation of the sociological facts that follow. There is a thunderous debate in our society over whether the family is simply changing or actually in decline. The facts that follow and the horizon of values I have just set forth lead me to affirm that the family is both changing and declining. The word "crisis," however, is the best metaphor to comprehend both of these dynamics. Of special importance for describing this crisis is the present-day situation of children and youth.

The 10 percent decline in the marriage rate since 1975 and the approximately 1.5 million abortions that occur in the United States each year suggest, some believe, a culture-wide decline of interest in marriage and children (Popenoe, 1989, 2:1-5). More directly relevant to the thesis of family crisis is the colossal increase in out-of-wedlock births—an increase from 5 percent in 1960 to around 30 percent of all births today (Popenoe, 1989, 2:1-5). In the black community, out-of-wedlock births have risen from 20 percent in 1960 to roughly 68 percent today (Taylor, 1992). But this rise is not just among minority communities. Twenty-two percent of all births in the white community are now to single women— the same rate that existed in the black community thirty years ago when the overall out-of-wedlock birth rate was, as you recall, only 5 percent. Single mothers, their mothers, sisters, and other female friends often end up caring for the children of these births. But it is not only out-of-wedlock births that help create the feminization of kinship. The increase of divorce contributes as well. In addition, both divorce and nonmarital births help create another phenomenon called the "feminization of poverty." In fact, the two feminizations—of kinship and poverty—are closely related phenomena. Take divorce. Lenore Weitzman in her ground-breaking *Divorce Revolution* (1985) states that within one year after divorce, women and their children experience a 73 percent drop in disposable income while their ex-husbands enjoy a 42 percent increase. Although these figures are probably exaggerated, even corrections have supported their general validity (cf. Jacob, 1988).

It is now becoming clear that the feminization of kinship and poverty is not particularly good for children. This is where Thomas's argument that the highly dependent human infant needs a definite father and mother rings true. Of course, this dependent human child and its parents need a variety of supportive human communities and networks as well. But this truth should not obscure the fact that these networks work best when they support a fully involved mother-father partnership. A recent federally sponsored study for the National Center for Health Statistics shows that one in five children under age eighteen has a learning, emotional, behavioral, or developmental problem. By the time they are teenagers, one in four suffers from one or more of these problems. For male teenagers, the rate is nearly one in three. What is this study's explanation of these trends? These researchers hold that a leading factor is the continuing dissolution of the two-parent family (Zill and Schoenborn, 1990). There is other highly suggestive although less than conclusive evidence that is often cited for the unfavorable overall effects of the decline of the two-parent family. Louis Sullivan reports that 70 percent of young men in prisons grew up without fathers in their home, that the children of single parents are five times more likely to be poor and two times more likely to drop out of school (1992, 34-36). Eighty percent of adolescents in psychiatric hospitals come from broken homes; three out of four teenage suicides occur in households where a parent (generally the father) has been absent; and children living apart from a biological parent are 20 to 40 percent more vulnerable to illness (Klein, 1992).

The trends suggested by these facts cannot be blamed solely on the deteriorating financial state of most families, although this is clearly important. Economists Victor Fuchs and Diane Reklis demonstrate that since 1960 almost all indices of teenage well-being have declined. SAT scores fell, suicide rates tripled, homicide and obesity rates rose sharply, and poverty rates, although declining between 1960 to 1970, rose for children while staying basically stable for adults. Fuchs and Reklis give a startling interpretation to these facts, especially for economists. Although the deteriorating economic base of children has contributed to these trends, they show that most of the material decline has occurred since 1980. They credit cultural shifts—individualism, divorce, changing sexual mores—with most of the prior decline in the overall health of children; these shifts are probably still factors today (Fuchs and Reklis, 1992, 41). The rise of single-parent families is an important expression of these cultural trends. To summarize these trends is not to denigrate single parents, many of whom are unbelievably heroic and doing a fantastic job. It is rather to speak frankly about a cultural and social trend brought about by a host of systemic social and cultural changes powerfully affecting the lives of individuals—a trend which, taken as a whole, is not good for children of Western societies and should not be idealized.

CAPITALISM AND BUREAUCRACY: SOCIAL SYSTEMS AND THE FAMILY CRISIS

These facts require a deeper interpretation. The decline of the two-parent family is itself a symptom of more profound social patterns. Without displacing my biblical and Thomistic angle of vision, I will review some supplementary social science frameworks. Three factors require attention—the spreading impact of capitalistic market systems, the penetration of governmental bureaucracies in the intimate matters of the family, and the deepening trend toward individualism in all advanced societies.

Both Marxists and Durkheimians place the blame for family decline on the social patterns of capitalistic, market-driven, industrial society. It was competitive industrial society that took men away from domestic farm life and the family-centered small businesses and pushed them into wage labor far removed from wife and children. Industrialization gave men a new kind of economic power over their families and relegated women and children into the so-called nonproductive confines of private domestic existence. Interpreters all the way from Marx and Engels (1985), to religious-socialist feminists such as Rosemary Ruether (1975), to Stacey herself put the blame squarely on modern industrial capitalism. Although feminists have been more articulate about the shortcomings of the modern industrial family, in many ways this family form put far more pressure on men than it did women. In this sense, modernity may be proving to have been a risky gamble for both sexes. Segregating paid work, as it did, from the rhythms of home life broke formal and informal initiation rites between fathers and their sons. Women were indeed discriminated against in industrial society, but men may have lost their way entirely. This is the message of the mythopoetic men's movement

77

led by Robert Bly (1990), Robert Moore (1990), and others. Erik Erikson and Kenneth Keniston (1965) investigated such themes long before but in less dramatic terms.* It is perspectives such as these that throw light on the remote, detached, and shadowy men and former husbands in the matrifocal families of Pam and Dotty.

MODERN BUREAUCRACIES AND FAMILY CRISIS

Marxist analysis can be equally critical of the bureaucratic machinery of the welfare state. Although I personally see a large role for a variety of state-supported family programs, it is important to confront how these welfare bureaucracies, whether in socialist or capitalist societies, sometimes contribute to the decline of families and the feminization of kinship. Jürgen Habermas in his *Theory of Communicative Action* shows how the patterns of what he calls the "systems world" of welfare bureaucracies create a growing dependency as government increasingly takes over family functions (1987, 153-97).

Alan Wolfe in his *Whose Keeper* makes a distinction between the "private" or market family and the "public" or state family (1989, 52, 133). The United States is the example par excellence of the private family, that is, the family driven and shaped by the market forces of American life. But this family is anything but private. Increasingly, the private space of this family is being penetrated by the calculating and cost-effectiveness logic of modern market forces.

Wolfe shows how the indices of family decline in the United States are effectively matched by the indices of family decline in Sweden. Sweden is Wolfe's best example of the so-called public family. Sweden's cradle-to-grave welfare policies were designed to support families. Instead, according to Wolfe, they have encouraged patterns of divorce, nonmarriage, and state familism (Wolfe, 1989, 142-58). In ways somewhat parallel to those in the United States, children in Sweden are increasingly being cared for by single women. Ironically, it is also women who are staffing the state-run child-care centers and public schools. In both countries, women are increasingly raising the children, albeit with better government subsidies in Sweden than are available in the United States. There is less feminization of poverty in Sweden, but there may be no less feminization of kinship.

---

*Much of Erikson's commentary on generativity has to do with the crisis of being a father in modern societies. For an interpretation of Erikson from this perspective, see my *Generative Man* (1973).

CULTURAL INTERPRETATIONS OF FAMILY CRISIS

The public family of Sweden is a less radical expression of Plato's vision of the relation of the family and the state. Although parents do not completely disappear from the lives of children as they did in Plato's republic, in Sweden's welfare state, according to Wolfe, they become progressively more ephemeral, detached, and unauthoritative. But this is true for modern societies in general. Both parents and children get more and more of their moral sensibilities from the logics and patterns of both state and market.

State and market forces not only combine to inject an alternating dependency and rational choice mentality in families, they also function to undermine the authority of parents in the socialization of their children. At least this is the argument of Christopher Lasch in his *Haven in a Heartless World: The Family Besieged* (1977). As the state and its schools, welfare organizations, and mental health experts more and more insert themselves into family life, parents appear more inept and the center of competence and authority passes to those outside the home. Market values, amplified by the seductive voices of television and other media of communication, also undermine the authority of parents. The market's consumer logic undermines so-called traditional family values. The market's appeal to sex, power, prestige, and the immediate fulfillment of desires through uncontrolled advertising undercuts the parent's capacity to instill values of discipline, focused attention, and long-term commitments.*

Lasch uncovers the consequences of the multifarious forces undermining the authority of parents in the lives of their children. The declining authority of parents, according to Lasch, produces a split between love and discipline in modern families (1977, 174-83). Under the impact of advice from the psychiatric and psychotherapeutic professions, friendship in the twentieth century became the new model for family relations—friendship between husband and wife and increasingly friendship between parent and child. More and more parents could be warm and supportive, but they could not give authoritative guidance. Lasch argues that it is precisely this split between love and discipline that

---

* This truth points to the myopia of the Bush-Quayle attack on the media elite during the 1992 election for undermining family values. They were right in placing blame on television, movies, and advertising elites. But they were wrong in failing to see how these elites simply give voice to market enticements, which the Reagan-Bush years had both encouraged and failed to restrain.

leads young people in modern societies to be so easily manipulated by outside forces, whether they be the forces of the market, the peer group, the video, the television, or the demagogue. Superegos are not deeply internalized in postindustrial society, according to Lasch. Children may love their parents, but they may not deeply internalize their parents' values. And on the whole, Lasch contends, they certainly do not hold their parents in deep respect.

For fear that the reader may believe that Lasch and I have undercut the credibility of all psychologically oriented helping professions, whether religious or secular, let me say this: It should be possible for all counselors to discover and publicly articulate the centers of authority and value out of which they make their interventions. If they were to do this, the parent's authority would not be subtly undermined. Parents would know more clearly when the values of experts vary from their own and be able to confront this directly. *It is the distinct advantage of pastoral counseling, I will argue, that it can more easily work out of a publicly articulate and testable tradition of values.* This testable tradition should be carried by the church. It is the pastoral counselors' relation to the values and authority of the church which may help them escape Lasch's criticism that the mental health professions, along with the market and the state, tend to undercut family cohesion and promote anomic individualism.

FAMILY CRISIS AND RELIGION

Lasch's views are important, but they have limitations. His analysis of the loss of family authority is convincing. It is disappointing, however, that he has no constructive proposals about how family authority can be reconstituted. Furthermore, although Lasch is fully aware of the role that the Protestant Reformation had in elevating families and parenting over the medieval idealization of celibacy, he makes no suggestion about how religion might play a role today (1977, 183-89). It is my conviction, however, that the church and its pastoral care can play a significant role in giving authoritative grounding to a family form that stands between the male-dominated family of the industrial revolution and the female-dominated family of Stacey's postmodern vision.

The crux is the church's capacity to elaborate a new authoritative love ethic. In recent papers, I have elaborated a love ethic of equal regard as the grounds of a family ethic that provides an alternative to the ethic of the passing "modern" family or the ethic of the feminized kinship patterns that Stacey idealizes. It is an ethic that can provide a new structure of authority that will help the family resist the undermining influences of state and market. It can be an ethic both for the dyadic relation of husband and wife as well as for the relation of parents to their children.

I rely on the idea of Christian love as equal regard advanced by the Yale Protestant ethicist Gene Outka but enriched by the teleological interests of the Catholic moral theologian Louis Janssens. When considering the command "To love your neighbor as yourself," these theologians interpret this to mean that we are to love our neighbor, be it friend or spouse, with the same seriousness as we naturally love ourselves (Janssens, 1977, 220). To love the other with equal seriousness as ourselves is a strenuous ethic, far more strenuous than either ethical egoist or utilitarian perspectives. But to love or regard the other as ourselves means we are entitled to love or regard ourselves equally to the other. This ethic does not allow us to regard ourselves more, but neither does it permit us to take the masochistic stance of regarding ourselves less. This is a rigorous and highly demanding ethic of mutuality.

Interpretations of Christian love as an ethic of mutuality have much to contribute to an ethics of families. They can help open the ethical space between the modern family where the husband still had most of the power and the alternative matrifocal family in which women have the power but also the burden of loneliness and full responsibility. The ethics of mutuality balances largely Protestant, self-sacrificial models of Christian love associated in the modern period with Anders Nygren (1953), Rudolf Bultmann (Hallett, 1989, 5-6), and to a lesser degree, Reinhold Niebuhr (1941, 84). Appeals to Christian doctrines of self-sacrificial love *(agape)* were used, in fact, by Paul, the author of 1 Peter, and even Luther to legitimate the patience, long-suffering, and obedience required of women in the Christian family.

Mutuality models of love have been of special interest to feminist theologians such as Mary Stewart Van Leeuwen (1990), Christine Gudorf (Andolsen, et al., 1985, 175-91), and others. To say that love as equal regard rather than love as perpetual self-sacrifice is the goal of the Christian life seems to women less susceptible to the manipulation of powerful agents, mainly men, who may use appeals to self-sacrifice to circumscribe and exploit them. Furthermore, mutuality models of love provide the ground for resisting the broad trends in our society which, despite the complaints of feminism, are increasingly releasing men from their family obligations and producing the growing feminization of kinship we have discussed. It may be noted that mutuality models of Christian love are significantly informed by *caritas* models of love associated more with the Catholic than the Protestant theological tradition, and that the New Testament scholarship of Victor Furnish (1982, 332) and Luise Schottroff (1975, 23) lends support to this interpretation of Christian love.

There is biblical support for a love ethic of equal regard. Although it is quite clear that much of biblical literature reflects the patriarchal character of the ancient Jewish, Greek, and Roman families, this is not the whole story. Walter Brueggemann argues that "there is a counter theme which suggests that the marriage relationship in both the Old and New Testament is understood as a covenantal relation which reflects mutual respect, concern and love" (Brueggemann, 1977, 14:19). Elisabeth Schüssler Fiorenza has found in the early pre-Markan material evidence for an ethics of mutuality between the sexes in what she calls a "discipleship of equals" (1983). This continues in a modified way into the letters of Paul, especially the baptismal formula of Galatians 3:28, which proclaims that in Christ there is neither "Jew nor Greek, . . . slave nor free, . . . male nor female." Furthermore, David Balch in his *Let Wives Be Submissive* detects in the return to the doctrine of female submission in 1 Peter evidence of the early church's apologetic attempt to hide before its Greek patriarchal detractors evidence for a heightened equality between husband and wife within the Christian house church (1981). Is it possible that the seeds of an egalitarian family ethic of covenanted mutuality were sown in early Christianity, which, although not fully realized then, has continued to work out its logic in human history?

This view of Christian love as equal regard does not eliminate the symbol of the cross and what it implies about the place of self-sacrificial love. Self-sacrifice is still very much a part of the Christian life in this ethic. But according to this view, it is not an end in itself but a transitional ethic in the service of mutuality and equal regard. Self-sacrificial love, in human relations or in the family, refers to the second mile we must often travel in a finite and sinful world in order to restore human relations once again to a situation of mutuality and equal regard.

THE CHURCH, MUTUALITY, AND THE CENTRALITY OF CHILDREN

The church's pastoral care must be guided by an ethic consistent with its theological tradition. I believe that an equal-regard love ethic accomplishes this. Then the church's care should surround this ethic with the ironic values of the doctrines of sin, grace, forgiveness, and redemption. The ironic character of these religious themes helps Christian ethics handle the tension between its demanding ideals and the realities of human frailty. Theology and the social sciences may show that some family forms are better than others for raising children. In fact, this is what I was arguing when I reviewed how certain aspects of the Aristotelian and Christian tradition articulate with certain aspects of the social sciences to support the importance of the mother-father partnership. This tradition provided a theory of the "order of the good" (the *ordo bonorum*), which the love ethic of equal regard further orders and enhances. But Christian irony suggests that all families, even the ostensibly equal-regard, mother-father partnership, can be corrupted under the conditions of finitude and sin.

In addition to the distinctly Christian element of irony, I want to introduce a life-cycle perspective into our understanding of love as equal regard. For instance, I want to ask, What does Christian love as mutuality or equal regard mean for the raising of children? How can the ethic of mutuality be adjusted with viable concepts of parental authority? It is my belief that for the love ethic of mutuality and equal regard to guide the raising of children, it must be supplemented with a theory of the human life cycle. This is the difference between an ethic serving the purposes of moral theology and an ethic serving pastoral care. It is in their knowledge of the dynamics of the life cycle that modern psychology and psychotherapy can make their most profound contribution to an equal-regard ethic relevant to the concrete circumstances of care. They help us understand that mutuality must take different forms at different points in the life cycle. Mutuality constitutes the ideal center of an ethic toward which everything in the life cycle points even though this norm is not always fully expressed at any one moment along the way.

A few illustrations are in order. For instance, mutuality between parent and infant occurs in anticipatory and preparatory ways. Although the human infant is highly dependent and often makes overwhelming demands, mutuality can still take the form of face-to-face and eye-to-eye contact in parents' interactions with their newly born children. In later phases of childhood, parents who live by an ethic of mutuality need not relinquish parental guidance and good judgment. Instead, they can treat their children with respect and permit ranges of freedom and responsibility appropriate to their ages. When an ethic of mutuality is at the center of a family ethic, parents raise children *to grow gradually toward* genuine mutuality. Attaining mutuality may not be accomplished fully until adulthood, but if this central value is firmly in place, children sense that patterns of equal regard are progressively being realized.

If mutuality in the sense of equal regard is central to a family ethic, elderly parents can more graciously accept the encroaching physical, and sometimes financial, dependency on their children that old age frequently brings. They can accept this partly because they know that a deeper equal regard and respect has been present in the family process from the beginning and undergirds their life together even in decline.

Obviously, within such a life-cycle theory of equal regard, there will be many moments of costly self-sacrifice, especially on the part of parents during the early years of their children's infancy and youth. But even here, self-sacrifice is that second mile required to empower children to move toward an ethic of equal regard and mutuality, even with their own parents. This is the ethic that should empower both men and women, husbands and wives, and the supporting structures of extended family, government, mental health profession, and church. This is the family ethic that should fill the growing vacuum between the traditional family and Stacey's "feminization of kinship" that her fascinating book failed to explore. This is the family ethic, nuanced by irony and a life-cycle perspective, that should answer Lasch's concern with the declining authority of families.

I believe that such an ethic is possible. Socialization patterns for children and youth should be guided by it. Religious and cultural institutions should accept it and find powerful ways of promoting it. Psychotherapy within a Christian context should uncover the developmental and value lacunae that prevent families from growing toward an equal-regard ethic between spouses and between them and their children. Pastoral psychotherapy should attempt to develop the insight and relational resources needed to help families move toward that goal. Although pastoral care and counseling should never use even the ethic of gentle equal regard rigidly and moralistically, it should still constitute the gently held and judiciously applied moral center of all of the church's care of families.

My argument has been that there are strong ideological and social trends working to create matrifocal families. This unrealistically releases men from the obligations of families and works to the disadvantage of both women and children, creating the feminization of kinship and poverty. Although the women who head these families are both heroic and worthy of empathy and support by both church and state, as a general societal trend the drift toward the matrifocal family should not be idealized. Theological strands stemming from the interplay of Aristotelian philosophy with Christian thought provide resources for cherishing as an important proximate good the mother-father partnership. And a love ethic of equal regard can provide a new ethic for the reordering of gender relations in this mother-father team. A life-cycle ethic of equal regard should guide the church's care with families and help restore their moral authority. In addition, an ethic of equal regard should guide the church's socialization of youth and its more specialized pastoral counseling with troubled families.

CHAPTER 6

Aging and the Conflict of Generations

K. Brynolf Lyon

In 1690, the twenty-seven-year-old Puritan theologian Cotton Mather wrote his first treatise on old age. In *The Old Man's Honour, or, The Hoary Head Found in the Way of Righteousness,* Mather reiterated two themes commonly found in the sermons and writings of the American colonies on the relationship of the generations: both reason and scripture accord honor to old age and the younger generations are to pay special heed to the wisdom of years. Older adults had special religious and moral obligations to be exemplars of the good life for those "less furnished in long experience." Younger generations, for their part, were expected to treat older adults with filial veneration in response to the depth of piety usually produced by so long a time in the faith. In a society and culture characterized by patriarchal gerontocracy both within and outside the church, Mather's readers had little trouble understanding what he meant—though they no doubt resisted a variety of its implications.

In the 300 years since Mather's essay, changes in the demography as well as the moral and political economy of aging in the United States have significantly reshaped the dynamics of social conflict between generations (cf. Cole, 1991; Achenbaum, 1978). The sheer number of persons now reaching later life, the rise of retirement as an expectable life stage, the socioeconomic realities of Social Security and Medicare, and the business world's discovery of older adults as consumers have precipitated profound conflicts on the landscape of American life. The cultural, emotional, political, and spiritual resources needed to make our way ahead are not readily at hand and only dimly perceived. In this context, the challenges to the church and its ministries of care are deep and broad.

SOURCES OF SOCIAL AND CULTURAL CONFLICT

Social conflict between generations is rooted in several interrelated spheres of life: the political economy, culture, and the psychodynamics of human development. The following overview of sources of social conflict between generations is not exhaustive. It is meant merely as illustrative and focuses on the social and cultural dimensions of such conflict. What will soon be apparent from this discussion, however, is that generational conflict is deeply conditioned by gender and ethnicity. The interaction of gender and ethnicity with the moral and political economy of aging makes the realities of generational conflict in our time extraordinarily complex.

The possibilities of conflict between younger and older generations today are significantly structured by the ways in which the life course has been influenced by the activities of the modern state in reshaping the economy (Mayer and Schoepflin, 1989, 15:187-209). The primary example of this is Social Security. Social Security is, in effect, a modification of the market by the state that has encouraged the development of a post-labor stage of life (retirement). (Wide-scale retirement in this country is a product of increased longevity in interaction with a certain set of cultural expectations and the demands of industry in a capitalist economy. My point is simply that the mechanism which makes "universal" retirement possible is Social Security [cf. Myles, 1989].) So profound has been this alteration of the life course by the state that retirement is now a nearly universally expectable life stage in this country with its own psychosocial and economic dynamics. While some persons retired during Mather's time, most "worked until they wore out" (cf. Fischer, 1978).

Social Security is often cited as the most successful of the "welfare state" programs in the United States. Though its long-term financing remains a vexing problem, it enjoys widespread support across generations: relieving many families of a significant aspect of the financial burden of old-age and guaranteeing some income constancy in an increasingly lengthy period of life spent outside the labor market. Yet,

87

even in this most "successful" of welfare state activities, we are already experiencing or are ripe for social conflict.

One of the most important reasons for this is the problem of what is now called "generational equity." On the one hand, Social Security has successfully helped reduce poverty among persons sixty-five years of age and older. In just the last twenty years the poverty rate for older adults has dropped from 26 percent to 12 percent. On the other hand, as has been frequently noted, this has been bought at a tremendous cost and resulted in significant disparities in public spending for various age groups. During most of the time in which the poverty rate for older adults was declining, for example, the poverty rate for children was increasing and now stands at approximately 20 percent. Indeed, about 40 percent of all persons who are poor are children (Wolfe, 1991, 6:23-28). This disparity in economic security between the young and the old has given rise to the call from some quarters for generational equity: a more equitable distribution of resources among the generations.

The generational equity debate takes a variety of forms today. Some versions pit older adults as a single group against children as a single group. Other versions pit wealthy older adults who nonetheless receive Social Security against impoverished children. Still other versions pit a largely white older population against the needs of ethnic minority children. Finally, some versions of the generational equity argument simply claim that we should not disturb the current Social Security program, but rather significantly increase government support for the poor.

In Mather's time, the question of generational equity arose almost exclusively within propertied families. Conflicts concerning the respective financial security of the young and old were, in effect, conflicts regarding who would inherit (and when they would inherit) property in exchange for providing for the well-being of the parents. The intervention of the state in this issue in modern times has meant that the question of generational equity is now posed across families. This has had both good and ill effects. On the one hand, financial security in old age is less tied to the politics of family life in the way in which it once was. Today, financial security is subject to more universal social criteria, which are worked out through the government's modifications of the market. On the other hand, these "universal" criteria are themselves products of a political process, a fact that has resulted in outcomes that are far from equitable: the generational equity issue is but one example. The growing concern regarding what constitutes a just distribution of medical resources between the generations given the escalating costs of long-term care for older adults is another example (cf. Callahan, 1987; Homer and Holstein, 1990).

Seeing these issues only in terms of conflict between generations, however, obscures some of the harshest realities of our situation. Although it is true that the poverty rate for older adults as a whole has dramatically declined over the past twenty years, the decline has not been experienced equally across lines of gender and ethnicity. Women over sixty-five, for example, are almost twice as likely as men in the same age group to be poor. Widows are two-and-one-half times as likely as men to be poor. Most strikingly, the poverty rate among older African American women who are heads of households is nearly 50 percent. The more sporadic work history of women (due in part to their taking time away from their jobs to bear and care for children and also to the fact that no Social Security credit is given for this care) and the lower pay they receive in their employment leads to comparatively lower contributions to Social Security and, thus, lower benefits in their older adulthood. This situation, combined with the fact that a greater percentage of women than men are employed in positions that do not provide a private pension which might supplement Social Security, leads to a large disparity in economic security between the sexes in old age. Even when women have access to a private pension they are likely to receive smaller benefits because of their work histories. Social Security and private pensions are, in effect, modeled after men's work history (indeed, middle-class, white men's work history), and the effect of this shows up clearly in the respective well-being of the two groups (this data is from Smeeding, 1990; and Quadagno and Meyer, 1990, 64-66). Thus, while the economic survival of the generations is less tied to the family politics of inheritance, it remains tied to the family politics of gender and ethnicity.

As the inequities of gender and ethnicity make clear, the political economy of aging in the United States creates social conflict through its interaction with broader cultural trends. One of the most important examples of this interaction of political and moral economy is the role of women as caregivers of elderly parents or in-laws. Children caring for elderly parents is not a new phenomenon, of course. During Mather's time and before, filial care of older adults was the primary form of nurture available. Yet, as Elaine Brody (1990, 13) has noted, "The increased number and proportion of very old people in the population, the rise in chronic ailments and the disabilities that result, and the falling birth rate mean that contemporary adult children provide more care and more difficult care to more parents and parents-in-law over much longer periods of time than ever has been the case before." Thus, while a good deal of emotional and financial support still flows from older adults to their adult children, the pressures of parent care on those adult children are rising.

The vast majority of this care (estimates suggest about 80 percent) is provided by women. The cultural expectation that women are to be the family caregivers coupled with the comparatively lower valuation of women's work in the labor market has meant that women are usually turned to for parent care. This is true even if the woman is caring for her own children at the time or if she is employed. Women, rather than men, are expected to adjust their schedules to accommodate the tasks involved in caring for elderly parents.

Parent care is a rewarding experience for many, of course. Yet, as Brody notes, more and more women are caught "in the middle" between the demands of their employment, caring for their own children, providing parent care, and the conflicting cultural values which pull them in these various directions. Indeed, as increasing numbers of persons live later into old age, the women "in the middle" include not only middle-aged women but also women in their own early old age who are caring for their own aging husbands. The emotional burden of these situations varies considerably from situation to situation and tends to have different emotional and moral valences in various ethnic groups where the values and practices around parent care have been stronger and more nested in communal support than is true of other groups (Yee, 1990, 39-42). Nonetheless, it is clear that women disproportionately bear both the financial and the emotional burdens of parent care. Generational conflict, in other words, is again gendered.

The final source of generational conflict to be noted here concerns the cultural resources available to older adults to make sense of their aging. The vacuum of meaning that has surrounded aging throughout most of this century is now often filled by the market. The increasing financial well-being of some older adults has led to their discovery by business as a consumer group (cf. Minkler, 1990). Indeed, in some ways, the image of older adults as having money to spend and lots of free time to spend it (a prominent version of the American Dream) becomes a way for a previously marginalized group of persons to re-enter the center of society: Though they do not produce, they can buy. In effect, the cultural resources older adults might draw upon to make sense of their aging are being "colonized," to use Jürgen Habermas' apt phrase, by the market. Our image of human fulfillment in old age, therefore, is increasingly marked by the image of older adults as happy consumers on a moral holiday.

This image does not reflect the life realities of millions of older adults in our time, nor does its own vacuity satisfy many others. Nonetheless, it suggests the paradox of much of what has been said in this section of this essay: *The socially legitimated incorporation of older adults into the center of society hinges on their status as consumers at the same time that the conflict precipitated by the inequities within and between generations makes the claim for that status in its present form problematic.*

RESOURCES FROM THE MODERN PASTORAL CARE AND COUNSELING MOVEMENT

Pastors confront the issues of generational conflict through the immediate, lived realities of persons: in the struggle of a poor elderly woman living alone, in the anguish of a middle-aged woman trying to sort out her responsibilities to her aged parents in deteriorating health, in the struggle for control between younger and older members of a congregation, in the questioning of a recently retired couple regarding what they ought now to do. Each of these situations is woven into a broader social and cultural fabric of which generational conflict is a significant thread. Whether we see the broader tapestry or not, it is nonetheless present: shaping and being shaped by the situation immediately before us.

What is required of the care of the church, we must ask, in the face of these issues? What resources do we have available to find our way ahead in pastoral care and counseling? Earlier theologians like Mather, Calvin, Augustine, and Chrysostom spent a good deal more time than we pastoral theologians worrying about aging in the context of generational conflict (Lyon, 1985). But no more than we have did they address the interrelationship of moral and political economy in shaping that conflict. In some respects, therefore, the issues of generational conflict push the care of the church into largely uncharted terrain.

We are not bereft of resources, however, from the modern pastoral care and counseling movement. For example, nearly all of the basic

91

elements of care as outlined by Hunter in chapter 1 of this volume remain relevant. Empathic listening, clarifying, and being a nonanxious presence will obviously continue to be important in the pastoral care of persons in the midst of generational conflict. While even these aspects of care need to be extended to deal with the social and political dynamics of generational conflict, they nonetheless provide important foundations for the care of the church. Likewise, the realities of conflict within and between generations ought not to compel us to forget what we have learned from those psychological and theological resources which have informed the development of the modern pastoral care and counseling movement.

Pastoral care and counseling have been profoundly influenced, for example, by psychodynamic theories of human development. Such theories place a great deal of emphasis on generational relations as central to the maturational process. Where Freud saw the central drama of development in the intrapsychic struggle between fathers and sons, object-relations theorists often construe the mother-child relationship as pivotal. It must be acknowledged, of course, that until quite recently psychodynamic theories of development failed to address development in older adulthood itself: seeing old age either as beyond the developmental pale entirely or as a largely regressive phase of life precipitated by the increasing and increasingly intense losses that accompany aging.

The work of Erik Erikson was a significant exception to this. In the final of his eight stages of life, Erikson posited a developmental crisis of older adulthood, which he called "integrity vs. despair." Erikson's work remains important in terms of addressing the issues of aging and generational conflict not only because of his discussion of the developmental crisis of older adulthood, but also because he clearly saw development in the context of wider social and cultural processes. Though Erikson himself did not extend his work very far in terms of political economy, his perspective on human life certainly opens out into those concerns.

The more recent influence of family therapies in pastoral care and counseling also will continue to be relevant. Family therapies point us toward the wider field of influences which maintain and transform behavior. As such, they will be particularly useful in helping pastors situate generational conflict within its immediate familial context. Object-relations family therapy, in particular, holds a good deal of promise for enabling us to make sense of the mutual influences of individual developmental processes and family systems. Although this latter body of literature has yet to be aimed at aging in particular, its general direction is promising.

The theological resources which have had the greatest influence on the modern pastoral care and counseling movement—Tillichian, liberation, and process theologies—also will continue to be of use. It must be acknowledged again, of course, that none of those resources was developed with issues of generational conflict (or even aging itself) explicitly in mind. While this is not the place to address the relative adequacy of these perspectives in light of issues of conflict within and between generations, their quite different ways of making sense of the relational character of existence, the centrality of grace, and God's concern for justice, for example, will continue to be appropriately mined for reflection on the issues discussed in this essay.

More important to the care of the church in the midst of generational conflict than the enduring influence of particular schools of theology, however, are the recent efforts of Charles Gerkin (1991 b), Don Browning (1983), and others to retrieve ethics as clinical hermeneutics. Generational conflict, as I have described it, is fundamentally about justice within and between generations. If those engaged in pastoral care are appropriately to minister in these situations, they must have ethical abilities that enable them to make sense of the broadest issues of social justice and they must have caregiving skills that allow them to nourish and renew lives in ways sensitive to those broader issues. While we are still in the early stages of learning what that might mean, recent developments in the modern pastoral care and counseling movement provide us with instructive beginning points (cf. Graham, 1992; Couture, 1991 a).

CHALLENGES TO THE CARE OF THE CHURCH

Although many of the insights of the modern pastoral care and counseling movement will remain important, there are significant ways in which those insights will need to be extended or understood in significantly different ways given the challenges of conflict within and between generations. I will focus my remarks on three such issues: extending the empathic imagination of caregivers to account for the influence of the political economy in the formation of selves and families, attending to communities and institutions as agents of care, and facilitating reflection on the moral callings of the generations in their relations with one another. Each of these issues pushes the care of the church to reconceive itself in a broader social and historical context.

First, the care of the church must come to understand questions of political economy as central to its work. Older adulthood is experienced as it is today in part because the interaction of the market and the state has reshaped the life course in extraordinary ways over the past sixty years. As noted, the impact of this is felt across the generations: creating new or more complex stresses and opportunities in regard to all generations than was previously the case. Pastoral care in these circumstances cannot neglect questions of political economy because those questions are thought to be external to the self, as something "out there," separate from the processes that constitute intersubjective reality. Political economy, rather, is ingredient in those processes and, therefore, is a constituent of the relational practices and inner worlds of us all.

Additionally, the realities of conflict within and between generations make clear that political economy cannot be understood as embodied in one dimension. Rather, it is differentially reproduced within selves and families by gender and ethnicity as these shape and are shaped by the emotional and spiritual histories of those selves and families. To recognize the importance of political economy in these ways is to claim for the care of the church the feminist and womanist notions that "the personal is political" and "the political is personal." It requires, in effect, an extension or deepening of the empathic imagination of caregivers to account for the fuller sociohistorical realities of the becoming of selves and families.

Second, as an implication, those of us engaged in pastoral care must come more fully to address *communities and institutions* as agents of care. The therapeutic model of pastoral care has largely focused on care for individuals and families. This work remains important, of course. I simply note here that conflict within and between generations is not only a product of intrapsychic or family dynamics. It is also rooted in and carried by the structures of community: the broader web of relationships, beliefs, and practices through which we reproduce the way we live our lives together. By helping us be aware of such things, the care of the church can help us see and act in response to the deeper ecology of care within which our lives are impoverished or enriched.

Conflict within and between generations, in other words, requires that the care of the church seek the transformation and renewal of congregations, neighborhoods, corporations, and the state as agents of care: as communities and institutions which foster or impede the flourishing of life. As the realities of generational conflict make clear, these broader structures cannot be an afterthought of the care of the church, to be dealt with after the real work of caring for individuals and families has taken place. They are, rather, constitutive features of the ecology of care in which individual and family development is sponsored and channeled. Pastoral care, in other words, must expand its own vision of itself and join with other aspects of the church's ministry to be about the task of communal and institutional renewal.

Third, seeking the transformation of communities and institutions and extending the empathic imagination of pastors to account for the ways the political economy becomes instantiated within and reproduced through selves and families is not enough. We must also come to understand questions of moral economy as concomitant with questions of political economy. In other words, the embodied norms of reciprocity that make sense of or stand in tension with the realities of the political economy of aging must become more fully available for critical reflection and transformative practice.

More specifically still, we must become life-course ethicists in this regard. We must be concerned not simply with universal ethical principles that are independent of stage of life, but also with the moral callings of the generations in their relationships with one another in the midst of the particular social, cultural, and psychodynamic contexts of their realization. We must ask, for example, what is a good old age given the contemporary realities of conflict within and between generations? What are the obligations of the generations to one another today? To ask these kinds of questions and to see them as important in individual and communal formation is to recover an older tradition of ethical reflection, one various aspects of historical Christian traditions, including Mather, knew a great deal about. Although we may be helped by recovering that tradition, we must also extend it in a way specially sensitive to the differential interplay of moral and political economy over the life span (the most extended discussion of these issues is found in Daniels, 1988).

Indeed, it is only by struggling with these questions ourselves and enabling others to struggle fruitfully with them that we will have a chance of having compelling cultural and religious resources that might be able to resist the powerful influences of the market in its colonization of the meaning of old age. But the three issues discussed in this section are interrelated precisely at this point. For we must not only have such cultural and religious resources, but also have individual and communal practices and forms of relationship that can sustain and make sense of those meanings.

This concern with moral economy in relation to political economy is required simply by our effort to enact the *care* of the church as the care of the *church:* our calling to nourish the conditions necessary for the *just* flourishing of God's creation. As Gerkin, Browning, and others have observed, the moral confusions and ethical uncertainties of our time do not make the kind of ethical reflection required here easy to come by. Likewise, the uncertainties within pastoral care and counseling itself regarding the relationship of moral vision and therapeutic practice make this task additionally complex. Yet, it must be done. We must be able to reflect ethically within the complexities of the caring event itself on conflict within and between generations with the kinds of issues here noted in mind, lest the care of the church simply reproduce the injustices that presently exist or create new and potentially worse injustices.

IMPLICATIONS FOR THEOLOGICAL EDUCATION

What then might this all mean for theological education in pastoral care? Given already overcrowded curricula in the area and tensions in the relationship of pastoral care to other fields, this is a difficult question. Nonetheless, two issues seem particularly pertinent: the first having to do with the kinds of knowledge necessary appropriately to care for persons in the context of generational conflict, the second concerned with the relationship of pastoral care to the care of the church more generally.

First, being able to understand the workings of political economy in the shaping of the life course and being able to have the kind of practical wisdom necessary for communal and institutional transformation can no longer be seen as optional for pastoral caregivers. Although some will specialize in these questions more than others, it is now clear that the market and the state internally influence and shape human experiencing and the structures of institutions and communities. In some ways we have known this for a long time. Yet, we have continued to develop and teach psychological theories which presume it isn't so. Systems theories might eventually provide us some leverage on these questions. Even lacking fully developed models for how to make sense of this in caregiving situations, however, we must make a beginning in the teaching of pastoral care.

Second, given the multidimensional character of generational conflict, pastoral care should form curricular alliances with other theological disciplines. This requires recognizing two things. On the one hand, it requires recognizing that pastoral care is an *expression* of the care of the church, not *the* care of the church. The care of the church is constituted by the whole variety of ways the life of the church seeks to promote the flourishing of God's creation as enactment of the gospel: through worship, prayer, Bible study, fellowship, social ministry, music, preaching, and so forth. On the other hand, it requires recognizing that the traditional divisions of the theological curriculum often do not well suit the way life presents itself. Most real-life issues, I dare say, do not come neatly categorized as "Problem in Christian Education" or "Problem in Pastoral Care" or "Problem in Systematic Theology." Life is distinctly messier than that.

While it is perhaps old hat to say we need to be able to think across disciplinary boundaries, that is nonetheless what we need to do. The problem of generational conflict is a problem for the care of the church, not just for pastoral care. Therefore, we need to find ways for the variously gifted theological disciplines to bring their distinct resources together for the transformation of the realities of our generational existence (I have suggested some of the implications of this for Christian religious education in Lyon, 1988, 4:243-54). This requires each discipline risking some of its own most sacred notions and the subversion of the competition between theological fields for students and prestige. Those familiar with the relevant discussions will know that this is no more than to make another plea for practical theology, properly understood, as the heart of the theological and congregational enterprises (cf. Browning, 1991). It is to make a plea for helping pastors and congregations understand the relationship, for example, between churches' efforts to influence the political processes that shape economic life, the most intimate forms of pastoral counseling with older adults, and the study of historical theology.

One ought not to assume from my earlier remarks in this essay, therefore, that pastoral care now needs to be the place where all questions of ethics and communal-institutional transformation are asked in the theological curriculum. Pastoral care must continue to have a distinct focus. Although it needs to extend its self-understanding in certain ways, it need not bear the burden of the whole care of the church. Rather, it

97

simply needs to promote, contribute to, and be enriched by the struggle with issues of generational conflict throughout the theological disciplines.

FINAL QUESTIONS

In 1726, when he was sixty-three years old, Cotton Mather wrote his second treatise on aging: *A Good Old Age; An Essay on the Glory of Aged Piety.* Mather wrote fervently about the importance of living a good life in one's old age, a goodness which showed itself in a piety that expressed faithful caring for one's own soul and for younger generations. What can that mean in our time? What kind of communities nurturing what kinds of intergenerational relations could help us make good sense of Mather's concern? What revaluations of gender and ethnicity—as these interact with the moral and political economy of aging—are we now compelled to pursue? The complexity of these questions is barely hinted at in these pages. But that they are right and important questions seems beyond doubt.

CHAPTER 7

Gender and Pastoral Care

Bonnie J. Miller-McLemore and Herbert Anderson

W e do not have to look far for signs of a dramatic gender paradigm shift in our time. Literature on gender, including more recent attention to men's studies, is everywhere. Gender is a prominent topic in the classroom, in professional gatherings, in political campaigns, in clinical case conferences, in some bedrooms, and occasionally in the board room. In the media, gender issues continue to grab the headlines. In 1991 alone, it was reported that women agonize over: the testimony of sexual harassment at the hearings to confirm a Supreme Court justice, the daring testimony of women celebrities about sexual abuse, women's roles in military combat because of Operation Desert Storm, the revelations of women who kill their abusers, the deceit of the manufacturers of silicone breast implants, inadequate family-leave policies and the government's reluctance to change them, the "rape" epidemic, and the "men's movement." We hear that men long for male mentors, seek to recover rituals of initiation, deplore the genocide of the African American male, struggle to make and keep male friendships, struggle with the responsibilities of fatherhood, and much, much more.

The transformation that has occurred in the relations between the sexes in the past three decades has radically shaken the very foundations of common life. Outside of race and sexuality, none of the other significant issues in this section of the book—aging, politics, economics, medical care, even the family—touch the core of personhood to the extent that gender does. The shift in standards for gender role behavior raises serious questions of personal identity, marriage and relationships with others, parenting, family, work, and justice between the sexes in all of society's institutions. In place of previously accepted traditions and roles, people now raise an unprecedented array of basic self-defining questions and related social, economic, political, and religious questions. What does it mean to be a woman or a man? Are family roles like husband, wife, father, mother gender-specific so that every family *must* have one of each? Are men and women more different than alike, or more alike than different? Given a few seemingly insurmountable reproductive differences, what does equality in the home and at work really mean?

Some people who like the changes in the organization of family, work, and gender roles credit the rise of second-wave feminism—the period of feminism dating from approximately 1966 (Lear, 1968)—while those who don't blame "bra burning" feminists. Both are wrong in different ways. While the feminist critique of the effects of domesticity on women served to undermine oppressive gender roles, this was not the only force at work. The increasing technical sophistication and rationality, service orientation, and individualism of postindustrial capitalist society canceled out many differences between genders required of a preindustrial, agrarian economy and broadened the possibilities for both women and men. As sociologist Judith Stacey suggests, gender changes were "coincident with the rise of second wave feminism" rather than caused by it (Stacey, 1987, 7-11). The modern nuclear family and its affective and instrumental gender roles would have come under increasing stress with or without a feminist critique. Certainly, feminism made a difference. It played the role of "unwitting midwife" to the massive social transformations of work and family life that have occurred in the post–World War era.

This gender paradigm shift has created new situations for pastoral care and a need to reconsider the framework of pastoral theology. Thus far, only a few persons in pastoral theology have addressed issues of gender directly. More attention to gender and pastoral care is needed. Alongside threats to the survival of our fragile earthly home and the shrinking of the planet to a global village, the gender paradigm shift is a fundamental change in modern life, fundamental enough to require a serious rethinking of pastoral care. This chapter attempts to explore problems of gender in our present social context and suggest some of the implications for pastoral theory and practice. Given what we can and must say about gender, how should we revise and expand our understanding of pastoral care?

Our experience of writing together illustrates the complexity of the topic. The two of us brought different concerns to this joint project. And yet we could not explain our divergent perspectives on this emotionally charged issue solely on the basis of gender. In fact, our perspectives were often, though not always, a reversal of traditional role expectations that women are primarily concerned about practical care and men are more apt to think abstractly. Even when our particular approaches reflected gendered ways of knowing, we also recognized that we are more alike than different. Indeed, our identities as white seminary professors in mainline church traditions and in marriages built on the ideal of shared responsibility gave us considerable common ground that will not be the same for women and men with other economic, familial, experiential, and religious histories. Gender makes a difference, but it is not the only difference. Although in this essay we attend primarily to gender issues and pastoral care, we are aware that the oppressions related to sex and gender are inextricably linked with other forms of oppression like racism, classism, ethnocentrism, imperialism, and heterosexism. Our focus here is on only one form of the abuse of power.

DEFINING GENDER

Until recently, many people considered the term *gender* interchangeable with the term *sex*. More current social scientific writing uses the term *sex* for biological givens and *gender* for the socially learned differences between men and women. This definitional nuance reflects a basic shift in cultural awareness and perception. We now recognize that what we had presumed as innate differences are more often the result of specific acts of socialization that dress boys in blue, with blocks and trucks, and dress girls in pink, with dolls. Gender attributions are more a construction of socially defined expectations, patterns, duties, and obligations than the result of biological givens.

At the same time, strict division between gender and sex is somewhat deceptive. Real life is far more complex. Gender always has biological linkage, just as sexuality never exists in some pure physical essence apart from social interpretation. The dualistic use of sex to refer to the physical and gender to refer to the social simply recapitulates problems of other binary oppositions of Western intellectual history (nature vs. culture, biology vs. environment, body vs. mind, woman vs. man) (cf. Griffin, 1978; Griscom, 1985, 85-98). While we use *gender* primarily to refer to one's socially constructed sexual identity and to learned differences in behavior and thought, we also believe that the particularities of physical givens and biologically shaped encounters significantly influence a person's sense of gender. *Sex* and *gender* are mutually influential.

Most people are preoccupied with personal, practical problems, not with such nuancing of a definition. Gender, like race and sexuality, is woven into the fabric of one's being. To think of my self is to think of myself as gendered. Even if it is largely socially constructed, the phenomenological fact remains that as early as eighteen months and usually by three years of age, through the complex interaction of genes and environment, a child sees herself or himself as a gendered person and not as a generic person. However, gender has an even more ambiguous relationship to genetic heritage than do race and sexuality. Where history and culture have constructed a portion of the meanings of race and sexuality, they have determined multiple and sometimes contradictory meanings and enactments of gender and of what it means to be a woman or a man.

Biologically and psychologically, women and men are more alike than different. Studies of differences in genes, hormones, and brain hemisphericity have yet to demonstrate irreducible differences in intelligence, emotionality, and behavior (Van Leeuwen, 1990, 54). Yet we simply do not know enough to be absolute one way or another. Research in the natural sciences and the social sciences does warrant a cautious acknowledgment of certain differences between women and men. Some sexual differences are inescapable. Some are even useful. Still other differences are in the nice but not necessary category. In order to care for men and women in the most effective way possible at this point in human history, we need to reconsider gender difference, correct the injustices created around the misuse of gender difference, and find ways to celebrate diversity.

RECONSIDERING GENDER DIFFERENCE
AND ITS MEANINGS

A headline in *Time* magazine proclaimed that "gender differences have as much to do with the biology of the brain as the way we are raised" (*Time*, 1/20/92, 42-51). While the headline may attract attention, the content of the article itself was not convincing. Some of the so-called innate differences between men and women such as height or amount of body fat may be true enough, but they are not remarkable. And a good deal of intellectual rubbish has been produced in support of innate mental differences between the sexes. Nineteenth-century biologists, for example, tried to prove that a woman's brain was too small for intellectual work but adequate for domestic chores; twentieth-century sociobiologists argue that a woman's ability to intuit other people's hidden motives and needs has evolved genetically to predispose them toward attending to infants. It is perhaps no coincidence, as Barbara Ehrenreich suggests, that studies of inherent differences receive funding and media attention precisely at a time of organized challenge to the ancient sexual division of power (Ehrenreich, 1992, 51).

Of greater interest are empirical findings about mental processing, statistical records of behavior patterns, and qualitative studies of emotional and moral development and experience. For instance, women tend to make more use of both sides of their brain as a result of a wider *corpus callosum,* the thick bundle of nerves that allows the right half of the brain to communicate with the left (Ashbrook, 1992, 46:174-83). Statistical surveys produce equally interesting results: female physicians, for example, see 36 percent fewer patients per hour than male physicians; men visit physicians 37 percent less than do women (*In Health,* 1991). These various studies do not presume to resolve the nature or nurture debate, a debate over the origin of gender differences that many researchers agree can never be fully resolved. Instead, many studies assume the influence of society as an inevitable variable. Greater access to the brain's imagery and depth, for instance, may help explain a girl's earlier progress in verbal activity. Or it may simply be that adults talk more to infant girls than to boys, which in turn influences brain development.

According to qualitative research, girls and boys develop differently because women have universally taken the main responsibility for raising children. Thus girls, identifying with mother, learn to define themselves through connection to and empathic identification with others, boys, moving away from mother, through separation and individuation (cf. Chodorow, 1978; Dinnerstein, 1976). Boys learn to make moral decisions according to abstract reason and rules of justice; girls rely upon contextual relationships and rules of care (cf. Belenky, et al., 1986; Gilligan, 1981). Again, while such studies confirm the power of gender differences, they also suggest the social malleability of human sexual nature.

So, for example, if fathers participated more directly in caring for children at the beginning of life, it might reshuffle these patterns, correct the built-in devaluation of mothers and female attributes, and provide alternative role models that would benefit women as well as men.

What complicates this picture of malleability is that which is more difficult to modify, namely, the procreative dimension of life: Females bear the potential of pregnancy and nursing; by comparison the role of males is more indirect. Due to the lengthy period of gestation, mothers are burdened longer than females of other species. Bodily, psychically, the woman may experience a more immediate, acute connection with her young. Hence, when persons remark that the "*only*" difference between males and females is simply that females bear young and nurse," that "only" continues to stand as an intriguing reproductive and endocrine difference that we have yet to grasp fully for fear of returning to unfair gender stereotypes and oppressions (Miller-McLemore, 1994, 72:229-47; Rossi, 1977, 106:9; Ruddick, 1983, 213-30).

Today not everyone wants to, can, or will choose to reproduce. People are more aware of the stereotypes and oppressions than ever before. In the past three decades many have recognized the costs of the institution of motherhood to women. Women have almost universally born the brunt of the labors of child care, often to their economic, social, and political detriment. Many have questioned the Victorian belief that if a woman is not a mother she is somehow incomplete. At the same time, a high percentage of women and men still become biological parents.

However people negotiate this particular life-cycle passage, the ability to reproduce the species, which is biologically unique to women, must be further understood. The responsibilities that have historically been a chief source of women's oppression must continue to be elucidated. While procreative potentials are partly given biologically, a mother's sole responsibility for the lengthy period of dependency of human infants is not. Although the biology of procreation is less than plastic, people have always modified who cares for children and how they are cared for. Unique to the scene now is the attempt to modify the degree of male participation in child care. Only greater understanding of procreative activities will make genuine relational and economic justice between women and men more attainable.

The gender-specific nature of family roles has been invoked recently in the efforts to revitalize the role of fathers. The instability of the family and the increase in neighborhood violence are blamed on the absence of the father-role that is specific to men. Children need fathers, the argument goes, because they love differently than mothers. The insistence on the unique role of fathers in families has become a political as well as a moral agenda.

This brief discussion of gender differences has led us to a far more important normative and philosophical question that falls within the territory of pastoral theology and care: Given the differences, however trivial or significant in actuality, whether nature or nurture in origin, what are we going to do about them? What do these differences mean or what ought they to mean for individual and communal sustenance and fulfillment? The question is not whether men and women are different, but rather what value we shall place on these differences and how we shall live with them. At stake is not just the question of gender but the question of the human capacity to live with difference among persons in a planet that continues to shrink. For that reason, we regard gender studies as a necessary endeavor in pastoral theology, because the celebration of diversity and respect for human uniqueness is at stake.

CORRECTING INJUSTICE AND RESPECTING DIFFERENCE

Historically, differences have meant opposition and oppression. Differences between women and men have been confused with an inequality between men and women, which has led to women's subjugation to men. Attempts to enact equality under the reign of this perspective on differences have meant simply a reversal of roles, which has failed to resolve problems of justice and fulfillment. In some cases, the legal and political implications of the definition of equality as sameness, in divorce laws or leave policies, for example, have only added to the economic and relational burdens of women, as studies like Lenore Weitzman's *The Divorce Revolution* (1985) indicate. Equality based upon a homogeneous standard of sameness with man as the normative model does not take into account pregnancy, the needs of children, or the ways in which the cultural and social environment limits opportunities for many women from birth onward.

Our legal, social, and economic constructions of equality need to embody a richer conception of the human that respects diversity and takes both sameness and difference into account, depending on the circumstances. Women and men are equal but different. From this perspective, acknowledging differences between men and women serves the greater cause of justice, fairness, and mutuality. Society is not yet genderless. Learning to live with difference means more adjusting and compensating justly for differences rather than suppressing women's ways of knowing and honoring men's. For example, Barbara Ehrenreich (1992) has suggested somewhat facetiously that the female advantage in reading emotions could be interpreted to mean that males should be barred from psychiatry—or that they need more coaching. A male advantage in math could be used to confine girls to essays and sonnets— or the decision could be made to compensate by putting more effort into girls' math education. In effect, we already compensate for boys' apparent handicap in verbal skills by making reading the centerpiece of grade-school education. In other words, why haven't we made similar compensations and allowances for girls? It is quite possible that if men menstruated and got pregnant, as Gloria Steinem once mused, we would have had different social structures and patterns to accommodate those realities. The question we need to keep asking is this: What difference should the gender differences make?

Considerable gender conflict remains hidden. Powerful gender subtexts still determine much of the interaction between women and men. Women file sexual harassment and rape charges, for example, but many social institutions, and sadly, religious institutions in particular, still fail to process the charges. Even more disturbing, the growing public attention to charges of harassment and violence toward women has not diminished the practice of it (cf. Fortune, 1989, 1983; Lebacqz and Barton, 1991; Poling, 1991). In fact, because women have more equality of opportunity for jobs previously held only by men, they are often vulnerable to the abuse of power and the violation of trust by men in positions of authority.

Some of the most painful conflicts over gender equality continue to occur in the family. Dramatic increases in divorce rates and substantial increases in the participation of women in the labor force have contributed to changes in "traditional" gender role divisions in the family. However, women are still subtly blamed for the dismal plight of today's children, for failing their so-called natural inclination to put family first, while many men continue to abdicate their parenting responsibilities. And it is a futile enterprise to persuade men to work harder at fathering and family relationships as long as American social and economic values continue to regard nurturance as a second-rate activity.

Gender conflicts internal to the family—Who will take the kids to

Little League? or, Who will write the holiday cards?—will never be fully resolved without attending to subtle conflicts inherent in the structures of our market economy. Perhaps the question, Who will move on behalf of the other's career? best exemplifies the fundamental contradiction between the family's division of labor and the market economy's view of labor. The market economy assumes, as Ulrich Beck has observed, the single individual, "unhindered" by personal relationships, marriage, or family commitments (Beck, 1992, 103-50). It is predicated upon home-maker-breadwinner roles of domination and submission. In familial relationships based upon equality, however, the market demand for individual mobility ignores the requirements of familial and social bonds and demands that they not interfere with the needs of the market. While few people publicly oppose equal opportunity or even equal pay for equal work or equality in the household, a workplace governed by traditional patterns and rules forbids equal involvement in family, relational, and domestic labor and continues to punish those, women and men alike, who carry such responsibilities. Until these contradictions are addressed, inequality between the sexes or more precisely, inequality between those in market labor and those in domestic labor—of either sex—will persist.

It is not easy in any society to maintain equality while at the same time respecting difference. What is different is frequently regarded as inferior. What is different may also be viewed as dangerous, and sometimes it is. Difference sometimes promotes disunity and often generates conflict. The inability to tolerate diversity has led to prejudice, isolationism, and self-protection based on fear. One of the most effective ways of seeming to dissolve conflict between persons is to maintain that differentness is an illusion. Another way is to dismiss the worth or significance of the other, hence the need to take them seriously, by claiming difference as an empirical proof of one's own superiority. Traditional definitions of humanness in white male terms have had the effect of maintaining gender superiority for men while at the same time defining women in male terms.

The biblical view of creation stands in sharp contrast to these efforts to diminish diversity or to turn difference into injustice and oppression. The diversity that is part of creation and human societies is a sign of the extravagance of God's creative love. And it is diversity, despite its diffi-culties, that fosters creativity and makes community possible. Within the human community of men and women, individuals are often able to help one another precisely because they are unlike one another. Creating false and oppressive differences between women and men is a violation of the relationality of creation. As Lisa Cahill puts it, the "hierarchy of the sexes is the consequence and perpetuation of sin, corrupting the dominator as well as the dominated" (Cahill, 1985, 55). Turning sexual difference into hierarchical gender categories is a rejection of the generosity of the Creator as much as is imposing unnecessary limits on the difference between genders. When it is rightly understood, difference is a gift of God and a cause for celebration.

IMPLICATIONS FOR PASTORAL THEOLOGY

Gender issues continue to evoke an undercurrent of tension throughout society. Hence, a central task of pastoral theology must be to examine the implications of gender differences, to define the hidden gender subtexts that permeate the culture and prevent human flourishing, and in some cases, to work toward reconciliation. Broadly stated, this means that pastoral theology must make gender analysis a more central part of its theoretical constructions. When only male voices determine the parameters and content of the discipline without attending to gender subtexts, the visions of pastoral and practical theology are limited. If men and women do indeed think differently, how can our vision and method of pastoral theology be broadened to include a variety of voices? The following attempt to answer this question borrows and modifies slightly a framework for the art of pastoral care suggested by Charles Gerkin (1991*a*, 45:399-408).

Attending to the social context. One of the legacies of Gerkin's work is the way in which he has turned our attention beyond the intrapsychic "therapeutic metaphor" to the social context for the work of pastoral care. As he argues in *Prophetic Pastoral Practice,* "The imaginative prophetic pastor will seek to both embody and respond to the wisdom of God as that wisdom has been made available to us in the stories of our tradition and as that wisdom reveals itself to us in the events and issues of our present life" (Gerkin, 1991*b,* 71). We must listen at many levels. Beyond the concern for the moral and historical context of pastoral care, we need to consider other contextual factors: interpretations of gender alongside those of race, ethnicity, class, and world view.

If we attend seriously to the social context, we are likely to discover that the practice of pastoral theology cannot avoid wider public implications. Individual healing does not happen apart from social remedies.

Pastoral theology must not disregard the power of the social context to undermine publicly the good that pastoral care has effected privately (cf. Graham, 1992). Women and men who have been scarred by oppressive definitions of gender will not finally be free until the gender subtexts that institutionalize injustice and gender inequality are eliminated. In a time of radical transition, those who engage in pastoral care not only need to sustain persons and communities through conflict and upheaval; they need to be engaged in efforts toward social transformation as well. It is necessary, for example, to challenge from pulpit and pastoral office alike the social norms of care that artificially separate public material achievement from private nurturance and then proceed to deny equal value for domestic and public work. It is equally important that pastoral theology be about the task of reshaping the ideal of love as self-sacrifice, under which women have traditionally lost all sense of themselves as persons, in order to move toward a new religious ethic of mutuality, reciprocity, and equal regard.

Listening with new eyes. One of our students observed at the end of a class that the readings were helpful but not the source of his greatest insight. "It was a cry. A cry that I just couldn't seem to get out of my mind. A cry that kept coming back to me again and again." This cry was the anguish of one particular woman in the class, recovering from an abusive marital relationship and struggling to define herself as a single mother and a woman. Although the student had been a pastor for twenty years, he had never really thought about the differences between the struggles of women and men in postmodern society. After hearing the cry of this woman, "Pastoral care took on a new perspective and a greater sensitivity. I began to hear things in a different way, to look again at what it means to do ministry and pastoral care with new eyes."

Listening with new eyes is different from the unconditional positive regard and empathic listening of the therapeutic paradigm that may have been part of this student's initial training. Gerkin makes a significant theological connection between listening and hearing. When we listen carefully to people, we hear their pain. Listening across gender, as well as listening across all differences that have spawned oppression, is the hardest exercise in pain we can perform. It is hard for men in particular to hear that they have inadvertently and sometimes directly been the source of this pain. Rather than believing he could understand through empathy, the pastor just mentioned had to admit that at certain points he could never understand as he wanted to or as he should. And this failure to understand across certain differences had all too often been a source of suffering, injury, and injustice.

In one of the first essays on women and pastoral care, Emma Justes concluded that "pastoral counselors who find that they are unable to travel the route of hearing women's anger, of exploring with women the painful depths of experiences of incest and rape, or enabling women to break free from cultural stereotypes that define their existence, should not be doing pastoral counseling with women" (Justes, 1985, 298). We concur. This does not rule out men *per se* as much as it rules out all those, men and women alike, who cannot, for whatever reason, perceive the pain of gender oppression and respond adequately. More recently, Maxine Glaz (1991, 17:94-107) has alerted us to the problem not of too little empathy but of too much indiscriminate empathy, which surfaces long-repressed sentiments that may overwhelm rather than help a person who suffered abuse. In some situations of sexual abuse, battering, and marital conflict, only women should care for women and men for men, while in other struggles over self-esteem, self-confidence, and competition, a man may speak more freely with a woman and vice versa. More often than not, however, the abuse of power by men and the resulting rage of women has seriously damaged any basic sense of trust between men and women. In many interactions across genders, simply reestablishing trust will necessarily take conscious behavior changes, improved means of professional accountability in the privacy of the pastoral office, a determination to work toward reconciliation, and considerable patience.

In critical instances, then, people have no ready entrance into the experience of the other. Listening in order to hear requires a kind of conversion to heretofore unrecognized, oftentimes harsh realities of another person's existence. Over against the relatively optimistic view of the human condition more common to the therapeutic ideal, this view of listening dares to see the face of personal and social sin and human exploitation and not look the other way. Blinded by the light of conversion, people who listen with new eyes will never see the same again. Ultimately, this kind of listening demands confession of one's blindness, narrowness, and complacency and the adoption of a new advocacy on behalf of the other. As Gerkin reminds us again and again, we must be listening for the subtle and not-so-subtle injustices that are inherent in the world as each person experiences it. This listening with new eyes implies much, much more than "lip service . . . to cultural, economic, and political aspects of human problems and the practical actions appropriate to addressing them" inherent in the therapeutic model of the past few decades.

What we may hear when we listen through pain is the promise of a presence that transcends our limited efforts at care. Human pastoral care is sustained by its participation in the healing care of God. Before God there are no hierarchies of differences; the ones giving care and those receiving care are all "broken hearted," women and men alike (cf. Brock, 1988). What we hear when we listen is "the voice of God as that voice speaks silently and mysteriously through all the other voices to which our ears give attention" (Gerkin, 1991a, 45:406), and that voice invites our participation in making all things new.

Advocating because of what we hear. Insisting on gender consciousness does not mean that women and men are irreconcilably different. Quite the contrary, such consciousness allows greater realization that people are people. For both men and women, if a pastoral caregiver is not aware of the changes that have taken place in sex-defined roles, a good many personal, marital, and communal conflicts will not be adequately understood. For women, if a pastoral caregiver does not know how to recognize the stark realities of incest and other violence toward women, only further damage and violence will ensue. All pastoral caregivers must sharpen their sensitivity to the stress women experience who are wage earners *and* homemakers (and men who do both), the economic disvaluation of women in the workplace, health issues specifically related to sexual differences, the violence against women, and the implications of female images of God for self-esteem (DeMarinis, 1993; Doehring, 1992, 46:23-31; R. Hunter, 1990, 1329-34; Miller-McLemore, 1989, 43:201-21; Neuger, 1992, 2:35-57; cf. Justes, 1985; Saussy, 1991). For men, the pastoral agenda is less obvious but equally vital. It needs to include an exploration of masculine role confusion, attention to the fear and anger that gender role changes have evoked, consideration of the tension between the expectations of work and family, and an examination of buried grief for losses of many kinds (Clinebell, 1977, 139-59; R. Hunter, 1990, 704-7; cf. Culbertson, 1992; Dittes, 1985, 1987; Keen, 1991).

From this perspective, pastoral care is never neutral about human suffering and injustice. Knowing and seeing the needs of the marginalized and the abuse of children and women, as Gerkin has observed, "brings with it tremendous responsibilities for widening the horizons of our care of persons" (Gerkin, 1991a, 45:403). This knowledge fosters a care that includes seeking stiffer penalties for domestic violence, greater awareness of sexual harassment and clearer modes of professional accountability, stricter means of enforcing male economic and relational responsibility for offspring, better public policy on behalf of leave-time to care for children, and so on. Pastoral care must be an immediate response informed by a Christian moral vision of community and vocation to persons temporarily or more permanently outside the mainstream of community life.

Seeking reconciliation. To celebrate and live with sexual diversity requires the ability to practice reconciliation, particularly as we discuss gender in the context of pastoral care and theology. Reconciling has been part of the church's practice of care for centuries. In the early church, it was thought of primarily as a means of discipline for the sake of community. With the development of the penitential system, reconciliation was privatized and the focus shifted to making peace with God. The recovery of aspects of the prior meaning of reconciling as a communal way of living is a necessary mode of care for our time. The potential for mass destruction, the globalization of neighborhoods, and the growing recognition of gender and other differences all converge to make it necessary that we learn to practice reconciliation as a discipline of the community for the sake of our common future.

Reconciliation as we use it here includes the desire for a restoration of relationships and hearts that have been broken. But it is more. It does not just right wrongs; it brings us to a place where we have not been before. It is about prevention of injustice and oppression more than restoration; it is an attitude or way of living and thinking more than incidental action. We must honor sexual uniqueness *and* promote the community of women and men. It may mean, for example, encouraging men to pay greater attention to the affective side of life while encouraging women to take greater part in the public sphere. As a way of living, reconciliation promotes the fuller enactment of dominion and procreation for both women and men.

If this is the case, reconciliation must never become a hasty peace that smooths over memories of violence toward women perpetrated by men on the presumption of gender superiority. Too many women have been told that it is their Christian duty to forgive the men who abused them. This trivializes and ignores memory; it denies human identity and dignity (cf. Schrieter, 1992). Reconciliation is not an easy truce created by certain psychological techniques of conflict resolution or religious rituals of confession and forgiveness. Nor is it simply an inner peace. Ritual and techniques help; inner peace is a side benefit. But reconciliation keeps its own timetables. It will take time to repair the gender damage of twenty centuries of abuse. Reconciliation must involve naming and expunging the structures that oppress men and women alike. Hence, those in pastoral care have a responsibility not to deny conflict and bitterness but rather to enable continued dialogue between women and men within the turmoil.

In the end, however, reconciliation is not always the goal; sometimes it is not even historically possible or desirable. When genuine reconciliation does occur, it is the work of God to which we lend a hand. And it may become a way of life that leads us into new lands. The adjudication and celebration of differences between men and women depend on it.

CHAPTER 8

Sexuality:
A Crisis for the Church

James N. Poling

This is a pivotal time in the history of sexual ethics in the United States. A Supreme Court nominee was confirmed to the highest court despite public charges of sexual harassment. Prominent ministers in both evangelical and progressive churches have lost their status and jobs because of sexual abuse of persons for whom they had spiritual responsibility. There is a spirited debate about "traditional family values" as a code phrase for differences of opinion about women's rights and gay and lesbian concerns. The level of conflict and sharp disagreement about sexual ethics is perhaps as strong as any time in this century. How did we get where we are?

There are at least two poles to the present discussion. One pole is the resurgence of concern for so-called traditional values (cf. Fishburn, 1991). Spurred on by the evangelical wing of the Christian churches and some conservative political and social analysts, many church members believe that sexuality should be confined to the family with strong sanctions supplied by legal authorities. In this view, sexual intercourse is limited to marriage. Premarital, extramarital, and same-gender sexual expressions are seen as immoral and perhaps illegal. Abortion is considered murder except when the life of the mother is in danger. AIDS is an excuse for controlling life-styles rather than only a public health emergency.

The second pole is a coalition of progressive views with a variety of interrelated ethical commitments: to listen to the victims of sexual violence in a different way (cf. Fortune, 1983); to consider the possibility that the requirements of love and justice can be met in covenantal relationships other than legally sanctioned heterosexual marriage; and to be open to the testimony of gay men and lesbian women that loving same-sex covenants including sexual expressions are morally appropriate (cf. McNeill, 1988). This coalition of ethical positions shares a commitment to the principle that marginalized groups such as women, African Americans, and lesbians should have a certain priority in ethical discussions (Nelson, 1978). The balance of this article will focus broadly on this set of moral commitments, giving a privileged voice to the particular concerns of African Americans. (For a summary of the claims of other ethnic groups in recent ethical and theological discussions of sexuality see Thistlethwaite and Engel, 1990. Also, for discussion of ethical and theological questions related to abortion and AIDS, which the present essay cannot take up in a substantive way, see Andolsen et al., 1985, 101-20; Shelp et al., 1986).

THE CONTRIBUTION OF PASTORAL CARE
ON ISSUES OF SEXUALITY

In a recent article, Charles Gerkin referred to his own clinical training in the 1940s when supervisors and students were motivated by a desire to accurately hear the suffering that was often denied by the larger society (Gerkin, 1991 a, 45:400).

> Those of us who were attracted to pastoral care in those days were convinced . . . that in significant ways North American culture had hardened its heart against the cries of those who were oppressed by the conformities that culture demanded. . . . Insensitivity to the pain of the guilt-laden, the oppression of those whose lives were set about by rigid conformities had come upon American culture, most particularly American religious culture. The listening ears of religious people had, so it seemed to us, become tuned only to moralistic ways of hearing. Self-expression had been stifled, even condemned by some who were in a position to set the tone of American religious life. The experience of the guilt-laden, the relationally conflicted, the inhibited in spirit was not being given credence. To us, their experience demanded to be heard, their quiet protest against the conformities of moralized religion deserved a listening ear.

This ethical commitment to listen to those unheard by the culture and to support their protest against moralistic conformity was the basis for reform of the church. In the beginning of the pastoral care movement, pastors and chaplains visited those who were marginalized: the sick in hospitals, the mentally ill in psychiatric facilities, and prisoners in the criminal justice system. Verbatim transcripts of pastoral conversations were primary instruments in creating the discipline necessary to hear what suffering persons were really saying, especially when the words and feelings created great anxiety and denial in the pastor. Such training was based on the assumption that what persons had to say about their suffering was important, even when it seemed to contradict social morality or theological dogma. Pastoral work was no longer understood as socialization and restoring deviant persons to acceptable behaviors and feelings. Anger and depression were seen as appropriate responses to the marginalization experienced by the ill, the mentally ill, and prisoners.

The basis of the reform was the empirical principle of the pastoral care movement, which required pastors to listen to the experience of suffering persons and give it validity in relation to theological norms. Implicitly, experience was understood as "the felt, bodily, psycho-social organic action of human beings in history" within which could be discerned the immanence of God (R. Hunter, 1990, 357). This principle had the effect of relativizing traditional authorities who set the terms of morality. The pastoral care movement understood itself as a reform of the church and culture away from authoritarian and moralistic theologies and toward empathic relationships with persons and communities in their practice of the Christian life.

Until the early fifties, sexuality was not an important focus of the pastoral care movement. The topic is hardly mentioned in its leaders' early books and articles. An early book by Richard Cabot (1913, repr. 1937) was written to allay the fears of the church that the new ideas of Sigmund Freud and Havelock Ellis would bring drastic changes in sexual ethics. In a lecture titled "The Consecration of the Affections," Cabot said, "The problem we are concerned with is, of course, the problem of chastity, the problem of purity as a virtue" (1913, 10). He spends much of his time reassuring his Christian audience that the new talk about sexuality is not a threat if the church remembers its commitment to certain values like chastity, honesty, family life and marriage, and so on. He speaks as one who is confident about the traditional morality of the church and for whom the "problem of sex" is not the burning cultural issue it would later become.

In the first two texts of our field in 1936, sex is treated as a minor topic. Cabot and Dicks barely mention it in their case studies (Cabot and Dicks, 1936). Boisen defends a sacramental view of sexuality:

> Instead of reducing religion to the level of the sexual, a correct under-standing requires that the sexual be raised to the level of the religious. . . . What true love wants is union with the idealized other-than-self, which is also what religion wants. Sex love thus seeks not just the finite love object but the infinite, and when it ceases to do so it is no longer love. . . . These positive values are to be found first of all in the home. This might involve a rediscovery of the sacramental character of marriage. . . . It would set up the ideal of a self-mastery and consecration of will on the part of the individuals concerned which would enable them to practice self control and to reserve the act of intercourse to such times and such occasions as would have for them a truly sacramental value and serve as the outward and visible symbol of communion, not merely with each other but with God. (Boisen, 1971, 278-79)

This quotation discloses a religious orientation that does not feel threat-ened by issues of sexuality. Some of the later texts in pastoral care follow this same lead by treating sexuality as a minor issue (cf. Dicks, 1944; Kemp, 1947; Wise, 1951).

In the early fifties, a dramatic change in the attention of the pastoral care movement to sexuality was signaled by two books, Hiltner's *Sex Ethics and the Kinsey Reports* (1953) and Doniger's edited volume, *Sex and Religion Today* (1953). Suddenly, sexuality was a topic that merited attention and theological reflection. It had become an issue too big to be ignored or assumed under other topics. Why?

There was evidently more going on here than the movement's attempt to respond to a change in the larger culture. In some parts of the church, for example, the cultural change on issues of sexuality brought forward *stronger* moralism and repression, whereas the pastoral care movement invested considerable time trying to *understand* it. What was happening?

The most likely explanation, I believe, is that sexuality provided a means by which the pastoral care movement could challenge the church's narrow moralism. The movement's empirical principle sug-gested that if persons in and out of the church are suffering because of conflicts between their sexual behaviors and the church's ethical posi-tions, this phenomenon merits careful attention and pastoral under-standing, not condemnation, even if this approach creates anxiety in church leaders. God is speaking through these new voices of suffering even if the church does not want to hear.

117

For some pastoral care leaders, Kinsey's research was explosive. He discovered in the 1940s that individual behavior deviated dramatically from the prevailing and accepted views of sexual ethics. Large pluralities and even majorities of persons in United States society engaged in premarital petting and intercourse, extramarital affairs, and homosexual behaviors. This information meant that individuals, in their private lives, were challenging the public consensus that sexuality was being confined to the family. This crisis was especially acute for the pastoral care movement because of its principle of taking such behavior seriously and asking socially critical questions about its meaning, unlike conservative churches that could account for such behavior as the continuing prevalence of sin, which needed only more vigorous enforcement of its traditional values of family life.

The pastoral care movement responded in three ways to Kinsey's research. First, it affirmed the empirical principle that experience was a source of God's revelation and often had priority over traditional morality and theological dogma. Joseph Fletcher suggested that the moralism of the past was actually responsible for much of the confusion about sexuality.

> First of all it needs saying that the Christian churches must shoulder much of the blame for the confusion, ignorance, and unhealthy guilt associations which surround sex in Western culture. (Doniger, 1953, 188-90)

Second, the pastoral care movement adopted the theme of covenantal relationality as a more adequate moral basis for sexual expression.

> There is another issue that the pastor must settle in his own mind. What is his goal in working with people who come with sex problems? Is it to seek behavior on the basis of civil or moral law? Is it to inculcate a "Christian philosophy of sex," by which we mean a set of intellectual statements about sex and the way it should be handled? Or is it to help people to achieve the capacity for love, so that their sexual impulses may come under the control of love and become the expression of love? . . . The goal of the Christian pastor should be that of helping people to develop their capacity for love.
> (Doniger, 1953, 164)

Covenantal relationality as a theological basis for sexuality was meant to challenge the narrow behavioral moralism of the past and to give a positive role for sexuality in human life. This direction was followed by most of the larger denominations in their later ethical statements about sexuality.

Third, however, covenantal relationality actually meant marriage and the family, which was considered the only appropriate social location for sexual expression. After carefully developing a covenantal ethic informed by developmental theory, Hiltner basically reaffirmed that the appropriate purpose of sexuality was the enhancement of marriage, and he feared that the promiscuity of the lower classes and the rationalizations of gays and lesbians would threaten the stability of society (Hiltner, 1953, 123, 226, 233). He was hopeful that a more adequate theology and courage to face the facts of the Kinsey report would eventually strengthen the family.

By the end of the 1960s, every large progressive church denomination had debated and passed statements on sexuality (cf. Genne, 1976; Wynn, 1966, 1970). Based on a cursory reading of these statements, they seem to be consistent with the three points just given: (1) criticism of previous moralistic approaches to sexual ethics based on the empirical principle of giving primary attention to experience; (2) affirmation of covenantal relationality as the theological basis for sexual expression; (3) reaffirmation of the family as the appropriate social location for the expression of covenantal relationality and sexuality. As the churches defined their sexual ethics in various official statements in the 1960s, the fears they most identified were premarital and extramarital sex and homosexuality. Psychologically, however, one wonders whether fearing that teenagers, single adults, divorcees, gays and lesbians might engage in unapproved sexual expression helped persons to focus their attention away from anxiety about their own sexuality.

Although the denominational statements on sexuality have held for almost two decades, the present situation in the churches is characterized by confusion and resistance to the liberation movements of women, African Americans, and gays and lesbians. Leadership for the church around issues of sexuality has not been coming from the established leaders of pastoral care. Although a new generation of feminist and other pastoral theologians is beginning to challenge the church again (cf. Couture, 1991a; Glaz and Moessner, 1991; Lebacqz and Barton, 1991; Poling, 1991; Rediger, 1990), the main leadership is coming from other disciplines and perspectives, principally feminist and womanist challenges to patriarchy (cf. Brown and Bohn, 1989; Fortune, 1983; and many others), African American challenges to racism (Andolsen et al., 1985, 121-42; cf. Cannon, 1988; Grant, 1989), and gay and lesbian challenges to heterosexism (cf. Heyward, 1989; Hunt, 1991; McNeill, 1988).

Why is the pastoral care movement not providing important leadership in the current debate over sexuality in the church as it did in the fifties and sixties? In one sense this turn of events is surprising given the pastoral care movement's commitment to reform in the church, its opposition to moralism and theological narrowness, and its concern to listen to the unheard voices of those who suffer. One might expect that the pastoral care movement would become a leader in the new attempts to reform the church's attitudes on sexuality. But in this new crisis of sexuality, pastoral care lags behind.

Marie Fortune has emerged as a leader in the movement to bring sexual violence to the attention of the church. What she says about the silence of the church may just as well apply to the pastoral care movement:

> The most significant reason for the silence in ethical discourse is that sexual violence is something which is perceived to happen primarily to women and children and, as such, has not been a priority for most ethicists. The limitations of the patriarchal bias and male experience (which for most male ethicists probably did not include sexual assault) have meant that sexual violence as an experience and as an ethical issue has been overlooked. (Fortune, 1983, 43)

Because most pastoral care specialists have been men, they have not really understood the theological significance of sexual violence as an issue for the church, and they have remained silent.

In like manner, African American womanist scholars have challenged the pervasive sexual attitudes, which function to reinforce racism in the church.

> Both black and white feminist groups that do not give explicit attention to the realities yoking racism and sexism will find that they can be easily manipulated by dominant males who appeal to unexamined class and race interests to achieve economic exploitation of all women. . . . Both in informal day-to-day life and in the formal organizations and institutions of society, black women are still the victims of the aggravated inequities of the tridimensional phenomenon of race/class/gender oppression. (Eugene, 1988, 32-33)

The connection of racism, sexism, and classism described by Toinette Eugene has not been addressed by the discussions of sexuality in the church. The preoccupation with whether sexual expression is allowed outside marriage prevents the church from seeing how the racist distortions of sexuality dominate and oppress African Americans.

The liberation movements of gay men and lesbian women also are challenging the church to change its analysis of sexuality.

> Heterosexism is the basic structure of gay/lesbian oppression in this and other societies. . . . Heterosexism is the *structure* in which are generated and

cemented the *feelings* of fear and hatred toward queers and dykes, and toward ourselves if we are lesbians or gaymen. Dialectically, such feelings serve also to secure the structure. They thereby strengthen not only such traditional patriarchal religious institutions as Christianity, which have helped set the structure of compulsory heterosexuality in place; but also more deeply personal "institutions," such as the self-loathing of homosexual youths and the hatred of such youths by others. (Heyward, 1989, 50)

Carter Heyward shows in this statement that the inability and unwillingness of the church to face its fears about gays and lesbians serves to maintain the patriarchal structure that depends on a myth about "traditional family values." The voices of gays and lesbians challenge this oppression that is built on the backs of marginalized people.

The study documents on sexuality commissioned by the United Church of Christ (1977) and the Presbyterian Church (USA) (1991*a*, 1991*b*) are examples of denominational attempts to take more seriously the views of the liberation movements of feminists and womanists, African Americans, and gays and lesbians. The fact that these statements are criticized so harshly is a clue to the depth of the present crisis.

Sexuality as a collection of ethical issues is here to stay. The anxiety about this topic has fueled discussion and conflict in the church. But the denominational statements approved in the past have hidden what we now know are much more serious dangers, namely, sexual violence against women and children, racist concepts of the body and persons of color, and oppression of gays and lesbians. As issues of sexual violence and heterosexism become clarified in our churches, the deeper polarizations will become evident. Ending sexual violence against children and women and ending heterosexism require more than merely tolerance of different behaviors and choices. What is required is confronting the powerful groups who benefit from these evils, namely, the leaders who benefit from male dominance. The awful truth is that traditional sexual ethics focused on controlling the sexuality of women, children, minorities, and gays and lesbians, but ignored the sexual behaviors of men, especially white, married, heterosexual men, for example, as witnessed in the recent disclosures about sexual abuse of children in the family and sexual misconduct by professionals, including the ordained clergy. In this new crisis, the power structure of male dominance is coming under challenge. Women are demanding the right to their own sexual integrity, which means freedom from sexual abuse as children, freedom from rape on the streets, on dates, and in marriage, and freedom to control the consequences of their sexual expression, namely whether to become pregnant or to carry a pregnancy to term. African Americans are challenging the church to see that the evils of oppression by race and class can only be changed when the white middle class is courageous enough to examine its own sexual pathologies. Gay men and lesbian women are demanding to be included in the full opportunities to exercise power and leadership and to have the same civil protection as other persons.

The empirical principle of the pastoral care movement requires that these new voices be heard, not only for their stories of suffering, but also for their social analysis and theological critique. The ethical imperative to the pastoral care movement is to organize in solidarity with these movements in the same way we supported those who were marginalized earlier in this century.

THE CURRENT CHALLENGE FOR PASTORAL CARE

The pastoral care movement has two choices. Either it is still a reform movement to change church and society, or it is a profession within the established patriarchal church and society concerned mainly with its own financial future, accreditation, and making sure it has a secure place for its members. The reason the pastoral care movement is not providing leadership on issues of sexuality is our inability to face male dominance within our movement. If the pastoral care movement decides to return to its earlier reformist goals, it must respond to the present crisis in the area of sexuality by focusing on issues of the liberation of women, African Americans, and gays and lesbians from the traditional sexual ethics that support male dominance. If male dominance is the current issue that threatens to polarize the church and the culture, there is much that the pastoral care movement needs to do.

First, we must make an ethical commitment to provide the resources of our field, principally pastoral counseling, at reasonable prices to the individuals and groups who are oppressed by the ideologies of church and society, namely, the survivors of sexual violence, women struggling against patriarchy, and gays and lesbians who are trying to cope with the oppression of a heterosexist society. Such a liberation-oriented care for those who are in serious danger from the society will require a reexamination of our traditional ethical positions, including the myth of neutrality in issues of ethics and morality. A liberation ethic will also require a reexamination of our usual ways of financing our work and will raise other questions about how our work is organized. Developing pastoral care strategies for perpetrators of sexual and other forms of violence will be necessary as this population begins to come for help. Special attention needs to be given to clergymen and male seminary students as they attempt to understand themselves differently in a changing world.

Second, such a commitment would mean revising our usual theories of care. As many recent scholars have clearly shown, all the standard theories of personality, family, and therapy harbor serious distortions in their assumptions of male dominance. Psychoanalytic thought usually treats women as subordinate to men; family therapy ignores the gender inequality that is acted out in the family; human potential theories assume that reaching one's potential is primarily a matter of individual effort and courage within a beneficial interpersonal web. These and other theories ignore gender and racial injustice in society by labeling women and minorities as deficient. The creative work being done by feminist, womanist, and gay and lesbian scholars needs to be taken into account in our theories of pastoral care.

Third, the pastoral care movement will have to examine its own organization of power and resources. Male dominance is aptly and sufficiently illustrated by the accreditation process, the selection of leaders, the decisions about programs and policies. It is no accident that 90 percent of chaplains, pastoral counselors, pastors, and other church leaders are men. And it is no accident that women, African Americans, and gays and lesbians complain that the accreditation process and the opportunities for leadership are stacked against them. Listening to the new voices will require significant administrative changes.

The pastoral care movement is a microcosm of the church, the ministry, and the seminaries. In this century, the church has become increasingly anxious about sexual matters. Seventy years ago, sexuality was only a small issue to be dealt with in passing. When Kinsey and others showed that individuals were not behaving the way the church expected, the pastoral care movement interpreted these data to mean that the moralistic approach to control of sexual behaviors had failed and the movement's leaders devoted twenty years of study to understand sexuality and confine it within the traditional family. Now we can see that this approach has failed as well. The branches of the church that never repented of moralistic solutions have intensified their efforts to control sexuality through evangelism, aggressive programs of family life education, and by lobbying the government for legal penalties for abortion, pregnancy outside marriage, and homosexuality.

The progressive branch of the church, of which the pastoral care movement is a part, is in crisis, and sexuality is one of the issues that begin to disclose the depths of this crisis. At first, leaders were confident that education and tolerance would be sufficient to confine sexuality in certain expected ways. But now we can see how wrong we were. While the church was looking for sin among teenagers, single adults, and gays and lesbians, the much greater evils of sexual violence against children and women and the oppression of gays and lesbians were being overlooked. Now that these evils are disclosed, the church must decide whether to respond with courage or denial. There is disturbing evidence that a majority of leaders of the church would rather define sexual issues in the traditional way and refuse to face the consequences of male dominance in church and society. If the church chooses such denial, the present crisis will be prolonged. The pastoral care movement could regain its prophetic role in the church by advocating its empirical principle that the voices of those who suffer be given priority in the ethical and theological debates about sexuality.

CHAPTER 9

The Challenge of Abortion

Christie Cozad Neuger

Pastoral theology has consistently refused to consider the paradox of abortion. In a recent computer search of the literature in pastoral theology, pastoral counseling, and pastoral care, I found only twenty-nine references to works on abortion over the past twenty-one years. Of those twenty-nine, ten had to do with genetic counseling. A recent study noted that only 3 to 4 percent of women considering abortion contact a clergyperson for advice, support, or resources (Rzepka, 1980, 28:168). In addition, introductory textbooks on pastoral care and counseling either do not mention abortion and problem pregnancies at all or use them as brief illustrations of crisis situations without any thorough discussion of the issues involved.

In contrast, the complexities of the abortion debate have moved to a central place in our culture. Political elections and appointments are frequently decided on the basis of the candidate's stand on abortion. The secular literature has exploded in an attempt to address the dynamics of abortion. Writings in theological ethics, in church history, and in theologies of the meaning and origins of life are burgeoning. Abortion is an extremely complex topic best understood as a deeply felt life-and-death issue on almost every level of personal, familial, and social experience. The field of pastoral care and counseling may grasp its significance only through a multiple fusion of political, legal, medical, religious, philosophical, sociocultural, psychological, and deeply felt personal horizons. Abortion crystallizes crucial issues for pastoral theology and pastoral care and counseling—the meaning and value of life, ways to understand family, the role and value of women and men, the cultural and personal splits between production and reproduction, and the meaning of spiritual discernment and ethical reflection in pastoral counseling.

THE CULTURAL CONDITIONS OF CONFLICT AROUND THE ISSUE OF ABORTION

Rachel Hare-Mustin reminds us that abortion is not a recent phenomenon (1989, 63). During the nineteenth century in America, somewhere between one fifth and one third of all pregnancies ended in abortion. In 1973, after abortion's legalization, one fourth of all pregnancies ended in abortion (Luker, 1984, 20). These data suggest that the frequency of abortion has remained relatively constant. Women have always had to find ways to deal with the responsibilities of reproductive power. As Beverly Harrison states, "Women's way of meeting the challenges of fertility, pregnancy, and childbearing is a most basic dimension of the true human story, even though it has been invisible in the tales the dominant histories tell" (1983, 157).

The view that abortion is equivalent to murder has not dominated history, either philosophically or theologically. Although abortion has generally been frowned upon both by early Greek philosophy and by the Jewish and Christian traditions, two ancient strands run through both of those traditions. One strand held that the fetus is the moral equivalent of the child it will become. The other purported that, although the potentiality of life grants a fetus some rights, the fetus is of a "different moral order" than already-born human beings. According to this viewpoint, the rights of a fetus become greater as the pregnancy progresses and viability is more likely (Luker, 1984, 11). Both of these perspectives have existed throughout recorded history and both are present in the debate today.

The most prominent belief throughout the early church was that abortion was not approved, but neither was it murder. Canon law suggested that the abortion of an "unformed" or "unanimated" (soulless) fetus was not murder and that fetuses were given souls at forty days for male and eighty days for female. Since the gender of all fetuses was, to the naked eye, physically indistinguishable until about the fourth month, all could be claimed to be female and so could be aborted until the eightieth day without committing murder (Whitney, 1991, 43). This position, most clearly articulated by Aquinas in the thirteenth century, was adopted by both church and secular society and held for many centuries.

In the United States up until the early 1800s, common law held that abortion before quickening, or the felt movement of the fetus, was permitted. According to Lawrence Tribe, abortion was common in America during the eighteenth and nineteenth centuries. In fact, the earliest statutes on abortion, which were written in the 1820s, had to do with prohibiting post-quickening abortions that endangered women's health. These statutes reflected concerns about illicit sexual activity that necessitated abortions and risks to women's health in having abortions but not about the morality of abortion itself (cf. Tribe, 1990). By 1840 only eight states had enacted statutes that restricted abortions in any way (Tribe, 1990, 29).

Several cultural shifts between 1840 and 1870 changed abortion legislation. The fertility rate for white, non-immigrant females dropped from an average of 7.04 to 3.56 children per woman between 1800 and 1900. The rate of abortion climbed to an estimated one abortion out of every four or five pregnancies. Abortion as an option became more public with considerable (carefully worded) advertising in public newspapers and catalogs. And, most important, the emerging medical movement was looking for ways to legitimate itself (Tribe, 1990, 29-30).

In the mid-1840s, the medical profession faced a dilemma. A group of physicians who were mostly white, non-immigrant, middle and upper middle class were attempting to upgrade the quality of the medical profession. They were unable to establish licensing until they could demonstrate that certain credentials gave medical practice higher quality than it had without those credentials. These "regular" physicians needed an issue on which to demonstrate their educational, technical, and moral superiority over the "irregular" practitioners (homeopaths, midwives, and others). As Kristin Luker says, "Unlike the other medico-moral issues of the time (alcoholism, slavery, venereal disease and prostitution) only abortion gave physicians the opportunity to claim to be saving human lives" (1984, 31). Certainly physicians were concerned about women's health and the high mortality rate from abortions. Luker suggests however that the medical profession also thought that American women were committing a moral crime based on their ignorance of the value of embryonic life. She contends, however, that women understood the processive nature of fetal development and that they evaluated the moral issues differently from how the physicians did (1984, 25).

At the same time as the medical profession was seeking to come into being as the American Medical Association, abortion was emerging as a social issue. As noted, abortions had become frequent in the nineteenth century and the birth rate for white women (non-immigrants) had dropped almost 50 percent during the century. At the same time there was a great influx of immigrants whose birth rate was and remained high. In addition, American culture was facing the paradox of both the first wave of feminism and the "cult of domesticity" (Baehr, 1990, 1). Thus, the medical profession began its massive efforts for legitimation at the same time as the dominant forces in the culture were worried about both race genocide and the trustworthiness of "their" women.

Consequently, physicians mounted a highly effective public campaign that resulted in a move from none to more than forty statutes outlawing abortion within twenty years. Many of those laws are still on the books in thirty states and would revert to their previous legal status if *Roe v Wade* were overturned (Tribe, 1990, 34).

This legal, medical, and moral history constitutes the central context of the abortion debate. When the AMA made abortion its context of legitimation, women were stripped of their own moral agency to address reproductive decisions. Physicians became the moral voice of reproduction and, as Luker says, "Abortion as a major social, political, and ethical issue could disappear beneath the cloak of an emerging profession's claims, there to rest quietly for almost a century" (Luker, 39).

The laws that resulted from the shift in cultural climate of the late 1800s did not change the rate of abortion. Instead, most abortions became illegal and were therefore often performed in dangerous and life-threatening circumstances. Class differences emerged quickly. Middle- and upper-middle-class women were often able to get physicians to name their abortions as necessarily therapeutic and perform them under safe conditions. For poor women, immigrant women, and women of color, illegal abortions frequently resulted in death or in tremendous pain and injury (Tribe, 1990, 35). Since abortions could only be legally performed by physicians, those who couldn't get a physician to support an abortion had to turn to those who were willing to break the law for profit.

Over the years, legal abortions (especially for privileged women) became much easier to obtain. Physicians began to realize that they disagreed with one another over what constituted a therapeutic reason for abortion and they began to ask for more clarity. In 1967 and in 1970, the AMA released positions stating that they were in favor of reformed abortion laws that would allow the complete freedom of a physician to decide whether an abortion would be the most helpful option for a pregnant woman requesting one (Tribe, 1990, 36). Also in 1967, twenty-one members of the clergy announced via the *New York Times* that they would be working to refer pregnant women who wanted an abortion to doctors they knew would perform safe (although, in this country, illegal) abortions. This clergy group, known as the Clergy Consultation Service, grew into an organization of thousands of clergy who helped women in crisis pregnancies between the years 1967 and 1973 (Carmen and Moody, 1973, 22).

Other cultural factors stimulated the reevaluation of abortion laws in the late 1960s and early 1970s. People began to reclaim their right to influence public policy on moral issues. Civil disobedience, consciousness-raising, and a sense of personal power in the political realm had surfaced in response to race relations, war, and poverty. Women were working outside the home in unprecedented numbers and feminist groups were emerging that understood women's lack of equality in reproduction. As race and class oppression were better understood by the larger public, the public realized that poor women and women of color were the ones who suffered as a result of abortion restrictions. Even in states where abortions were legal, the costs were often prohibitive. Consequently, at the same time physicians were saying that they no longer shared common criteria about abortion decisions, various factions of the culture were claiming the right to address those moral and legal decisions themselves. Activists emerged who through various kinds of consciousness-raising, educational, and social action processes, greatly influenced the legislative decision making.

In 1962 the Sherri Finkbine case came to public attention. Finkbine, a mother of several children, found out that she had been taking thalidomide during a vulnerable part of the pregnancy, creating very high odds that the fetus would be severely damaged. She was about to be granted a therapeutic abortion when she notified the local newspaper about her situation out of a desire to let other women know the risks of thalidomide. Luker suggests that the resulting public outcry demonstrated that "both extremes on the continuum had assumed that their views were representative of public opinion; the case of Sherri Finkbine

129

demonstrated how great their differences really were. Each side began to mobilize support for claiming that its own view of abortion was, in fact, the common one, the historically correct one, and the morally proper one" (1984, 65). The debate now moved from the medical consultation rooms to the general public.

By 1967, twenty-eight state legislatures had considered bills which liberalized abortion and by 1970 twelve states had passed such laws (Tribe, 1990, 42). In 1973, the Supreme Court decided via *Roe v Wade* that women have a fundamental right to decide whether or not to terminate a pregnancy based on a right to privacy. Because of that fundamental right, the court can only interfere when there are compelling reasons. Fetal viability and the woman's medical safety were both decided to be compelling reasons and so certain medical restrictions based on the development of the pregnancy were made. The court said two things: that the right to abortion was not an absolute right for women, and that the decision about abortion could not be based on any particular theory or theology of when life began, for example, that life begins at conception (Tribe, 1990, 11).

This Supreme Court decision allowed middle- and upper-middle-class women to be able, for the most part, to get abortion on demand; it did not help poor women get abortions that they couldn't afford. As a result of the 1976 Hyde Amendment, which restricted federal money for abortions except in life-threatening circumstances, the same class distinction that had always existed in abortion availability was made even more clear. The Supreme Court decision also spawned a powerful right-to-life movement made up of Roman Catholic, evangelical, and conservative religious groups. Many of the early pro-life activists stated that they were shocked by the Supreme Court decision in 1973; they believed that the values they held so deeply about the beginning of life and the essential right to life were universally held in American culture. They reacted strongly against the variety of viewpoints about fetal life and women's rights. In contrast, the pro-choice side of the debate relaxed after the *Roe v Wade* decision, feeling that they had accomplished what was needed.

THE THEOLOGICAL DEBATE

The debate over abortion, dominated by the medical profession from the late 1800s through 1970, now shifted to the theological world. The debate took on, as Luker suggests, the quality of a "holy war" at this point because the pro-life decision was based on the sacred right to life of a fetus from conception on.

The history of theology and theological ethics demonstrates a much broader diversity of theological opinions about abortion than the current debate suggests. Theology has consistently valued all potential and existing life. Even so, life has been valued developmentally, not absolutely. Even the Roman Catholic position on fetal life has shifted over time. And, as Harrison points out, "The ebb and flow of Christian anti-abortion teaching parallels too closely . . . the resurgence of negativism toward women to sustain the illusion that the chief element in Christian teaching against abortion was an exclusive or overriding concern for the real value of life" (1983, 129). She also suggests that one of the strongest concerns in the church's anti-abortion teaching was a pastoral concern for the safety of women and that this pastoral concern, which would now be more likely to support procreative choice for women, is often missing from theological debates. In similar fashion, Virginia Ramey Mollenkott notes that at a recent Evangelical Round Table discussion on the sanctity of life she was "struck by the absence of any acknowledgement of the sanctity of women's moral agency and the general unconcern about the well-being of women" (1987, 17:290).

A survey of both the pro-life and the pro-choice sides in the theological literature shows much more discussion about the precise beginning of life than about the questions of meaning and public support for those who are already born. The debate tends to leave out the historical contexts in which the theological debates were formed. Since pastoral theology is primarily concerned with helping people in the larger contexts of their lives, these theological debates provide minimal assistance in devising faithful approaches to pastoral care and counseling in abortion crises.

The theological debate has also become somewhat "sloganized" in such a way that theological thought is restricted to one of three or four positions (cf. Ellingsen, 1990; Enquist, 1985, 5:414). The primary ethical question pits rights against rights in a framework of individualism: What are the fetus's rights to be born over and against the woman's rights to determine if and when she will give birth? This kind of moral reasoning works not only in a very narrow framework but also pits woman against fetus in a win or lose, polarizing struggle.

Harrison suggests that the real work of ethical reflection on abortion must include the full context surrounding the decision. This context includes the entire history of abortion practices, philosophies, theologies, and debates. It includes analyses that reveal who benefits from the dominant points of view. It includes the dynamics of the culture in which those debates take place: of our particular culture and its place in the larger world culture. And, most important, it includes the personal story and the various cultural, familial, and individual particularities of the woman facing the decision to abort.

THE CONTEMPORARY POLARIZATION IN THE ABORTION DEBATE

What is it in our culture that keeps us from being able to tolerate the ambiguities of abortion and instead forces violent and unyielding polarization? At least three characteristics of late-twentieth-century American culture inhibit collaborative approaches to the abortion issue.

Quest for Quick Answers

First, our culture likes quick, clear, unambiguous answers, especially in matters that have to do with scientific knowledge. For example, the authors of a number of theological articles applied the most recent studies in embryology, genetics, and obstetrics to church doctrine so that an unambiguous answer about the origins of unique personal human life resulted (e.g., Shannon and Wolter, 1990, 51:603-26). As a culture, we tend to look for static and fixed rather than ambiguous answers to our questions.

Since we are evolving creatures in an unfolding creation, most of life's realities require us to tolerate decision making that needs continuing reevaluation. Pastoral care and counseling has faced this reevaluation at its deepest level; in fact, one of the hallmarks of good pastoral counseling has always been to help our counselees learn to do processive evaluation rather than give counselees an answer that they must live with. Pastoral counseling has consistently considered the ability to value ambiguity as a mark of mental and spiritual health. Helping counselees recognize the balance between static realities and continuing process is a natural part of pastoral counseling and is a critical part of working with any decision about abortion. A crisis pregnancy offers no ideal solutions. Each decision-maker has to live with the continuing consequences, with all of their ambiguity, forever.

Gender Polarization

Second, we live in a culture of gender polarization in which the abortion question is as much about the value of women as it is about the value of fetuses. Women, especially women of color and of working and poor classes, continue to be devalued and harmed in economics, career tracking, physical abuse, pornography and body exploitation, and mandatory motherhood. The abortion debate painfully pits woman against woman, as well as woman against her unborn, so that no matter what happens, women lose. Women on both sides of the abortion issue have attempted to choose what will give them the most power, prestige, and safety in a culture in which adequate amounts of these are denied them. And, because of the limited number of choices for women in terms of achieving worth, both pro-choice and pro-life women make decisions about their lives that do not allow either compromise or the ability to value their counterparts' choices (Luker, 1984, 199).

In her research about activists on both sides of the abortion debate, Kristin Luker paints a clear picture of the world view each side holds. The world views of the women activists are strikingly different. Luker portrays the average pro-life activist as middle-income, unemployed outside the home, high school educated, married, religious (often Roman Catholic), and with three or more children. She demonstrates that the average pro-choice activist is high-income, at least college educated, working outside the home, often in a high-paying career, with one to two children, and nonreligious (Luker, 1984, chap. 7).

What becomes clear via this profile is that these women live in extremely different worlds with very different options for being valued. Each world carries with it a particular view that necessitates a limited but clear way that women get their worth. The pro-life woman with few economic options and few avenues for self-expression primarily gains both safety and respect through mothering. The pro-choice woman knows that mothering, especially unplanned mothering, may destroy her economic and employment security and leave her vulnerable to sex discrimination in the workplace. No compromise is possible for either side when options for women's worth and women's safety are so limited. We must attempt to understand the polarization in the abortion debate in light of the world view risks that women on opposing sides face.

In addition, women who are the most at risk in a time of restricted abortions are not carefully represented by either group of activists in the debates. These women are poor women and women of color who are

133

often denied access to safe, legal, and affordable abortions and are often pressured into sterilization rather than given access to abortion.

Pastoral theology has only recently begun to understand and integrate the systemic and systematic oppression that women consistently experience and its impact on their mental, physical, relational, and spiritual lives. We are only now beginning to move away from an adjustment-oriented theory and theology of pastoral counseling to one of empowerment (Neuger, 1992, 2:35-37). As pastoral theologians we must learn to hold in tension the polarities of rights and responsibilities in the context of a world that consistently devalues both women and children. As we seek to empower women, men, and families, the culture and its assumptions, which look so much like reality, must constantly be held in suspicion. Given pastoral theology's general commitment to teaching women and men how to live in faithful and accountable ways as moral agents, we need to be engaged in changing *culture* so that women have the options that give them the power to be moral agents in their own lives.

Modernity and Postmodernity

Third, we live in a culture which is in transition characterized by some as the move between modernity and postmodernity. According to Kenneth Gergin, a contemporary social constructionist, modern society was built around the need to contain disruptive forces and to build walls around chaos. Freud's work in the destructive power of unconscious forces and the need to make them conscious (and thereby manageable) would be a paradigmatic example of modern cultural dynamics. Behavior modification and its offshoots constitute another example of "the need to render chaos predictable" (cf. Gergin, 1992). The primary belief that comes out of the modern period is that objective knowing is possible; thus, a single voice can represent that knowledge.

Postmodern society is characterized by the concept of multiple perspectives rather than by objective knowledge. Gergin suggests that we are "populated by others" in such a way that we are exposed to countless opinions, personalities, and doubts (1992). The result is that there is no single organizing truth but multiple perspectives. The postmodern person is aware that paying attention to the particularities of people means recognizing different shades of truth.

The dilemma, of course, is one that Charles Gerkin has explored in pastoral theology. In a culture of multiple perspectives and unending ambiguity, what can people share that allows them to be about the work of collaboration in their common life? Both Gergin and Gerkin would suggest that it is the narrative process, the sharing of perspectives and, out of that, creating new and common perspectives, that will bring common ground.

In terms of the cultural struggle with the issue of abortion, this sharing of perspective is both necessary and difficult. Luker suggests that both sides founder on the same point—that each side expects its point of view to be the universal one (1984, 190). The fact that we are in the midst of this cultural transition from believing in objective knowledge to acknowledging multiple perspectives, I believe, is nowhere clearer than in the abortion debate.

Pastoral theology must continue to work with this tension. Pastoral counselors have been willing to accept multiple perspectives and relative truths to a certain extent. However, we have tended, at least in the back of our minds, to form an objective measure of truth and health and wholeness, which we have used to measure ourselves and our counselees. In considering abortion, the belief in *multiple perspectives* of truth, and the hope in some *absolute, objective* truth, are in constant battle. In a 1990 poll, 73 percent of Americans were in favor of full abortion rights and 77 percent regarded abortion as a kind of killing, if not, indeed, murder. This is a clear symbol of a culture acknowledging the reality and even validity of ambiguity and of a culture in the pain of that acknowledgment. We, as pastoral theologians, must be willing to jump into that struggle with people and with the culture as a whole, learning both to live with ambiguity and to find what is shared and secure in the midst of that.

TRENDS IN PASTORAL THEOLOGY AS RESOURCE TO THE ABORTION DEBATE

As Roy Woodruff says in his article on abortion and pastoral counseling, "Counseling is a person-centered, as opposed to an issue-centered, arrangement" (1975). This has been both a strength in pastoral counseling and a problem. In terms of its strength, pastoral counselors have been willing to see the concrete contexts of any situation and understand it in the life of the person in need. Pastoral counselors have also been willing to be "open to the larger conversation" and to join perspectives with counselees in the effort to help people broaden the parameters of their own conversation. They have suspended judgment so that the counselee can strengthen and move toward her or his own capacities for moral

135

reasoning and make decisions that can be owned. In this counseling process the wholeness of the counselee, with her or his multiple dimensions of psyche, spirit, body, relationships, cultural location, and so on have been appreciated and the whole has been seen as sacred.

These qualities, which are integral to modern pastoral care and counseling, are crucial in working with women and families in the crises of unplanned and unwanted pregnancies. That situation requires the largest possible lens through which to appreciate the concrete particularities of each individual crisis.

Pastoral theologians are also prepared to bridge worlds in ways that are extremely important at this point in time. In particular, the secular and sacred tension that Rodney Hunter and John Patton discuss in chapter 2 is especially valuable in this time of cultural crisis around abortion rights and responsibilities. Since the abortion debate has polarized theological thought, for the most part, into pro-life as religious and pro-choice as secular, pastoral theology has the opportunity to reclaim a religious world view that can surround the whole process of discernment in these issues. Given the immense ambivalence that most Americans feel about abortion, theological perspectives that shift from static to processive categories and which move from ethics built on rights or duties to those built on responsiveness and responsibility would be welcome.

Finally, pastoral theology's tradition of critiquing both church and culture, as pastoral theology bridges the secular and sacred, is a necessary resource to each. Pastoral theology must continue to be willing to tolerate its own ambiguity in standing on this middle ground, not of belief, but of perspective. It can speak to both worlds as each attempts to substitute absolutes for options and static dictates for evolving perspectives.

THE CHALLENGES TO PASTORAL THEOLOGY IN THE FACE OF ABORTION

Pastoral theology and pastoral counseling can address four basic areas in order to be prepared to help individuals, families, and society with the dilemmas and possibilities of abortion. All of these already exist, at least in nascent form, within the current pastoral theology movement but are not yet at its core.

1. *The understanding of cultural dynamics as central to our theory building and clinical practice.* In tending to accept dominant assumptions as truth and locating the problems that people bring to us inside their own

psyches and spirits, our field has inadequately appreciated the power of a dominant culture to shape its members in ways that perpetuate the rules and power dynamics of the status quo. We consider deviation from this dominant system as individual or relational pathology rather than adaptive response to cultural dictates. If we are to be about the work of empowering those who have been marginalized in that culture, we must find ways to be critical of the assumptions we have taken for granted. Without understanding and critiquing the oppressive dynamics of racism, classism, and sexism, we will be unable to contribute to the abortion debate in empowering ways. We will tend to duplicate the slogans and the harm. Since abortion is primarily about women and children, and especially poor and working-class women and children and women and children of color, our work in theological and psychological discernment around abortion issues is relatively meaningless until we can see the dynamics of the culture in their appropriate place, and unless we can become person-centered *and* issue-centered.

2. *The movement from individual to systemic thinking.* So long as we limit ourselves to looking at the individual alone in her consideration of abortion and we are unable to see how the multiple systems in her life constrain her decision, we will be unable to help her. For example, studies indicate that disclosure for the sake of support may or may not be helpful, depending on the context. We have to be able to explore the woman's whole social and cultural system with her. Or, there might be times when we are unable to see why a decision is not clearer for the pregnant woman, because we have not taken the time to look at the family and cultural rule systems in which she lives. The movement from an individual focus to a systemic one means not that we lose the individual, but that we place her in her concrete circumstances.

3. *The development of multiple theoretical and theological perspectives.* If our task is to enlarge the conversation and to bring perspectives together for the sake of enhancing the narrative possibilities for our counselees, then it is important that we bring as many potential conversations as possible into the counseling room. We cannot be content with only one theoretical approach with our counselees, either psychologically or theologically. We must be able to shift perspectives and languages for the sake of understanding the issues, of bridging worlds, and of enlarging our repertoire of therapeutic discourses and possibilities.

4. *The willingness to gather knowledge about the specifics of abortion.* We need to know as much as we can about the psychological and spiritual dynam-

ics of the abortion decision so that we can offer the widest possible set of options to those who come to us for care. For example, many clinical studies have developed profiles of the kinds of women who are most at risk for longer-term psycho-spiritual distress during the abortion decision process and after abortion procedures: Women who are extremely ambivalent about their decision, who have minimal support, who have abortions later in their pregnancies, or who don't believe that they will be able to manage this crisis well are all at higher risk for psychological and spiritual distress after having an abortion (Adler, et al., 1990, 248:41-44; Armsworth, 1991, 69:377-79; Lemkau, 1988, 12:461-72, and 1991, 61:92-102; Major, et al., 1990, 59:452-63; Mueller and Major, 1989, 57:1059-68; cf. Speckhard, 1987). In addition, numerous studies discuss the consequences to mothers and children when women are forced to bear an unwanted child. If pastoral counselors stay alert to the research in the area of crisis pregnancy resolution, they will be able to find the best ways to help people in crisis pregnancies to engage in ethical reflection and decision making in light of the various complexities of the abortion question. Care during the decision-making process and planned follow-up work, especially with high-risk women, should be considered a standard part of any pastoral counselor's work with women in crisis pregnancies.

IMPLICATIONS FOR THEOLOGICAL EDUCATION AND MINISTRY

The implications of this material for theological education and ministry are clear. First, seminary students and pastors must be exposed to the myriad complexities in the abortion issue—the historical, political, legal, philosophical, clinical, theological, racial, class, and gender dynamics. These dynamics become background for seeing each crisis pregnancy in its particularities with the inescapable tensions about value, rights, and needs. We need to train pastors and pastoral counselors to avoid individualism while respecting individuals.

In addition, each ministry practitioner needs to be able to explore the various ethical dimensions of the abortion question in frameworks that promote reflection rather than close it off. The questions about abortion are, in many ways, more important than the answers, especially as we prepare to offer ministry to women and families in crisis.

Second, seminary students and pastors need to look at the issues raised here in terms of the assumptions of the culture and the dominant value systems and reflect upon how those interfere with the healthful and faithful resolution of pregnancy dilemmas. Those who benefit most from the values of the dominant system must learn to listen to those who are most marginalized by it. Those who are best able to reveal the injustices of a system are those who have been most harmed by it. They must be the teachers as we reflect on assumptions that have been seen to be truths.

Third, we must understand the issue of reproduction in larger terms than conception, pregnancy, and birth. Reproducing ourselves involves long-term commitments to provide care and support to those we bring into being. Those who are responsible for that care must be able to have the clearest voice in making careful decisions about reproduction. Pastoral counselors need to be about the business of empowering those voices in a debate which often ignores those who are most concerned.

And, fourth, abortion must be given its central place as an issue that crystallizes deep and symbolic concerns within our faith traditions. Abortion asks us to consider such deep faith questions as God's plan for creation, the meaning of free will, the responsibility of good stewardship, the deep existential issues of being, and the purpose of women and men as co-creators with God. Pastors and pastoral counselors must be helped to tolerate the power of this kind of reflection with its inherent ambiguity and angst. We cannot afford either "sloganized" theology or polarized theology if we are going to be able to help those who come to us with these issues. We must become comfortable enough with the challenges of the abortion question to begin to find ways to invite women who are struggling with unplanned pregnancies into trustworthy pastoral relationships so that the process of exploration and decision making may enhance their faith lives.

CONCLUSION

Finally, it is important to consider that pastoral counselors must always stay alert to how their own value systems and ambivalences are playing into the care and counseling process. The issue of abortion has deep psychological and spiritual meaning for each of us. No matter what our position is on the rights and responsibilities of abortion, it is impossible for us to be disinterested in the process by which people reflect on their pregnancy decisions. At some level, we are always asking ourselves about the meaning and value of our lives and at what stage that value emerged. In the abortion debate, lives are on the line, symbolically and really. Whether we believe that fetal life gains value as it moves toward independent viability or that it has absolute value from conception onward, we need to gear our efforts toward helping our counselees engage in ethical reflection to the end of making their own faithful and healthy choices. This is not to say that those choices will be ideal or without regrets. It is normative to experience both ambivalence and sadness in any decision about an unplanned or unwanted pregnancy. Experiencing ambivalence and distress does not indicate a poor choice. It only indicates the need to tolerate the ambiguity of being human in a world that calls for us to try to use our freedom responsibly. Pastoral counselors need to help equip women, men, families, and, indeed, cultures, to live with that freedom and its ambiguity in the healthiest possible ways.

CHAPTER 10

The Politics of Pastoral Care:
An Alternative Politics of Care

Roy SteinhoffSmith

The Gadamerian hermeneutic through which Charles Gerkin proposes to reform the field of pastoral care and counseling assumes a politics of dialogical mutuality. "Politics" is "the science or art of . . . government" *(Random House Dictionary of the English Language)*. Two issues are closely interwoven in any "political" analysis: power and participation. Government requires the direct or indirect participation of people in the wielding of power. A political analysis focuses on how people in a particular situation do or do not participate in the exercise of power over their own and others' lives. Thus, in Gerkin's reformulation of the pastoral dialogue, the fusion of the personal and the pastoral horizons can truly occur only if both truly participate. Absent such mutual power to define the shared horizon, one person imposes his or her interpretation of reality on the other, and no dialogue or fusion takes place.

Charles Gerkin's project implicitly requires a political analysis of the power relations in the current practice of pastoral care to determine if such practice promotes dialogical mutuality. Such an analysis seeks to answer two questions: Who participates in the continuing definition of pastoral care events and who does not? Second, How is this power to define these events used?

THE POLITICS OF PASTORAL CARE

Power disguises itself in ideologies which claim to be descriptions of realities but which actually cover over the specific and particular ways power is experienced. In order to get under the ideologies which obscure the political realities, we must examine what actually occurs in specific pastoral events. I have chosen two such events, one from today, one biblical.

The Homeless Caregiver

My wife and I host an "open meal" each Sunday afternoon at our church. Most of the people who come are destitute and without homes. My wife, Carolyn, is also a member of a "team," made up of church members, who care for people living with AIDS and their family members. When this event occurred, Jerry, who was homeless, had been coming to the meal regularly and had helped cook and set up for it. He is gay and in his forties. When Carolyn talked with him about the care team, Jerry said he'd like to join it. She told him she'd find out when the next training session was and make arrangements for him to attend.

When Carolyn told the leaders of the team about Jerry's interest, they expressed reservations about his participation. The care team shouldn't be burdened with the care of a homeless man, with the necessity of finding him transportation. Besides, he wasn't a member of any of the churches sponsoring the team.

Carolyn did not accept these objections. After some thought, she told Jerry what the leaders had said and asked him if he still wanted to be part of the team. He said he did, and Carolyn made arrangements to pick him up for the next training session.

This session was held in the evening, from seven to nine. Jerry was staying at the Salvation Army shelter. They usually did not admit people after seven. Jerry asked the Salvation Army officer on duty at the shelter whether he could come in late because of the meeting. The officer said, "No. Transients should not be involved in social or community activities because then they have no reason to get off the street." We invited Jerry to stay at our place for that night, and he accepted.

Carolyn took Jerry to the training session. In a small-group meeting, he spoke about the reaction of his friends on the street to his coming to the meeting: "You can't do that. You can't hang out with people with

AIDS." Another member of the training group remarked that he had felt the same way about being with homeless people.

After the training session, Carolyn and I took Jerry to several meetings of the care team. One time we were out of town and arranged for one of the care team leaders to pick him up. They missed connections and he did not get to the meeting. Since then, Carolyn has been less active on the team. Jerry has moved off the street, has been working, and we see less of him. He is no longer active with the care team.

The Lawyer and the Samaritan

Just then a lawyer stood up to test Jesus. "Teacher," he said, "what must I do to inherit eternal life?" He said to him, "What is written in the law? What do you read there?" He answered, "You shall love the Lord your God with all your heart, and with all your soul, and with all your strength, and with all your mind; and your neighbor as yourself." And he said to him, "You have given the right answer; do this, and you will live."

But wanting to justify himself, he asked Jesus, "And who is my neighbor?" Jesus replied, "A man was going down from Jerusalem to Jericho, and fell into the hands of robbers, who stripped him, beat him, and went away, leaving him half dead. Now by chance a priest was going down that road; and when he saw him, he passed by on the other side. So likewise a Levite, when he came to the place and saw him, passed by on the other side. But a Samaritan while traveling came near him; and when he saw him, he was moved with pity. He went to him and bandaged his wounds, having poured oil and wine on them. Then he put him on his own animal, brought him to an inn, and took care of him. The next day he took out two denarii, gave them to the innkeeper, and said, 'Take care of him; and when I come back, I will repay you whatever more you spend.' Which of these three, do you think, was a neighbor to the man who fell into the hands of the robbers?" He said, "The one who showed him mercy." Jesus said to him, "Go and do likewise." (Luke 10:25-37 NRSV)

William A. Clebsch and Charles Jaekle's definition of "pastoral care," first offered in 1964, continues to be an accurate description of how pastoral care is frequently practiced in the mainline white North-American church: "The ministry of the cure of souls, or pastoral care, consists of helping acts, done by *representative Christian persons,* directed toward the *healing, sustaining, guiding,* and *reconciling* of *troubled persons* whose troubles arise *in the context of ultimate meanings and concerns*" (*Pastoral Care in Historical Perspective,* 1975, 4).

According to Clebsch and Jaekle, pastoral care did not take place either in the case of the homeless caregiver or in that of the good

Samaritan. In the former, no "troubled person" sought or received "healing, sustaining, guiding, or reconciling" from a "representative Christian" "in the context of ultimate meanings and concerns." In the latter, the shock of Jesus' story resides in its portrayal of "representative" religious persons as not caring and of the enemy Samaritan as caring. But even if the Samaritan had been a "representative [religious] person," his care is not "pastoral" because it is not done in response to "troubles aris[ing] *in the context of ultimate meanings and concerns.*" Both these stories describe what Clebsch and Jaekle call "other helping acts," which do not possess the "dignity" appropriate to acts of "pastoral care" (1975, 7-8).

I have chosen these stories precisely because they uncover the limits of not only Clebsch and Jaekle's definition, but also the common understanding of "pastoral care." People with power use it to define such boundaries, which in turn designate who is to be recognized and valued for what kind of acts—that is, who can participate in the determination of the community's activities.

The "lawyer" who questions Jesus reveals what is at stake in the control over such definitions.

> The lawyer sets a trap for Jesus. The trap concerns the definition of "neighbor" or the kinds of people it is appropriate to associate with. Jews did not socialize with Gentiles, and pious Jews kept their distance from less pious Jews. Jesus was known to associate with riffraff of all kinds. If he could be trapped into a definition of neighbor as shockingly broad as his practice, he could be accused of breaking the law. (Patrick, 1984, 56)

If the lawyer is successful, he destroys Jesus' power to affect his audience and augments his own. The stakes are political. Control over definitions of a community's boundaries—in this case, of the limits of "neighbor"—is equivalent to the power to govern a community's activities. The lawyer assumes the following hierarchy. At the top are the religious authorities, who possess the power to "love" and so to define both what "love" is and who the "neighbor" or proper recipient of "love" is. Then there are these "neighbors," those who are worthy to receive the "love" possessed by the authorities. Outside the hierarchy, with no access to "love" and so with no possibility of "eternal life," are those who are not "neighbors": the unclean lawbreakers and unbelievers.

Clebsch and Jaekle assume a similar hierarchy. Pastoral care is the activity of "representative Christian persons"—religious authorities. They are the only ones who actually perform caring activities—"healing, sustaining, guiding, and reconciling"—in the care relationship. They care for "troubled persons," but only those whose "troubles" are about "ultimate" things. Clebsch and Jaekle reflect the tendency to equate "ultimate" troubles with psychological ones when they agree with Viktor Frankl "that most—if not all—human [in this context, psychological] troubles point eventually to issues of ultimate meaning" (1975, 6). They also exhibit one kind of "pastoral" thinking when they use this ambiguity to reinforce the authority of "representative Christians." They assume that the sheer presence of "representative Christians" converts what might otherwise be merely a psychotherapeutic relationship into a "pastoral" one. Only "representative Christians" finally decide, without any clear criteria, which troubles and solutions "involv[e] God" and which do not (7). Left wholly outside the definition of "pastoral care" are those with "worldly" or nonpsychological troubles and those who respond to such people (4-10).

Clebsch and Jaekle's implicit hierarchy accurately reflects the structure of much practice of pastoral care in the mainline white North-American church in ways other than those already indicated. Theological and clinical writers describe pastoral care as the activity of pastoral professionals, who diagnose and treat the spiritual or "ultimate" (which are indistinguishable from "psychological") troubles of parishioners and clients. Pastoral care, in this understanding, does not encompass responses to material or social suffering—that caused by physical illness, poverty, or oppression. The church, theologians, and clinical professionals usually classify such responses as prophetic or social, not pastoral, ministry.

The story of the homeless caregiver further reveals the limits of this understanding of pastoral care. First, ministries with people living with AIDS or with people without homes are not considered part of pastoral care, unless such ministries involve "counseling" about ultimate or psychological issues. Such ministries fall outside the recognized ministerial or practical theological functions: preaching, worship, religious education, church administration, and pastoral care. This exclusion results in their neglect not only by ministers, but also by the church as a whole. By definition, such ministries are, at best, peripheral to the church's mission. At worst, they are considered to be dangerous distractions, luring the church away from its true "spiritual" mission into "social work." Clebsch and Jaekle reserve their harshest judgment for "professional ministers [who] delude themselves and abdicate their pastoral responsibilities when they assume that, since all ministerial acts are, at least by intention, helpful, therefore all these acts are pastoral" (8). In Luke's lawyer's terms, people with AIDS or without homes are not "neighbors" and so are not worthy recipients of "love." A pastor shouldn't associate with them.

Second, those "prophetic" church members who, in the service of a different understanding of love or care, seek to serve such "marginal" people tend to reclassify them solely as recipients or objects of care. The leaders of the care team and the officer at the Salvation Army shelter had great difficulty conceiving of Jerry as a care-giver, rather than merely a homeless care-receiver.

Recognition of this tendency to classify people as either active care-givers *or* passive care-recipients illuminates the difficulty socially active congregations often have with suffering members. Characteristically, such members often complain that such congregations do not care well for them. "Prophetic" pastors are "too busy" to visit hospitalized parishioners. Committed church members may take communion and tapes of the Sunday morning worship to homebound members, but they do not do much else to help them. Even churches with vans often do not pick up disabled members to bring them to church services and activities.

The problem with such members is that they do not fit fully into the category of either the active care-givers or the passive care-recipients. As church members, they are expected to fulfill the role of activist servant of the suffering and oppressed. But their affliction identifies them as in need of service. Like Jerry, they are caught between the categories and so tend to be neglected (Adams and Hiltner, 1970).

In either its more traditional or its "prophetic" mode, pastoral care tends to reproduce and support the existing political hierarchy, which protects the power of the privileged and excludes those who are suffering and oppressed from participation in the decisions which determine their own and others' lives. If the afflicted remain passive and submissive, the pastoral hierarchy may reward them with some care, especially if their problems can be construed as "ultimate" or "spiritual" (or psychological). If they attempt to participate in the care relationship, to use their power in it, if they seek to care rather than just to receive care, those with power in the pastoral hierarchy may tend, in blatant and subtle ways, to exclude and punish them.

This analysis suggests that the current politics of pastoral care does not provide the necessary conditions for carrying out Gerkin's project.

Pastoral professionals who adopt Gerkin's model without first changing the politics of their practice risk enforcing the existing power relationships in the field of pastoral care and counseling. Rather than fusing their horizons with those who suffer, pastors may impose theological or psychological diagnoses, interpretations, and treatment plans on those who suffer. They may try to be the primary interpreters of the "texts" of their parishioners' or clients' lives, who, the pastors think, will get "better" only to the extent they accept the pastors' interpretations. Meanwhile, pastors may unconsciously continue to exclude from the caring dialogue all those whose suffering does not meet the "ultimacy" criterion or who do not have the economic power or religious status to enter it.

AN ALTERNATIVE POLITICS OF CARE

Contained in the two case studies is a vision of an alternative politics of care, one that would support Gerkin's project. I say of *care* rather than of *pastoral* care, because, in this vision, the pastor is not the sole or primary participant in care; power is shared, all participate in the activity of care.

Five figures inhabit and contribute to this vision. The first is *a homeless caregiver*. This politics abolishes the differentiation between active caregiver and passive care-recipient. It recognizes that those who are suffering and oppressed are also valuable participants in a caring community. They too have gifts to offer others. They too have the power to care.

Implicit in the first figure is the second, its complement, *the privileged care-receiver*. To break down the differentiation between the active caregiver and the passive care-recipient is to realize that the former also suffers and is in need of care. No person is without need or suffering. In this alternative politics of care, people with power—who are privileged to participate in the decisions affecting their own and others' lives—do not lose their power if they identify themselves or are identified as suffering. Nor do they have to give up their power in order to receive care.

The third figure is *the privileged servant*. In the first case, Carolyn and I are privileged. We are valued members of a church. We are "ministers" of the "Open Meal," which serves primarily people without homes. I am an ordained minister, formally recognized as a "representative Christian person." In response to Jerry, we found ourselves in the role of "servants." Our task was to do the mundane things—finding out the time and date

147

of the training session and care team meetings, mediating between him and the leaders of the care team, driving him places, providing him with a bed for a night—to support his participation in the care team. This figure suggests that, in this alternative politics of care, the role of those with power is to do what is necessary to support the participation in the caring community and society as a whole of those who have been excluded from participation, who are suffering, and who are oppressed.

The fourth figure is *the good Samaritan*. To Jesus' Jewish audience, the Samaritan is an evil enemy of God. Yet, Jesus' story presents him as the only one faithful to the love command and so to God. This figure suggests that the alternative politics of care values those who practice love, no matter what their professional, ethnic, religious, or moral identity. If a non-Christian or even "enemy" of Christianity proves to be a loving neighbor, then we are to value and learn from his or her practice.

The fifth figure is *the afflicted judge*. After telling the story of the good Samaritan, Jesus asks the lawyer to judge who is loving from the perspective of the half-dead man. In the alternative politics of care, one defines love and determines who is loving from the afflicted person's point of view (Patrick, 1984, 59-60). This figure places at the authoritative center of the alternative politics of care those who are excluded or treated merely as passive objects of pastoral care in the existing political structure. Their perspective and participation become central to the definition of care.

This alternative politics results in a new definition of "care." Care is the activity of a person or a community that supports the full and powerful participation in communities and societies of those who are suffering, excluded, objectified, or oppressed.

The alternative politics reorients those Christians who decide to participate in it. In the traditional politics, Christianity is equated with special or privileged knowledge about "love" and "care." Clebsch and Jaekle assume this equation when they define "pastoral care" as the activity of "representative Christian persons." Current pastoral professionals also assume it when they equate the capacity to care with ordination and "pastoral" education. This assumption results in the already-discussed hierarchy, through which Christian pastoral professionals protect their privilege. They focus primarily on maintaining the "dignity" of pastoral care by carefully differentiating it from "other helping acts." They implicitly define "care" as an activity by which those with power and privilege maintain their superior position over those who are assumed not to have the knowledge or capacity for care.

The alternative politics requires the relinquishment of this claim to privileged knowledge about care or love. Rather, Christians follow the Jesus of Luke 10, who placed the power to define love in the perspective of the sufferer and the power to practice love in the activity of an unbeliever. In this politics, rather than focusing on differentiating themselves from non-Christians, Christians join with and learn from sufferers and any who practice love.

In this politics, care is not a function of "pastors" or experts, but rather is the mission of the whole church, a communal praxis. Nor can it be confined to a particular kind of activity—for example, counseling about ultimate or psychological troubles. Rather, it is a norm governing all of the church's activities.

The new politics defines care as responsive to all kinds of suffering, not just "ultimate" or "spiritual" or psychological problems. More radically, care becomes an activity which requires the participation of the afflicted, no matter what the causes—physical, psychological, social, or religious—of their suffering. Care then becomes an activity done *with* not *to* others. It is a relational activity.

In the traditional politics, pastors diagnose and treat parishioners or clients. In an alternative politics, Christian practitioners join with the afflicted and others who respond to suffering in devising strategies aimed at destroying the barriers which prevent the afflicted from fully participating in society and in constructing or supporting communities in which the afflicted exercise power.

Such strategies may include more traditional psychotherapeutic techniques, as long as these are oriented toward validating the sufferers' perspectives and insights, freeing them from the internal or psychological mechanisms that prevent them from exercising their power as participants in history, and supporting their entry as powerful agents in communities and society. Such appropriation of psychotherapeutic techniques must be critical. It must not replicate the clinical politics through which professional therapists or caregivers retain the sole power to define what care is and to determine the course of therapy. It must eliminate the economic and social barriers that prevent those who are poor and suffering the most from fully participating in the therapeutic relationship.

In an alternative politics of care, such therapeutic strategies will be

149

joined with economic, social, cultural, political, and religious ones. Christian practitioners of care must join with those who seek to construct an economics in which all have what they need to live and thrive, a social order which encourages all to develop and contribute their particular gifts and abilities, a cultural matrix which includes and values diverse ways of viewing and constructing worlds, a political system in which all participate as agents or subjects of history, and a religious canopy which celebrates the reality of every person and being—the whole of creation.

Finally, those who seek to participate in this alternative politics of care must not become so intoxicated by such grand visions that they neglect or devalue mundane practices. For most of us reading this essay (the assumption being that most of us are privileged), participation in the new politics also means doing things like providing transportation for those who don't have any, providing a place to sleep, a telephone or simply an address other than a shelter for a homeless person applying for a job, buying groceries and cleaning up the house of a person living with AIDS, providing space for people who have no space to meet together and organize themselves, providing materials—paper, pens, computer terminals, copy machines, telephones, fax machines—needed by such communities of the dispossessed when they get organized and launch campaigns to make themselves heard, using our access to those with power to support such campaigns, providing child care for dispossessed organizers, and other seemingly "worldly" activities. This list should not be taken to be exhaustive. A central principle of the new politics of care is that any caring act done by any person deserves recognition as being an act of love. Changing a diaper or washing dishes or preparing a meal—each, when done with care, possesses all the dignity that God and humanity can give.

While an alternative politics of care requires the renunciation of *"pastoral"* care, there is an important role for a "care specialist," including an ordained minister or pastor, who develops skills in facilitating the formation of communities of care within and outside existing churches. Such a care specialist will focus specifically on fostering the participation and leadership of the dispossessed in these communities. While, as indicated, psychotherapeutic techniques, especially those focused on the formation and maintenance of groups, will be helpful in some aspects of this work, such a minister will likely also learn a great deal from community, union, and political organizers.

This alternative politics provides the dialogical mutuality necessary for carrying out Gerkin's project. In this politics, a true fusion of horizons between caregivers and sufferers can take place. Because the latter have the power to participate in the praxis of care, they determine it at least as much as the caregivers.

CHAPTER 11

Race, Ethnicity, and the Struggle for an Inclusive Church and Society

Charles W. Taylor

I began writing this chapter around 9:30 A.M. Thursday April 30, 1992. The previous afternoon I had heard the announcement that the four police officers who had savagely beaten Rodney King were acquitted. Wednesday night, April 29, from midnight until dawn, I alternated between napping and watching Los Angeles go up in flames on TV news. Shortly after 7 A.M. Thursday morning, on the "Today Show," Bryant Gumbel interviewed one of the Simi Valley jurors who had voted the officers not guilty. In a calm and measured voice, which usually indicates a complete command of one's faculties, she explained that Rodney King, who was lying on the ground surrounded by a score of officers, at least four of whom were pummeling him, was in charge of the whole situation.

I lost it. I began to scream wildly and jump up and down; suddenly I found myself face down on the floor beating and kicking the hardwood and crying in a pool of spilled coffee. Fay, my wife of almost twenty-nine years, came into the room. Thinking that my behavior, which frightened me, must have scared her, I apologized. She turned aside my confession with a plaintive reply, "I understand, it just makes [one] feel so power-less." There we were, two African Americans in despair, mourning the loss of our illusions about America's ability or willingness to include us or our children.

I got up and went downstairs. There I paced and fumed, my mind ablaze with homicidal fantasies toward white police and jurors. I wended my way into the kitchen, turned on the TV news, and began to scream my indignation at one of the L.A. cops' defense lawyers, who was saying something about trusting the system. The phone rang. It was the Dean of my seminary asking if I would preach at the Seminary Eucharist service that night as a response to this tragedy. I told this white friend that my voice was hoarse from screaming and I was still wondering whether I was composed enough to face students today; but in spite of all of that, I would consider preaching and let him know my decision later.

About 8:30 A.M. I drove my wife to work and stopped by the school to check my mail and test my responses—would I be able to respond civilly to the overwhelmingly white population of our school? It was there that I opened a letter from Rodney Hunter and Pamela Couture, which asked me to write an article that addressed four questions. The first of these questions was: "What are the cultural and societal conditions which create the potential for conflict between races and ethnic groups in the struggle for an inclusive church and society?" After nearly an hour of doing various small tasks at school, I returned home about 9:30 A.M. I knew then that I had just experienced the conflict as real, not potential. I had also experienced some of the cultural and societal conditions that create that conflict.

In this chapter, I will share my responses to Hunter and Couture's first question and their three others: "What do the theory and practice of care as it developed in the late twentieth century have to contribute toward guidance in ministry in these situations? What changes in the theory and practice of care need to be made in order to minister in the situation? What are the implications of these continuities and changes for theological education and ministry?"

THE CULTURAL AND SOCIETAL CONDITIONS

I believe that readers need a full understanding of the cultural and societal conditions which create conflict between races and ethnic groups in order to understand "what is going on" in the incident just described. Further, readers need a solid grasp of the situation to consider the adequacy of the theory and practice of care, the changes that need to be made, and the implications of both the present way of caring and the needed changes for theological education and ministry. Therefore,

I chose to spend a little more than half of this chapter on discussing these cultural and societal conditions.

The Multicultural Society

The first cultural and societal condition that creates conflict between races and ethnic groups in the struggle for an inclusive church and society is the multicultural nature of American society. People often miss this obvious point: We have conflict because we have different races and ethnic groups—and we have them in profusion. For example, I read somewhere that in the fall of 1992 children from more than one hundred twenty language groups entered school in the Los Angeles area.

The recent struggles between the various races and ethnic groups that made up the Soviet Union and its empire illustrate the potential for conflict within a multicultural society. Surely, the debilitating series of battles between the Serbs and each of the other groups that were a part of Yugoslavia provide the most heart-wrenching example of the problem. Yet in this situation all of the participants share the same race—Caucasian—and the same geographical roots, the only differences being tribe and religion. By contrast, the ethnic groups that populate the United States come from different races and different regions as well as various tribes and religions.

The Strategy for Inclusion

The American melting pot strategy for resolving the problem of including various cultures in one nation is the second cultural and societal condition that creates conflict between races and ethnic groups in the struggle for an inclusive church and society. In the United States we have been able to bring together an unprecedented number of immigrants into one society. All of the warring tribes of Europe—Croats and Serbs, Russian Orthodox and Russian Jews, Irish Protestants and Irish Catholics, Czechs and Slovaks, French and Germans, Latvians, Lithuanians, and Estonians and Russians—have come here and become one people. This is a miraculous and marvelous feat. We have solved Europe's problem with hard work, Yankee know-how, and Native American land. When we see the conflicts in Europe today we can rightly celebrate American inclusivity, even though there is a price for it and a limit to it.

The Price

The price for American inclusivity has been the loss of the various ethnic heritages. We have become one people by all of the peoples' taking off much of their ethnic identities and putting on a White Anglo-Saxon Protestant (WASP) identity. In addition to learning American English, each group learned to devalue its own ethnic and family traditions: interdependence, extended families, reverence for tradition and mystery, integration of church and state, respect for human limits and tragedy. The various ethnic groups replaced their ways of living with WASP values: rugged individualism and competitiveness, the small nuclear family, a pragmatic preference for results, and the separation of church from state. A fierce emphasis on possibilities and hard work, which drives Americans to join Englishmen and mad dogs in the noonday sun, tops that WASP value hierarchy. The price of the melting pot strategy is that all the distinctive ingredients are reduced down to a bland vanilla pudding.

Though the melting pot process has been slower among some ethnic groups than others and in some neighborhoods than others, it has worked. Irish Catholic and Irish Protestant, Croat and Serb, Lithuanian and Russian have been freed enough from their past antipathies to join together as Americans to work, play, defend the country, live in common neighborhoods, and intermarry.

The Limit

The limit inherent in this American strategy of inclusivity creates much conflict between races—the melting pot only works for Europeans. The way to fit into America is to become generically white; only Caucasians can be melted into WASPs. The fact that Native Americans, African Americans, Asian Americans, and those Latino Americans with visible African, Asian, or Native American heritages cannot physically become white constitutes the main cause for conflict between races and ethnic groups in the United States. Thus, the unbelievably successful strategy for including all manner of Caucasians has within it an exclusivity which blocks the incorporation of other races. This limit creates a fundamental problem because America defines itself as a melting pot.

The Separation

The limit separates Americans. Non-whites structure their lives in response to the limit, while Caucasians live free from its bounds. Further, whites and non-whites fight with each other and among themselves about the correct way to describe and address the limit. The resulting charged separation constitutes the third cultural and societal condition that creates conflict between races and ethnic groups in the struggle for an inclusive church and society.

Non-whites and the Limit

Since the test for full membership in American society consists of looking like a WASP, only a few non-whites of mixed parentage can pass. Those non-whites who have the good education and the ability and luck to survive in white institutions are granted *associate memberships*. We associates are allowed to hold the type of positions that full members decide to give us. These jobs pay so much more than those of other non-whites that we associates can afford to move out of the non-white ghettos. This causes a physical separation within the non-white community between the associates and the underclass.

A large number of non-whites do not meet the requirements for associate status because of poor education, difficulty (or unwillingness) in behaving like whites, or the bad luck of running afoul of the white power structure. They live their lives significantly underemployed or unemployed (the percentage of non-white unemployment is always higher than it is for whites, the incomes of employed non-whites are always lower). Excluded from full participation in American society by race and bereft of the exemplary and supportive presence of successful non-whites in their neighborhoods (a resource that was available in previous times), they have little chance to get the needed education and the requisite training in white institutional behavior. The underclass has little power to change its situation.

In the same way that the power differential between a supervisor and supervisee makes any sexual advance by the supervisor harassment, the power differential between white members of the society and the non-whites makes most actions by whites exploitative of the underclass. Thus, the underclass experiences the majority of whites (and associates) as preying on them as landlords, spying on them as welfare workers, neglecting them as teachers, and beating on them as cops. They are angry. They feel no positive connection with white America and little connection with the associates. They are ripe for conflagration.

Associates and whites experience the pain of separation also. When they come into contact with each other in schools, jobs, churches, and neighborhoods, they make a startling discovery: All but the most superficial of contacts are usually taxing and often uncomfortable. There are many reasons for this phenomenon: the normal awkwardness of communication across cultures, the knowledge imbalance between non-white associates who know two cultures and whites who usually know only one (but know that one very well), the unconscious assumption of privilege by most whites and the angry consciousness of white privilege by most non-whites, the strange interplay between white guilt and denial by conscious whites and non-white anger and denial, and the irritation that both feel about the other's being given unfair advantages.

This discomfort has led many non-white associates to band together for support in white situations. This banding leads to further separation and uncomfortableness between whites who feel excluded by the caucuses and non-whites who become more conscious of their rage by participating in these groups.

Divergent Stories

The fundamental American story asserts that the United States is the land of opportunity for all; the melting pot open to all those willing to contribute. The racial limit to participation forces modifications to this story.

Americans divide according to the modifications they accept. Some forcefully conserve the story by emphasizing the "willing to contribute" part and the successful inclusion of many people; they maintain that underclass non-whites exclude themselves by their unwillingness to contribute. Others radically liberalize the story by downplaying the contribution side and focusing on the exclusion of non-whites from a society that claims to be "open to all." It seems that most whites tend toward the former version of the story and most non-whites toward the latter. However, there are many exceptions to these tendencies. This disagreement about the correct interpretation of America's defining story creates a great gulf between and among whites and non-whites. Thus the separation around "the limit" is exacerbated by the clash of stories.

A Case in Point

The responses to the Rodney King beating and the subsequent upheaval (riot to some, rebellion to others) illustrate the depth of this separation. Some whites saw the police beating of Rodney King as an awful aberration of justice that must be addressed by the rule of law.

157

Other whites, for example the Simi Valley jurors, perceived the freedom of the police to use great force as the necessary and too-thin blue line that protects them and their property against black "non-contributors" and criminals such as Rodney King. Further, many of those whites who disapproved of the verdict, saw the subsequent upheaval as a simple case of taking advantage of the situation, whereas many blacks saw the upheaval as a justifiable reaction (Ellis, 1992, 26-29).

In addition, many non-whites recognized both Rodney King's beating and the jury's response as a more or less regular occurrence, not an aberration. We saw Rodney being beaten, not as a criminal but as a black man; and most of us have had personal experiences that have convinced us that all our civility, training, and years of responsible service in WASP institutions are no protection against that law and those police. (Recently, I was stopped and questioned by the police for being black in the wrong neighborhood. I was doing a "prayer walk" as part of a spirituality program at the San Francisco Theological Seminary [SFTS] in San Anselmo, California, which is in Marin County immediately north of San Francisco. Many of the participants took "prayer walks" in the neighborhood around SFTS; I was the only black participant and I was the only one stopped. The police officer stated that he was not on his regular rounds; he had been called by a resident to investigate this black person in the neighborhood. After questioning and showing my identification papers, I was let go without being assaulted, further proof that the Bay Area is liberal.) And we are angry because we have played by the rules (the price) and we are still harassed and excluded (the limit).

Fay and I were despairing shortly after 7 A.M. on Thursday April 30, 1992, because the fires of Los Angeles had burned away the fog from our eyes and we saw that the issue in America is race, race, race. In spite of our education, sterling behavior, and acceptance by most persons at our white places of work and our white place of worship, we and our children were not full members of this society. We mourned because the issue is still the color of our skins and not the content of our character; thus our lives and our children's lives are always at risk.

THEORY AND PRACTICE OF CARE

What do the theory and practice of care as it developed in the late twentieth century have to contribute toward guidance in ministry in this situation? What does the pastoral care movement think or do that will help in the struggle for an inclusive church and society against the separating forces of race and ethnicity?

Many different persons and systems cried out for ministry in the example with which this paper began: Fay and I as we sat mourning on the floor that Thursday morning; the students in the Introduction to Pastoral Care course; the students, staff, and faculty of the Divinity School that the Dean wanted me to address that night; the Los Angeles community in the midst of upheaval; the church as it endeavors to desegregate; the United States as it struggles for a racially and ethnically inclusive society.

The pastoral care movement focuses more on ministering to individuals or couples like Fay and me than on larger systems like the Los Angeles community or the American society. Likewise the movement concentrates on the intrapsychic and interpersonal problems of individuals and couples more than on their cultural and societal troubles. However, I did find that some of the movement's commonly accepted resources helped me minister in this situation.

Commonly Accepted Resources

With the help of the insights of radical therapy and liberation counseling (cf. Miller, 1976), I diagnosed my "losing it" as a sane reaction to the anguish of being black in America rather than as a psychological problem. On this basis, I decided that my anger was gold to be mined, not dross to be destroyed. So I went back to school and taught instead of withdrawing until my "bad mood" passed. The class was Introduction to Pastoral Care, which met in groups on Thursdays for instruction in and practice of pastoral skills.

Bonnie Ring and I led the class that morning (because the students in my "Intro" class are overwhelmingly white and usually 40-50 percent female, I have made a practice of inviting a white woman to team teach the class with me). We called the class together to get permission to change the agenda for the morning. The class agreed to use the listening skills they had been learning to help one another express their thoughts and feelings about the L.A. upheaval. We sent them off into groups with a solemn pronouncement against lecturing to one another either directly or by asking rhetorical questions. Each of the three groups of eight had at least two non-whites in it.* Many students, both non-white and non-colored, reported this exercise of pastoral listening to be transformative.

We still had the sermon for the Thursday night Eucharist to decide about. The Reverend Fran Toy, a Chinese American woman who is our Director of Alumni/ae and Student Affairs, suggested a trialog sermon— one in which Dean Perry and I would introduce the subject and make brief presentations, then invite responses from the congregation. Thus we combined patriarchal and feminist process in this sermon event. Community response during and after the service was overwhelmingly and glowingly positive; they felt that both the content of our presentations and the process of trialog ministered to them.

Gerkin's Contributions

Gerkin challenges the pastoral care movement to make its care more theological, community-based, and oriented toward society. He prods us to become more theological by advocating a style of pastoral care that concentrates on helping people find meaning through interpreting their stories in the Christian framework (1984, 1986, 1991*b*). He asks us to move our locus from the counseling relationship to pastoral care within the parish and surrounding community (Gerkin, 1986, 19; cf. 1991*b*, chap. 5), thus making our care less individualistic. Gerkin orients care to society in two important ways. First, he gives a central place to the influence of societal and cultural conditions in personal, interpersonal, and group problems. Second, he proposes that "pastoral care . . . be directly linked to facilitation of the various ministries of the laity in the world" (1986, 102; cf. 1991*b*, chap. 6).

I did not think about Gerkin's narrative pastoral theology in ministering to the CDSP community on that Thursday in April or in my own self-care in the months thereafter. It was only later, in writing this chapter, that I noticed two parallels to Gerkin's themes in my actions. First, the trialog sermon in the context of Eucharist was a way of placing the upheaval and our reaction to it in the context of the "narrative themes, images, and metaphors" of the Christian story (Gerkin, 1986, 85-86). Part of the care the trialog provided was narrative pastoral care. Second, one of the ways that I cared for myself during the period after

*It is very unusual for us to have six non-whites among the twenty-four students in this course. We normally have only one African American and one or two Asian Americans or Latino Americans in the student body. In the fall five African Americans had entered the seminary, a record number for us. Their entrance precipitated a crisis, which led to a community-wide daylong workshop on cultural and racial sensitivity. This workshop happened before the L.A. upheaval.

the upheaval was by attending black Baptist churches a number of Sundays. Never before had I spent so many Sundays without worshiping in an Episcopal church. Upon reflection, I know that I attended black churches because I needed the nurture of the black narrative tradition, which addresses the struggle for an inclusive society every week and always places it in the context of the Christian story.

Gerkin's contributions to the pastoral care movement could have enriched my ministry to the Introduction class and to the community. A subsequent class meeting or community discussion might have been devoted to reflecting on the upheaval and our reactions to it using the following questions: (1) What is going on here? and (2) What are the narrative themes, images, and metaphors that may further illuminate our hermeneutical reflection? (Gerkin, 1986, 82, 85-86). In a third meeting the group might have worked out practical community responses to the issues and narratives surfaced in the second session. These two sessions would have helped the ministry to be more theological, community-based, and oriented to society.

What did the theory and practice of care as it developed in the latter twentieth century have to contribute toward guidance in ministry in this situation? The radical and liberation understandings of anger helped me accept my anger and use it in action. The emphasis on listening skills, empathy, non-judgmental regard, and genuineness enabled the non-white and non-colored students in the Introduction class to talk to and listen to one another about a strongly charged topic. The care movement's understanding of group process helped the Dean and me to recognize the wisdom of the Director's suggestion and then successfully lead the discussion. Thus, the generally accepted theory and practice of pastoral care gave me considerable guidance for interpersonal ministry in this situation.

Consideration of Gerkin's contributions might have brought more conceptual clarity to the trialog sermon and it might have led to further pastoral activities that would have ministered to the class and community in a more consciously theological, communal, and societally oriented manner.

CHANGES IN THEORY AND PRACTICE

The present theory and practice of pastoral care adequately deals with individuals, couples, families, and small groups. We need concepts, tools, and settings for addressing large systems and widespread understandings. Thus, the organizing question for this section is: What changes in the theory and practice of care do we need to minister to the Los Angeles community after the upheaval, the church as it struggles to desegregate, and the United States as it struggles to be a racially and ethnically inclusive society?

Linking the Personal and the Social

The pastoral care movement needs theories and methods that harness our in-depth understandings of individuals and small systems for use in societal change. Such theories would show how the two are interrelated; how race, culture, and society influence personal and familial issues and vice versa. These formulations would describe the dynamics of large-group behavior including large-group expressions of defensive behavior. They would illuminate the interrelationships between social action and personal growth. The theories' ability to guide practitioners in making interventions that effect profound personal and social change provides the best test of their adequacy.

Pastoral care also needs a setting in which personal growth and social action can be connected. By their tradition of concern for people individually and their ministries to groups and to the society, congregations link personal growth and social action in a way that pastoral counseling agencies, hospitals, prisons, and social action groups do not. Further, congregations have access to a greater cross-section of people than other pastoral settings. One can well imagine that many of the antagonists in the L.A. upheaval belong to congregations: the Simi Valley jurors, as well as their critics; the law enforcement personnel; the minority underclass; the minority associates and the middle-class whites. The congregation's ability to link the personal and the social underscores the importance of Gerkin's suggestion that the locus of pastoral care be moved from the individual to the congregation.

Both Howard Clinebell and Larry Graham have developed theories that attempt to meet the aforementioned standards. Clinebell expands his "Holistic Liberation-Growth Model" (1984, chap. 2) in *Well Being* (1992). Larry Graham's *Care of Persons, Care of Worlds* (1992) makes a significant contribution by going beyond Clinebell's expansion of personal growth theories and developing a thoroughly systemic viewpoint. These theoreticians provide the movement with direction in linking the personal and the social, and they challenge the rest of us to devise better theories. Both Clinebell (1984) and Graham emphasize the congregation as the normative setting for pastoral care, and both suggest methods for helping congregants to relate the personal and the social and to engage in social action.

An Intervention

I propose a systems intervention that would test Gerkin's narrative approach, utilize the parish setting, and address the main block to a racially inclusive church and society. In the Epilogue to *Widening the Horizons,* Gerkin suggests that "empirical studies that seek both to verify and detail the manner in which deep narrative structures shape and inform the narrative life of persons at all levels of sophistication should be undertaken" (Gerkin, 1986, 128). I recommend a three-phase intervention that applies Gerkin's suggestions to the issue of racial inclusivity.

The intervention's first phase would focus on discovering and bringing to awareness the stories that support the racial limit to inclusiveness. The second phase would entail working with images and metaphors from the Christian tradition to find those that transform congregants' exclusive stories and empower parishioners to desire a racially inclusive church and society. The third phase would involve designing and evaluating congregation-based support frameworks for congregants as they work for a racially inclusive church and society.

In sum, to better promote racial and ethnic inclusivity in church and society, the pastoral care movement needs to address large systems. To do this we need three things: theories that link persons and small systems with large systems, utilization of the parish setting and empirical research to test the adequacy of the theories, and interventions for changing the stories that limit inclusivity.

IMPLICATIONS FOR THEOLOGICAL EDUCATION AND MINISTRY

This final section discusses the separation between races by limit and the division between and among races by story; the care movement's present resources for ministering to individuals, families, and small groups; and the needed concepts, tools, and setting for addressing large groups and widespread understandings. This segment responds to the editors' question, What are the implications of these continuities and changes for theological education and ministry around the issue of race, ethnicity, and the struggle for an inclusive church and society?

This chapter describes the struggle for an inclusive church and society as both difficult and necessary. The difficulty lies in the deep separation between non-whites and non-coloreds, which is caused by the exclusion of non-whites from the melting pot. This rift is exacerbated by passionately held divergent stories. The necessity arises from the threat to society posed by exclusion-based non-white rage. This anger simmers continually, periodically bursting into flames as in Los Angeles. In between riots non-whites steam, whites protect themselves from the heat, and the opportunities for a peaceful inclusion boil away.

The difficulty and necessity of this struggle for an inclusive church and society require that theological education prepare people for the ministry of inclusion and that churches engage in it. Pastoral theological training for inclusion would build on the present pastoral resources of listening skills, knowledge of individual and small-system (couple, family, small-group) dynamics, and theological understandings. It would incorporate needed concepts and tools such as: large-system (congregational, workplace, community) dynamics, methods of systems intervention, and the interrelationship of small and large systems.

Training for inclusion would include the following four phases: (1) becoming aware of the stories and behaviors whites and others use to cooperate with the limit in both small and large systems; (2) finding Christian themes that transform those stories and challenge those behaviors in whites and others; (3) practicing sharing the new stories and living the new behaviors in small and large systems; (4) practicing helping others through the first three stages of this training. During the L.A. upheaval of 1992, Rodney King made a plaintive plea for peace by asking, "Can we all get along?" This chapter identifies the culture of racial exclusion as the cause of the upheaval and suggests a ministry of racial inclusion as our contribution to "all getting along." It describes that ministry as doing pastoral care in a manner and setting that (1) uses pastoral skills to deal with small and large systems; (2) engages the stories and behaviors that support racial exclusion with the transforming Christian narrative; and (3) supports converted persons in working toward racial inclusivity.

PART III
PRAXIS

CHAPTER 12

Pastoral Care with Congregations in Social Stress

Joretta L. Marshall

ongregations embody the fabric of human life, complete with the complexity of issues addressed in the foregoing section of this book. Pain and chaos emerge in individuals and families, as well as in the broader settings of congregations and denominations. Competing understandings of what it means to be faithful surface in perplexing visions for the church and its ministries.

It is fitting that a festschrift for Charles Gerkin would address pastoral care with congregations. Throughout his writing Gerkin reminds readers that communities of faith emulate the struggles of a broader social complexity. Multiculturalism, pluralism, the loss of a moral center, fragmentation created by interrelated and complex issues, and competing theologies generate communal confusion and pain. Consider the following:

• Several church members become uncomfortable as the new pastor uses inclusive language during the worship service to refer not only to humanity, but to God.
• An inner-city church struggles with how to retain its suburban membership while at the same time being a vital ministry for persons in the inner city. The values and needs of the suburban middle class conflict with those of the multi-ethnic urban poor.

• The father of a church family has been accused of sexually abusing one of his children. He has been one of the leaders of an adult Sunday school class. Pain, anger, confusion, and compassion emerge within the congregation.

• The denomination has released a statement that it will not support the presence of lesbians, gays, or bisexuals in the leadership of the church. A lesbian who has been an active member in the church has gifts for ministry and has asked your congregation to support her as she attends seminary.

These reflect the reality of congregations in the postmodern world. They represent not only places of individual conflict, but potential arenas for polarization within communities as theological and moral issues surface in the guise of individual and communal pain.

The congregation remains the primary context for pastoral care. As participants seek to make sense of the complexity of the world, they turn to the church and its pastoral representatives for care and guidance. Parishes seek perspectives on the chaos of their corporate lives and expect pastoral caregivers to respond with theological centeredness and moral sensitivity.

An exploration into congregational care illuminates three particular aspects of pastoral theology: the utilization of multidisciplinary tools already apparent in the literature, theological questions important for conceiving of the task of caring for communities of faith, and implications for theological education. This chapter approaches each of these facets with the hope of providing some context for pastoral theological reflection around care with congregations in social stress.

Two assertions remain prominent throughout the following remarks. The first claim is that pastoral care with congregations requires planned theological reflection, not merely techniques, to assist in managing the chaos, confusion, and pain of communities. I assert that it is imperative for pastoral representatives to offer an orientation to congregations centered in theological reflection. As communities of faith discern how to make sense of and bring meaning to the challenging issues of their communal life, they assume that pastoral caregivers might assist in that task from a particular theological perspective.

The second claim is that those engaged in congregational care need to continue to look beyond the clinical paradigm toward a more communal framework when constructing a framework for pastoral theology.

I do not mean to suggest that individual clinical material is irrelevant to care and counseling. However, one of the mandates for pastoral theologians is to consider what communities of faith offer to our constructive efforts, inviting a broader relational framework than is apparent in individual care and counseling.

CURRENT THEORIES AND METHODS

Two arenas of thought, psychodynamic theory and the more recent literature in congregational studies, have guided pastoral care and counseling in the last several decades. The theories and methodologies represented in the literature of these two areas of study have been adapted to our understandings of congregational care without much critical reflection. A cursory deliberation of current theories and methods offers insight into some of the dynamics of caring for congregations in social stress.

As has been evident throughout this book, psychodynamic theory in its various forms continues to be one of the most influential perspectives in the literature of pastoral theology. When reflecting on congregational care from a psychodynamic vantage point two factors emerge. The first component is a focus on how individuals manage internal struggles and how these dynamics appear in the context of congregations. The second component is a consideration of the role of pastoral representatives and their relationships with parishioners in the midst of congregations where conflict and polarization are manifested in the life of the community. An approach that relies upon psychodynamic theory is often centered almost exclusively on individuals and not on the community.

A fundamental strategy for communal care has been that of individual counseling or care. One perceives that pastoral caregivers have hoped the care of persons who present themselves in counseling would coincidentally alleviate some of the communal pain. Personalized care, though speaking to individuals or smaller subgroups and families, glosses over significant communal issues.

For example, the dynamics of transference and counter-transference have been a traditional vantage point through which pastoral representatives have come to understand their relationships to individuals within the congregation. The utilization of psychodynamic theory makes it possible to analyze why persons have negative reactions to particular pastors, why individuals do not get along with one another, or why congregational leadership sometimes erupts into conflictual energy. Indeed, such dynamics are clearly present and this framework does assist in diagnosing some of the energy behind some dissensions. However, the utilization of psychodynamic theory does not always invite pastoral theologians to address the complex reality that conflict not only reflects personal issues but also reflects core theological concerns, which may be divergent and competing. To deal with the conflict as if it could be explained sufficiently by principles of transference and counter-transference denies the community the potential of engaging with the essential theological and moral arguments, which may rest at the core of a controversy around social issues.

Other psychodynamic perspectives utilized in pastoral care have included group dynamics, developmental theory, and the broader concepts of family systems. Perhaps one of the more refreshing movements has arisen as a result of dialogue with family systems theory. For example, the work of Edwin Friedman in *Generation to Generation* (1985) presents intriguing and helpful insights into the dynamics of congregational life as persons interact and relate as the "family" of God. Yet, even here I would argue that to engage congregations as if they were only extended family misses the richness of discernment about what it means to be the church and to offer reflection on issues of theological consequence from a particular perspective of faith.

Illustrative of the appropriation of psychodynamic theory is the utilization of metaphors from the addiction model in reference to communities of faith. In this culture one hears pastoral caregivers refer to the church as a dysfunctional family or an addictive organization and to its ministers as codependent people. It is a curious phenomenon when pastoral theologians and representatives have little hesitation in referring to the church and its families as "dysfunctional" and yet have a great deal of anxiety and theological difficulty thinking about such theological concepts as sin or justice in the context of the community of faith.

The urgency in the pastoral care of congregations now is to renew our sense of theological focus while not dismissing the realities to which psychodynamic theories and methodologies attend. The theoretical constructs of individual psychodynamic, developmental, and family systems theories have highlighted the fact that congregations are made up of intricate stories and lives. Indeed, it is through the individual psychodynamic and systems theory approaches that one begins critically to understand the depth of the psychic pain of individuals. The concepts offered through reflection on human dynamics and the inner world will continue to engage those who envision the future of pastoral care, and yet we cannot afford to allow these theories to narrow our scope and understanding of communities of faith. The task for pastoral caregivers is to offer a genuine pastoral theological perspective informed by psychodynamic theory, but not dependent upon it.

A second set of perspectives useful in pastoral theology has evolved in the literature of congregational studies. Here issues are examined from the vantage of sociocultural realities, the analysis of power, conflict theories, and management concepts. This literature has been helpful in thinking about the narrative structures of communities and the richness of symbol systems that congregations adopt. The work of persons such as James Hopewell in *Congregations: Stories and Structures* (1987) challenges pastoral caregivers to consider the context and reality of communal history and vision. In this material, careful attention needs to be given to the dynamics of authority, power, and the reality of patriarchal hierarchy. It is imperative that such considerations persist as those within the pastoral care movement offer reflections upon just and right relationships within communities.

What is missing, however, in both the psychodynamic and the sociocultural congregational perspectives is a clear theological understanding of the congregation as a lived reality of faith. At the present time theories on how to manage conflict or diagnose mental health within communities are helpful, but what is more necessary are methodologies that engage the fertile theology of the congregation. The challenge to contemporary pastoral caregivers is that of reconceiving theological constructs within the context of caring for congregations in the midst of social conflict and stress.

CHALLENGES TO THE TRADITIONAL MODELS

If pastoral representatives are to face the complexities of a postmodern world, they need a rich and multiperspectival theological vantage point. Caregivers must be as versed in the literature of traditional and today's theology as they are in psychodynamic theory. A shift in emphasis from the one-on-one counseling modality to a genuine pastoral theological concern is imperative for congregations. Communal pastoral care should become as commonplace and valuable as individual pastoral counseling. Without an integrative theological core, pastoral repre-

171

sentatives are in danger of becoming part of the fragmentation rather than part of the creative presence of a discerning and justice-oriented community.

Charles Gerkin suggests that "the pastor is a listener and interpretive guide. The pastor's goal is to help persons find meanings in what goes on in their lives that stitch those events and relationships into the central meanings of the Christian story" (Gerkin, 1986, 107). Communities of faith, like individuals, attempt to create meaning from the events of their common existence. Care for congregations ought to continue to be guided by the offering of a moral viewpoint on social issues which seeks to represent a particular faith perspective in the midst of a multifaith world, asserting an identity which carefully responds to difference and diversity.

Insisting upon the primacy of theological reflection does not seem bold or particularly creative, yet it is one of the essential elements often relinquished by a focus on individuals and internal psychodynamic processes. The multiplicity of issues raised in this festschrift requires either that pastoral caregivers become experts in all of the social issues of our day, or that pastoral persons offer a theological perspective which remains sensitive and informed on as many concerns as possible. Theological inquiry around issues of ecclesiology, justice, and the congregation as pastoral representatives to the broader community suggests topics for continuing discourse. Thoughtful constructs centered in theology assist in maintaining a purposeful framework within communities rather than participate in further polarization by offering a smattering of diverse and divergent perspectives not integrated around a core of communal faith.

Theology is not just another language or symbol system, or one of the many lenses through which pastoral representatives see issues within the social world. Theology operates as the core perspective around which other vantage points are interpreted. Maintaining the primacy of theology is not intended to be a pejorative or elitist attitude. Instead, claiming one's theological center while at the same time listening to the voices of others and participating in continuing cross-disciplinary dialogue which is multicultural and diverse offers the caregiver a core around which to think about social issues. Those who would venture into congregational care must be constant and vigilant in their theological reflection without ignoring other perspectives.

ECCLESIOLOGY AND CONGREGATIONAL CARE

Pastoral care with congregations requires an articulation of what it means to be a faithing community. In traditional terms this theological activity is the content of ecclesiology. What is needed in our world is a return to concerns about the nature of the church, but not a recurrence of a narrow vision of the church. Indeed, as Peter Hodgson suggests, a "new paradigm" which is "nonhierarchical, nonprovincial, and nonprivatistic in its ecclesial vision" is imperative (Hodgson, 1988, 18). Pastoral theologians can continue to elaborate on the nature of the church and its ministries.

An initial ecclesial concern focuses on pastoral theology as a communal activity. Since congregations operate as the context for pastoral theology's constructive efforts there has to be an actual engagement and valuing of local churches. Congregations become places of accountability to both the tradition and the reality of everyday life for those who would conceptualize and participate in the care of communities of faith. Minimal, or even daily participation in the life of a congregation is not enough. Pastoral caregivers, particularly those who would venture into scholarship and the more formal activities of teaching and counseling, must value the local community of faith as central to pastoral theology.

Tensions arise between the ideal vision of what the church ought to be and the reality of communities that are limited and human. Some persons have found the need to leave the institutional church and have established other contexts for community based upon their experience of patriarchy or marginalization within the structures of the local congregation or denomination. Indeed, the church has not lived up to its claimed ideals. Often there is little sense of hope in these alternative communities that the church can remain a redemptive entity for persons. Illustrative of this tension is the movement known as Women-Church, which seeks to offer a place for women who feel the tradition has not been helpful for their worship, leadership, and communal life. Rosemary Ruether, in *Women-Church* (1985), has articulated a contemporary vision of the church and its ministries through liturgy and communal events. Valuing the local community of faith means, in part, reckoning with the fact that there are persons for whom congregational life is painful and, at times, abusive.

One necessary component of congregational care is to address the pain that is created when the expected ideal is not matched by reality. A caregiver in a congregation listens to the voices of those who painfully feel the oppression of the institution. Communal care is sometimes the act of listening, valuing, and honoring the experience of others without denying or dismissing an ecclesial vision, which continues to hold the ideals of the church. Valuing the local community of faith does not imply a denial of ways in which communities participate in unjust or destructive practices through the reality of racism, patriarchy, or the abuse of power. The pastoral person has the task of holding up the vision of the church while, at the same time, working to eradicate the structures that diminish the church's movements toward justice.

A second ecclesial issue emerges as pastoral representatives purposely engage congregations in reflection on who they think they are as the church. Part of the task of Gerkin's interpretative guide is as one who offers a framework for thinking about identity. Congregations need opportunities to think about who they are and what they represent in this broader culture. Similarly, divergent groups within the congregation ought to wrestle with what it means to be participants in the same church and to maintain a common or communal vision in the midst of the conflicts of diversity. It is clear that congregations cannot be all things to all people. To establish a coherent and consistent vision for how congregations reflect upon the fundamental issues of identity ought to be present if communities are to offer something particular to those who participate in its structures, liturgy, and worship.

Finally, from an ecclesial perspective congregational care requires not only an articulation of the story of one community of faith, but a willingness to listen and hear the voices of the marginalized, the quiet, the oppressed, and those who make us uncomfortable. In Gerkin's most recent book on prophetic pastoral care, he suggests the utilization of a centrifugal model for care. In essence, this imagery suggests that persons in the faith community are expanding and broadening their boundaries in ways that encourage them to become more inclusive (Gerkin, 1991*b*, 116-42).

Advocating that congregations look outward as much as inward means that more conflict will be created in an attempt to become an inclusive church. Listening to the voices of those who threaten one's comfort is a painful task. There is an awareness when congregations move out into ministry with the world that new tensions and competing visions will arise for communal pastoral care. Hence, one of the essential tasks for pastoral theologians is to assist the congregation in articulating an ecclesial understanding that guides the church in living with the ambiguities and tensions of such diversity. Without such a vision the risk of polarization and fragmentation is increased.

The inherent danger of suggesting ecclesiology as an important place for discourse is that of being stuck in a traditional approach to these matters. I am not talking in this essay about a cozy ecclesiology which emphasizes a wonderful and caring community, but an ecclesial framework which is challenging and, at times, may be quite painful. Communal pastoral care becomes more intense as those who would guide congregations in the task of being the church share in the shaping of a cohesive theological core out of which to lead communities in theological reflection.

PASTORAL CARE AND THE COVENANT TO DO JUSTICE

One of the central motifs in preceding chapters has been justice-oriented pastoral care. While this term is in danger of becoming so over-used in our vocabulary that it risks losing meaning, it is nonetheless fundamental to the concerns of congregational care. Genuine pastoral care is about the task of overcoming the dualism of prophet and priest as congregations embody an ecclesial vision, seeking to participate meaningfully in structures which seek justice rather than perpetuating injustice.

Carter Heyward suggests that "justice is the shape of mutuality in our life together, in our societies and relationships . . . the 'righteousness' of God . . . is reflected in human justice to the extent that we are willing participants in creating God's justice on the earth among ourselves. . . . Justice is the actual shape of love in the world" (Heyward, 1989, 190). How congregations and caregivers participate in creating justice-oriented communities says much about their theological commitments and persuasions. Indeed, the covenant to care is a covenant to seek justice on behalf of all persons, not only those who appear at our office doors or who can afford to pay for our salaries.

Pastoral care of congregations is a moral activity, and the call to participate in justice will create tension and conflict within congregations. The important notion is not to do away with the conflict but to utilize it to create opportunities for communities to engage in theological reflection about what it means to be an inclusive and meaningful faith community in a complex world. Congregations fractured by the issues of class, race, sexual orientation, or gender need opportunities to enter into moral discourse and not merely to dismiss those with whom they disagree. Caring for communities of faith means being vulnerable as leaders who risk the pain and alienation that may surface as persons honestly confront one another and in the process wrestle with their images of God, church, and world.

Attention to issues of power must continue to impinge upon our theological reflection. Activity on behalf of those in the community of faith with the least amount of power will result, at times, in conflicting visions for the church. Seeking to be forces of liberation within communities where persons suffer under tremendous pressures of class, race, or sexual orientation requires of pastoral persons an awareness and careful utilization of pastoral authority and power.

Finally, as pastoral caregivers we are called to continue to attend to the multiple structures of which we are a part. Questions related to denominational structures as well as organizations such as the American Association of Pastoral Counselors and other certifying groups ought to be brought into focus. How do these institutions participate in seeking justice on behalf of those within the culture who have less opportunity and access to caring systems? How can those organizations of which we are a part become responsible advocates for justice within the kingdom of God? Do we seek to minister with the under-served and those who are marginalized by our social structures, inviting them to participate in our local communities of faith even when this might create some risk to our financial security?

The concerns of justice are essential to a grounded pastoral theological framework with congregations. Integral to pastoral caregivers is not only a reflection about justice but an actual commitment to and participation in the vision of being just in relationships to the communities of which we are called to be a part.

THE CONGREGATION AS PASTORAL REPRESENTATIVES TO THE COMMUNITY

Congregations deserve to be valued and recognized not only by those who serve as pastors but by themselves. Communal care through the informal structures of communities has always been present, yet it has not always been valued by those of us who have been trained in the sophisticated theories of pastoral counseling. Many congregations have discovered how to care for one another and those beyond their walls in the midst of social stress. For example, communities that thought they would never have to deal with persons living with AIDS have discerned how to reach out and offer substantive forms of care. These congregations have wrestled, at least covertly, with the complexity of issues which surround this painful arena of living and dying. Communities of faith have incredible strength to overcome polarization when they meet pain and courage in human beings.

Traditionally the pastor has been understood to represent the church, yet the reality is that congregational members are persons of remarkable representational power. Rosemary Ruether suggests, along with others, that it is time to dismantle the clerical paradigm (Ruether, 1985, 75-95). Ordained clergy need to reckon with the fact that they are not the only ones who offer congregational care. Indeed, it is often through the work of laity and persons within the community that others feel the embrace of a particular congregation. This suggestion is not an attempt to deny the need for representatives who have the special function of pastoral care in a daily and continuing manner, but it is an affirmation that human beings care for one another in the congregation in ways that are beyond the clergy's control. Honoring those places of natural care in communities offers an opportunity for the congregation to confirm and interpret its own ministry.

One aspect of congregational care rests in clarifying what it means to be a clergy or professional pastoral counselor. The role of the clergyperson is not to do all of the care and counseling. Instead, one's role is to articulate and maintain a theological steadfastness so that as communities of faith struggle with conflicting social issues there is a language and perspective which remains central and faithful. This agenda is equally imperative for persons who see their vocation as full-time pastoral counselors. The task of pastoral counseling is not only to offer individual psychodynamic or family systems therapy to persons, but also to extend to those with whom one ministers an invitation to consider their connection to the community of faith. Similarly, one of the ministries of those in full-time pastoral counseling is as an advocate in the broader church on behalf of those whose stories of oppression and hurt they have heard personally.

TOWARD THEOLOGICAL INTEGRATION

As pastoral caregivers sustain a primary commitment to theological reflection, the community of faith will find it more natural to contemplate its task and ministry in the world. The three theological concerns of ecclesiology, justice, and representational ministry shape a part of what I understand to be important for congregational care. They are not all-inclusive theological constructions, and there are caveats to be uncovered and thought about carefully. Yet these foci represent a genuine theological approach to congregational care, which can be illustrated by looking at one of the examples from the beginning of this chapter.

Local congregations increasingly struggle with responding to sexual misconduct and abuse. Theological questions arise when considering this situation, which focus on the nature of the church, the structures of justice, and the movement toward care by congregational members. Is it possible for the church to be a place of reconciliation but not easy grace? What is the role and task of the church in the context of ministry with this family, this community, and systems of justice? Can a community of faith be expected to uphold in its care both the abuser and the victimized survivors? How does a congregation care for the perpetrators of violence in ways that encourage just ways of relationship? How do those who hear the stories of pain and violence in the context of counseling encourage pastoral response in communities of faith? How does a church deliberate on the issues of sexual abuse, violence, and justice from a theological perspective? Are there ways for the community to respond in the context of the broader church systems and denominational structures to work toward prevention and healing for persons caught in the dynamics of sexual violence? These are significant questions central to pastoral care with congregations.

THEOLOGICAL CURRICULA AND CONTINUING EDUCATION

Several implications for theological education arise as one takes seriously the realities of congregational care. First and foremost, seminaries and divinity schools must return to the task of training pastoral theologians rather than practitioners who specialize in counseling. For the most part pastoral counseling remains an urban phenomenon while local congregational care is the lived reality of the majority of persons. Churches depend upon the pastoral person to help interpret social crises. The representative cares for communities by offering a theological perspective on important issues on a consistent and daily basis.

Second, education needs to continue to offer cross-disciplinary work both within the fields of theology and outside the traditional parameters of religion. The centrality of theology as an interpretative guide cannot be overestimated. A variety of perspectives is important for generalists who become pastoral persons in local communities. However, at the core, the pastoral representative must retain the ability to think theologically.

Third, continuing education is an emphasis important for congregations and denominational structures. Persons do not integrate a core theological perspective during a three- or four-year Masters program. Continuing reflection upon the chaos, pains, and hopes of congregations assists pastoral persons in the task of theological constructions.

Fourth, the laity are essential participants in the constructive efforts of pastoral theology, and those within the fields of the academic structures are obliged to seek out methods for integration. Laypersons ought to be included in training and educational concerns since the local community of faith is the primary context for pastoral theologians to construct and reflect about particular situations. In like manner, congregations become, in reality, the primary caregivers. Parishioners need not be taught how to do care as much as be offered an opportunity to engage in critical reflections about the nature of their care. Congregations have much to teach professional pastoral caregivers about the natural ways they have learned to care for one another.

Finally, the institutionalization of pastoral counseling has resulted in a loss of ecclesial context. Often pastoral counselors have become part of a separate entity supported through a primary interest in psychodynamic theory. It is time for pastoral counselors to grasp once again their ecclesial center and for the church to utilize the gifts and graces of those who have clinical training to care for the souls of communities, not just those who happen to walk through the doors of an office or a counseling center.

Congregational pastoral care is an essential element of the church. How those within the field of pastoral theology continue to reflect, construct, and offer methodologies for communal care remains a pivotal issue for the future.

CHAPTER 13

Clinical Pastoral Education and Supervision: Emerging Issues and Changing Patterns

Maxine Glaz

The Problems in our society are writ large in hospitals.
(Farley, 1991, 87)

The hospital presents the clinical pastoral education student with a microcosm of a world besieged by pain and loss, by trauma, diversity, technological change, rapid changes in the health-care system, and by the economic reality of limited resources. It is a world of conflicting values and ideals, of power structures, insurance conglomerates, government regulations, and debate over private and public values in which every issue, every human problem described in the earlier chapters of this book, intersects.

How do we minister and provide education in a place that represents such a complex and rapidly changing world? How well does the therapeutic model of ministry, which evolved within the nexus of the religion and health movement, work in an increasingly complex and confusing organization? Is the pastoral care tradition adequate for our time, or must pressing issues of justice supersede attention to mercy—to ministries of emotional support and therapeutic growth that have been the preeminent theological concerns of the clinical movement?

It is my contention in this article that the institutional, social, and cultural conditions of the clinical settings in which most CPE is done require something like a paradigm shift in pastoral care and supervision, from a primary concern for therapeutic care to a more encompassing concern that includes moral counsel and guidance from within a religious perspective. While a deep understanding of persons (of ourselves and our patients) is a norm for clinical learning, it is a norm that today must be augmented by re-articulating the moral dimensions of our work as ministers. We must understand how therapeutic conversations contribute to the processes of ethical discernment as we address the relation of pastoral care to questions of justice (cf. Browning, 1983; Gerkin, 1991*b*).

EMERGING ISSUES IN THE HOSPITAL

In the sixties, Charles Gerkin and his students ministered to patients who illustrated the social and cultural diversity that has increased throughout America in the nineties. Persons of white European descent are less representative of our country's changing population. With population shifts, technological changes in health care create a new focus for pastoral care to patients. CPE students of thirty years ago visited patients who were in the hospital for days and weeks. Some died. More got well. Pastoral conversations could become richly meaningful, even life-changing.

Since the sixties, physicians have developed the capacity to give cardiopulmonary resuscitation with a corresponding explosion of means to keep people alive: Sometimes it works. Our patients are sicker as a result and fewer can talk during a hospitalization. Pastoral conversations are frequently organized by loss and decision making rather than by the patient's potential for restored health. These technological changes in medicine are accompanied by rapid changes in the health-care system. Health care is more expensive, consuming increasing dollars of the gross national product. It is more complicated and highly regulated than it was just a few years ago. The rationing of care that is essential to maintaining a decent system of health care has not been accomplished; nor do many communities plan efficiently for health-care insurance or hospital specialization. (Rochester, New York, provides an exemplary exception. The results have been enormous savings in health-care costs. The *Denver Post*,

September 21, 1992.) Capitalism, not cooperation, reigns and rules the health-care "market" (cf. Relman, 1992).

The Patient Self-Determination Act of 1991 reminds us that patients are to be involved in making their own choices about how much health care to accept during a terminal illness, but persons outside the hospital do not realize the mounting pressure on physicians to provide unwarranted health care on demand. Death does not seem inevitable; it is managed, and it creates enormous strains on the family who make ultimate decisions at the bedside of a loved one. In the midst of their agony, some medical treatment is continued only as a kind of terminal psychotherapy for the family. At other times physicians act as if everything must be done to keep the patient alive, or they assume a militant posture toward the enemy who is death (W. May, 1983, 63-86), or if there are baser motives, they continue treatment because they will receive payment for the service in any case. Lopsided visions of the purpose of medicine augment the cacophony in society about health care, which is itself in critical condition (Mermann, 1992, 337; cf. W. May, 1983).

Health-care decisions are more obviously value-laden economic decisions today than they were a generation ago, but, as decisions with ramifications for the public welfare, they are made either by families in crisis or by persons whose training predisposes them to be guided by technological formulas. Intelligent and well-intentioned health-care professionals navigate by norms in which private obligation supersedes commitment to the public good (D. Smith, 1990, 275-94; cf. Curtin, 1992), while the families they talk with navigate by tolerance for pain and by intuition. The illusion of individualism orchestrates many hospital conversations.

EMERGING ISSUES IN PASTORAL CARE

Hospital ministry is more complicated as a result of these extensive changes in culture and in health care. We cannot presume that either patients or staff are religious, or that they are rooted in a sustaining community, or that their values adhere to a commitment larger than immediate reward (Furniss, 1992, 349-59). A thoughtful ministry within the hospital involves us in considerations beyond the patient's prevailing feelings and wishes to the context and social implications of our care. But what does this mean as we work with patients? Consider this case:

The wife of an alcoholic man is angry with her husband because she believes he should be punished for his drinking. He is deathly ill. She believes his suffering is God's plan for his salvation. She wants him kept alive, although the staff says that continued treatment is inhumane. His condition is irreversible. The patient himself cannot speak and has no capacity for self-examination. He is withdrawn but communicates nonverbally that he wants no more medical care. For days his wife becomes more rigid as the staff talks to her. She is antagonistic: They think her religious purposes are questionable, at best. His writhing pain does not affect her. His punishment and his salvation are all that matter.

The woman's position in demanding continued care is not reasonable in the eyes of the staff or from a more liberal theological perspective. Complicated differences of world views and experience exist, such as problems in continuing treatments that cause harm, and concern for the broader question of the just use of resources. The chaplain experiences the feeling of being caught in the middle, struggles with the woman's conscience and his own, with his irritation and with hers toward her husband.

As a minister he offers attention and mercy in the midst of overwhelming chaos, and, in this case, the ministry culminates in healing. To the chaplain's amazement, an alliance with the woman allows her to soften her position and to terminate care. In the midst of pastoral conversations, issues of social, cultural, and religious differences and questions about the benefits of care are not discussed, yet they are resolved. The woman's loneliness, which is at the center of her conviction that the hospital is a secular institution with no interest in her husband's soul, shatters, and she meets his death with gratitude to the staff for their care.

RITUAL PRESENCE AS ETHICAL REINFORCEMENT

In the crux of changes in health care, clinical experience in the hospital enables students to experience cultural change "writ large," while they embrace the symbolic power of the pastoral role in conversation and in ritual presence. Clinical Pastoral Educators continue to emphasize the importance of listening and presence, of attention and mercy, as essential to this ministry, while the involvement of a chaplain in the patient's hospitalization enables patients to meet the questions of loss and death with greater comfort and with clearer moral resolve.

Families frequently speak about the mystery that pervades dying; of the awesome difficulty of consenting to stop treatment and of letting a loved one die. Many of them are terrified by the feeling that they are asked to play God in these moments. Their talk acknowledges a confusion about what medical treatment can and cannot accomplish. Perspectives about care are created by a longing for "the best of everything," perhaps particularly when a family is deprived in other life circumstances. Over my desk I keep the thoughtful prayer of an eight-year-old discovered in a chapel hymnal:

Dear God, I dont know wether I want my Grandma to live or die. If she lives I can to be with her. If she dies shell be out of misery. Please make the right chose,

Amen

This youngster's words express what is heard many times from the families of patients. They do not want to make life or death decisions, but they must. "Chaplain, what should we do? What would you do in our shoes?" Religious direction is often more reassuring than speaking in the unfamiliar language of principle ethics, "You seem to realize the time has come to let go but it is not easy. To terminate care is not to wrest the matter from God but rather to return it to God. I would let him go."

CPE and the style of hospital ministry it evokes induce staff participation in treatment questions so that medical and moral decisions regarding care are resolved in the context of community. In private, ministers preside at the bedside. More publicly, we are involved with staff and serve on the hospital's Ethics Committee. In and beyond the hospital we demonstrate civic and political involvement. Our ministry thus invites and supports moral reflection and action in numerous ways.

Characterizations of therapeutically oriented pastoral care as essentially individualistic and nearly secular, focus too narrowly on method and tend to overlook the direction by which hospital ministry serves ethical ends. As Rodney Hunter suggests, the therapeutic tradition of care recognizes the inherent tension between the symbolic power of the pastoral role and the relational capacity of the minister (see chapter 1). Currently, chaplains have less time to develop a therapeutic relationship with patients, and they draw more on the religious transference as a vehicle for healing. At the same time the problems of patients and their families are more practical: "What should we do? Chaplain, would you be with us and pray for us as we disconnect life support?"

A minister offers a historical religious perspective in the heart of modern crisis. Often this perspective is communicated through prayer and ritual presence. Ralph Underwood describes these means of grace as the essence of pastoral care (1993). Bedside rituals of committal include faith language and narratives that support people who wrestle with their own ambivalence about keeping a loved one alive or causing further suffering. Doubts about the morality of difficult decisions are partly resolved in the minister's presence and in the rehearing of a larger story of God's abiding love.

By means analogous to the parent who provides moral guidance, the minister acts as a reinforcer of religious values through participation in rituals. In childhood, parents help a child toward optimal involvement in social living with others through gentle but firm questions, by presenting generalizations or principles which can be retained to guide future action, and by enhancing the child's empathy for how others will feel if these social expectations are not met (Damon, 1988, 51-72). Insofar as the parent's teaching is itself offered empathically, the child absorbs such lessons with a greatly deepened sense of self and other (Damon, 1988, 115-28). Moral strength is thereby reinforced. If parents are authoritative, not dogmatic, or laissez-faire, or harsh and punitive, and when they themselves demonstrate concern for their behavior and its impact on others, they reinforce the child's developing moral sensibility (Damon,

185

1988, 54-64, 115-28). However, when the parent's style of managing the child's moral development is less than optimal, the child's conscience may instead skew toward harshness, or subterfuge, or self-indulgence (cf. Damon).

In the heat of crisis patients may be vulnerable to the ineffective working of a distorting conscience, but they may also be, more than usual, influenced by the authority of others. Representative acts of ministry thus allow us to affect the moral sensibility of those we serve. Particularly in ritual presence we act much as parents do in mediating culture; we attend to the moral situation or dilemma, we imbue actions with meaning, we organize principles for behaving, and we confirm the participants as standing within community. We serve as religious and ethical guides although we rarely give direct moral instruction in the course of liturgy.

A DEATH IN THE GANG

A patient or a family may not ask us to perform church or religious rituals, yet as ministers we are also involved in enhancing moral reasoning through ordinary conversation that is not particularly religious in nature (cf. Wallwork, 1991). I can demonstrate this conviction in a clinical vignette from the hospital. It illustrates well the complexity of ministry in the midst of secular pluralism, although, at least superficially, it does not represent a successful outcome:

The patient is a nineteen-year-old male. He appears to be Hispanic. He is on life support, but brain damaged. He took a pistol to his head and released the trigger to end a three-week depression. Gang members come two by two, to say good-bye: They are grieved and shaken. Race, color, sex, and sexual orientation of the visitors are as variable as the youthfulness of the faces is consistent. They are black, oriental, Hispanic, white, male, female, straight, and gay. Resignation holds them together.

They tell me the patient is unemployed and full of self-doubt. They tell me he is worried that he will never have anything, never get anything. His young visitors are mostly unemployed, at loose ends, and as filled with anxiety as he had been.

The patient's mother, I learn, is not Hispanic, but Filipino. His step-father is white and aging. His siblings are as racially different as is the larger community, the gang, of which they are a part. The mother tells my CPE resident, "We knew he had a gun, of course. He had threatened to take his life, but we just told him, 'You have to make your own decision.'" She believes she did the right thing, but what does she think of his decision? She cries very hard. She does not understand that ultimately she must consent to remove him from life support. Although he appears to be alive, he is already dead.

His blond girlfriend is pale with pain. She cries in the hallway across from our main elevators. "Why, why, why?" she says, repeating herself. "Why did he do it? I loved him but I could not help him." We retreat to my office to talk. She tells me she had broken up with him several weeks before because his drinking and the fighting between them had become intolerable. She had a job. He did not. She bought some cute white leather sandals with her fifth paycheck and he became irate about her purchase. She had something. He had nothing. It seemed like a little indulgence to her. He spent what money he had on booze and drugs. She avoids both. She feels that she is to blame for his death because his siblings accuse her with silent, vacant stares.

He had beat her up and pushed her down the stairs the night before he shot himself. When he came to her house the next morning, pounding to get in, she would not let him enter. "Oh," she cries, "If only I had opened the door and talked to him, I loved him so." She walks to his room again with me to say "Good-bye."

The staff allows the family several days to come to acknowledge the finality of his life before they become insistent. It is an unbelievable death when it comes so suddenly and while a machine breathes for the patient. After a long wait the patient is removed from life support. The family does not want to consider organ donation; this death is a tragedy in every imaginable way. The staff is annoyed with the family, but quietly so. They say they understand.

For days on end every conversation brings its own issues of discernment to the family, staff, and to the chaplain. The family does not immediately understand that their son and brother is dead. It takes time for the shock of what has happened to subside. The parents cannot comprehend how depressed their son was, for they saw his anger before they saw his fright. They did not hear his plea for help. He was to stand alone and figure it out himself. In his late adolescent rebellion he was hard to stand beside. The mother suggests she responded to her son's questions about suicide in helplessness or hostility, but could it be something else?

The patient's friends feel out of control and out of sorts, and that has come to be regarded as normal by all of them; they are frightened and disfranchised. Questions of personal adequacy, of ethnic and family identity and uncertainty permeate their relationships. Economic deprivation, social deprivation, and racial disrespect merge in an ugly pattern that has undermined character and hope. From a moral point of view it is interesting that the gang members tell me they were concerned, even desperate for him, and had nowhere to turn, and of all the parties to this drama they feel most responsible for what has happened.

The mother is burdened and out of touch. When did she give up on her son? why? She appears to be more relieved than I want a mother to be that her son is now gone.

My student and I talk about the mother's words to her son, "You have to make up your own mind," until we have our own dismay about them under some control. We agree the family could have been more helpful. We wonder about the mother's cultural background. Is this the way a Filipino mother ordinarily talks to an adult male son? Was she being deferential? Did she have other feelings she wanted to speak of to him? Or, was she trying to accommodate American culture with its notion of freedom of choice? Could her boy have been in trouble before? If she had consulted with a psychologist or social worker previously, might someone have said to her, "Our children have to make their own decisions." We conclude we cannot understand her motives. What appears to be indifference may have been prompted by her concern to do the best for him. We decide that what we can help the mother explore is how she felt when her son presented her with his dilemma about taking his own life, not how she feels because he killed himself. The student says, "I can talk with her about that!"

Initially the staff is frightened by the potential explosiveness of the gang. As the chaplain, do I diffuse their aggression or should I organize it in some way that benefits them? Deserved or not, my student and I hang around knowing the name "Padre" means we have the gang's attention and respect. They will not blow, but they do cry. We provide some structure for their grief. Trying to look cool, they talk about unemployment and despair. What hope can we offer except to agree it shouldn't have been this way for him? As a child of God he deserved justice. A gang member responds to this simple affirmation with tears.

I talk to the girlfriend because she is so obviously distressed. I listen in the ways I learned to listen in verbatim conferences many years ago, and now I hear her struggles with her conscience, her guilt, and seek to assess what kind of person she is before I respond. I work to help her regain a sense of proportion for her responsibility in the relationship and, though I rarely do so, in this case I point her toward therapy so that ultimately she can learn how to avoid repeating what has happened. As she departs from the hospital I know she is still sad, but relieved. She wants to find friends who aren't into killing themselves; six of hers have committed suicide this year. She looks for a different way.

The staff and the physician feel a terrible sense of helplessness too. They want very much to make something good come of what is so obviously awful. They put their efforts into trying to obtain organ donations—harvesting body parts. They cannot do anything else for the boy, but they hope that a good grief might result in consent that will have beneficial consequences for someone. Ultimately they are thwarted. Nobody is going to take anything more away from this family!

Layer after layer of conversation with family, friends, and staff requires the chaplain's attention, and each of them involves persons thinking aloud about moral questions. Bedside ministry is so often like this—a quiet and unpreachy kind of participation in practical ethics. It is most effective when it is practiced in Socratic fashion by asking questions that help parties develop principles, but inevitably those questions betray my pre-existing beliefs and values. Listening and unhurried presence and a certain persistence are essential to this process just as they are when good parenting contributes to moral formation. In this form ministry is not noisy or intrusive, and it may or may not be direct. Attention to words, process, and their narrative and ethical meaning is essential whether in listening or in speaking.

THE CLINICAL MOVEMENT AND THE QUESTION OF CONSCIENCE

At the same time, the pastoral care movement has focused too much attention on persons with over-developed consciences (Holifield, 1980, 39-53) and has tended to ignore others whose problems suggest other distortions of conscience; the cunning, the domineering, the victimized, or the self-indulgent. Can we be more aware of and helpful to them?

The girlfriend and the gang members represent persons who have consciences that are organized around taking responsibility. In crisis they will often manifest pain about what they did not do or what they did that they should not have done, even when they could do nothing else.

The young man's parents are not so easily categorized. We can only acknowledge that in this circumstance they did too little to guide or protect their son. As a mother myself, I wonder whether this mother's passivity had been a part of her pattern of managing her son from early in his life, because he had shown little capacity to delay gratification and to avoid self-destructiveness. We can speculate about the mother's motives, but we cannot know what they are in so brief a period of time. Nor can we discern what other social relationships have been influential for him, in her management of him, or in her inability to manage. So, we are still left to wonder about what kind of conscience she has, and what multicultural pressures reduced her sense of agency to the point that she abrogated supervision of her son when he did ask for it. Is she only a victim, or a victim and a victimizer as well (Glaz, 1991, 103-7)?

Through the history reported by the girlfriend, we learn that the young man himself struggled with aggression and tried to dominate her in order to regain some sense of control over his life. Because he had so little personal control he had almost no ability to manage the inherent complexities of racial prejudice, a broken family, and the identity confusion that was especially potent as he left home. He could not possibly muster the necessary strength to manage the class deprivation and economic hardship he also endured. He was lost before the gunshot that took him. Ultimately his aggression toward himself overtook his aggression toward his lover. He was victimizer and victim.

As we listen, we hear each of these individual stories differently and respond to them differently in conversation. We are attuned to feelings, certainly, but also to the moral feelings: empathy, shame, and guilt. We observe how people manage them; when they do seem to or do not seem to feel them. Over time, personality styles and character become clearer (Mitchell, 1988, 239-70; cf. Shapiro, 1965, 1981). We can discern what kind of conscience is in place or what deficits there may be and what kind of human being we may be talking to. With education we come to recognize the developmental journey and identificatory objects in human experience that account for other differences between people. "Not every wound is healed with the same plaster" (Ignatius of Antioch, 1953, 118-19), nor is every conscience the same. As we understand "the more difficult brethren," therapeutically oriented pastoral care emerges as a ministry with moral force.

However tentatively, pastoral conversations begin to account for and respond to differences in culture and in character. When there is a moral failure in empathic consideration for others or an absence of appropriate guilt, we can consider what might be asked that can help the patient and me, or the student and me, look at the problem together. The question, "How was it for you when he talked to you about taking his life?" gently presses the patient's mother. Her apparent indifference has had a devastating effect, but may reflect her caughtness as much, or more, than it reflects her apathy. Yet her response became the final tragic perceptual lens for her son's fragmented experience in the world: "No one cares what I decide." Can she be guided toward a greater awareness of her own confusion as her son talked to her about taking his life? The uphill struggle of her life and of her son's is not depreciated, nor is her capacity to learn through pain to reflect on past events and to experience renewal. A basic sense of agency, which a thoughtful question may restore, can help.

FROM THE INDIVIDUAL TO THE CONTEXT

A chaplain also observes the systemic interactions of people who are as dissimilar as these individuals are and their impact on one another for good and ill. Each level of observation, along with our own implicit values and goals, creates direction for intervention and change. Certainly we are concerned about social, cultural, and institutional issues raised by the family and their immediate dilemma. In the moment I cannot do much about the larger realities of this family's life, but as we interact within the vital field of the hospital I have some understanding and authority that I try to manage on their behalf.

Every pastoral conversation, every intervention, it seems to me is filled with potential for redemptive investment and interaction. At times, as in this case, the actual accomplishment seems minimal. So much more is needed for everyone's sake. Tragedy may have the day, as the staff fears, but even as I am devastated by the enormity of the difficulty I encounter, in the midst of it I know I cannot concede defeat. Like the consequences for the mother who should not have said, "Whatever you decide," the stakes are too high. I also must hope against hope that what little I can be, say, and do, matters.

PASTORAL CARE AS A PRACTICE OF MERCY AND JUSTICE

The hospital ministry of pastoral care demonstrates profound connections to concerns for justice, even though mercy is its prevailing norm.

Margaret Farley suggests that love is only love when it is grounded in justice (1991, 85-88). So with mercy; we are truly compassionate when our concern is proximate to equity and justice. Even though there is a flavor of mercy in prolonging medical care as compensation for earlier deprivation as in the gang member's death, there is little justice in using resources at the deathbed that would have served him far better in some other way. Yet once disaster befalls, mercy serves and heals.

In the midst of the hospital, a well-trained pastoral caregiver thinks in many directions at the same time: intuitively, interpersonally, ethically, systemically, historically, empathically, and in light of the faith tradition (the patient's as well as our own). Our thinking allows us to be immediately helpful without the illusion that we are beneficent to a social order in which, if anything, the problems are "writ larger." Kindness and mercy establish a presence with others, but it is only a generous presence when it is informed by concern for the moral dimensions of experience, including the concern for truth and justice.

Over and over again patients, their families, and staff confirm for me that they understand the significance of what ministry accomplishes for good within the hospital. The kindness and charity we demonstrate as educators and students of ministry does represent the gospel to those in acute need. It is not enough for the world outside our hospital doors, as it is barely enough for the world inside our doors; but how much better when we touch others with the conviction, "You matter in this world!" than to intimate in whatever misguided ways we may do so, "Whatever you think or decide!"

CHAPTER 14

Pastoral Counseling and Pastoral Psychotherapy: The Impact of Social Change and Social Difference

A. J. van den Blink

INTRODUCTION

Pastoral counseling, understood as an activity by representatives of the church for helping people in spiritual and emotional distress, has been going on from the very beginnings of Christianity. Pastoral psychotherapy, understood as a separate profession of clergy and specially endorsed lay people who have received intensive psychotherapeutic training and engage in this activity for remuneration, is a twentieth-century phenomenon. Social change is significantly reshaping the practice of pastoral counseling as pastoral psychotherapy.*

CONTEXT

After floating downstream for many years in the quiet waters of relative obscurity, pastoral psychotherapy has found itself navigating some very

---

*In preparing to write this essay I have also talked to and consulted with Gary Hellman, Roslyn Karaban, John Karl, Margaret Kornfield, Christie Neuger, James Poling, Mary Ragan, Douglas Ronsheim, Robert Svenson, James Walkup, Roy Woodruff, and James Wyrtzen. All of them are experienced psychotherapists, supervisors, and teachers of pastoral counseling.

turbulent rapids. Previously, the debate in pastoral psychotherapeutic circles had centered on how to define pastoral psychotherapy from various psychological and theological perspectives; what to require in pastoral psychotherapy training in terms of supervised experience, theoretical grounding (mainly in psychodynamically oriented psychotherapies), and personal psychotherapy; and whether to admit those who are not ordained to the profession of pastoral psychotherapy, provided they receive ecclesiastical endorsement.

Now the pastoral psychotherapy profession finds itself in a very different environment. The profession is challenged by proponents of new therapeutic orientations, such as family systems therapy and cognitive therapy; by advocates for adopting spiritual, rather than just psychological, perspectives; by critics who charge that pastoral psychotherapy is centered on male, white, middle-class norms and values; and by practitioners who question the necessity of ordination for practicing pastoral psychotherapy.

Previously, pastoral psychotherapy was relatively unknown in the church and society because of its small number of practitioners and the confidential nature of their practice, its problems of definition and identity, and the often dubious regard in which the profession was held by others. Secular therapists, if they were aware of the existence of pastoral psychotherapists at all, tended to regard them as too religious and insufficiently value-free. Ironically, pastoral psychotherapists' denominations and faith groups often regarded them with equal suspicion as too secular.

Now pastoral and secular therapists are more interested in ethics and values as secular therapists increasingly abandon their value-free posture. Eligibility for insurance reimbursement has become a pressing matter. Pastoral psychotherapists are being sued for sexual abuse and exploitation of their clients, thrusting the profession into the limelight and making the general public more aware of its existence. Legal liability and state licensing are affecting the profession in ways that were unthinkable just a short while ago.

Although stressing the importance of context has become a truism, the radical implications of the contextual perspective are only beginning to be understood. From this perspective we are always in a multidimensional (e.g., psychological, biological, relational, and societal) and multilayered (e.g., what is conscious and what is out of awareness) context. We can no more step out of our context than we can choose to leave our bodies temporarily. We can determine, within limits, how to relate to and deal with our external and internal environments. Indeed, our ability to relate in more authentic and loving ways to one another has the potential of transforming us from contextual beings to human beings.

The realities of the present context are catching up with pastoral psychotherapy. The pastoral psychotherapy profession, like the culture in which it is embedded, is being forced to take note of what is happening in the world and of the challenges that this new awareness is posing. Pastoral psychotherapists, individually and as a profession, are no longer dealing only with the usual kind of struggles for identity and predictable developmental changes that any new movement or profession has to go through. We are also faced with a complex and multifaceted crisis, partly societal and partly idiosyncratic to its ecclesial and therapeutic milieu, a crisis which appears to be demanding something in the order of a transformational change if pastoral psychotherapy is to survive with integrity and viability. Pastoral psychotherapy and the pastoral counseling movement, if my hypothesis is correct, will look quite different in the future—in theory, in structure, and in practice.

CURRENT TRENDS

At the risk of oversimplification, I would like to delineate three overlapping and interconnecting trends that are important to understand if one is to grasp what is happening to pastoral psychotherapy. First, consciousness raising that has been going on for some time now in our whole society is also evident in the pastoral psychotherapy movement. Most of us are, for example, becoming more cognizant of the way in which we have been and are being shaped in manner and degree by the values and assumptions of our culture. Second, the movement is learning to acknowledge and rectify systemic injustice in which pastoral counselors themselves, both as individuals and as an organized group, continue to participate. Third, the pastoral psychotherapy movement is having to deal with large changes in society and in the church from a position which is no longer privileged.

Examining Implicit Cultural Assumptions

The challenge of raised consciousness compels us to see more clearly how the prevailing cultural assumptions about, for example, gender and race and class, have shaped our behavior as pastoral psychotherapists in ways that we unconsciously or uncritically perpetuate in our theory and practice. Often we do not become aware of this until a difficult encounter with clients or colleagues brings our hitherto unexamined assumptions to the surface.

A case may illustrate this more clearly. The pastoral psychotherapist is a white, married, middle-class male in his forties, son of a recently immigrated European Protestant patriarchal family, taking training in family systems therapy after having practiced many years with a psychodynamic orientation. The clients are an African American, middle-class, divorced, professional woman and her son, who is underachieving in school. This woman is a survivor of sexual abuse who is quite outspoken and challenging, has worked her way up the economic ladder, comes from a large matriarchal family, speaks without embarrassment about her religious faith, a conversion experience which has changed her life, the importance of the church to which she belongs, and the many barriers that men and society place in her way as an African American woman.

The pastoral psychotherapist, like most of us born in a white American or European culture, is accustomed to acting on the basis of an individualistic paradigm, which is now being challenged by his training in family systems therapy. His client has internalized a more organismic paradigm. Whereas the pastoral psychotherapist would value individual autonomy over family, or nuclear family differentiation over family of origin, his client might have different values.

Depending on whether he diagnoses this situation from a psychodynamic or family systems point of view, he will organize his interventions around personal differentiation and insight into transferential patterns, or around helping this woman achieve appropriate boundaries and functioning in the mother-son dyad and between the two of them and the school. Either way he may miss the importance of the extended family and kinship network in the lives of mother and son.

If he ignores or discounts her conversion experience or religious affiliation, he may miss or pathologize an important source of strength and empowerment. If he holds only the two-parent family as normative, he may undermine her efforts at being a competent solo parent, no matter how good his intentions are. If he is not aware of the importance of matriarchy in this woman's life, he may get into an unnecessary power struggle. If he does not understand the pervasive and degrading presence of racism and sexism, he may read her anger and upset solely in terms of her own, unresolved, personal, and interpersonal conflicts rather than as an appropriate response to being victimized by extrafamilial forces. And if he is not aware of his own privileged position in terms of his race, gender, and class, he may fall into the trap of an unwitting paternalism and thereby add to his client's problems. Because more and more pastoral counselors are having similar experiences, the consciousness of many is being raised (van den Blink, 1988).

I do not want to overstate the degree to which this is happening. Indeed, since the majority of pastoral psychotherapists are politically and theologically liberal white men, a persisting difficulty and an important contributing factor to the present dysfunctional stasis in the pastoral psychotherapy profession is the degree to which so many fail to understand their own internalized cultural biases. The most enduring and influential of these cultural particularities are noncontextual thinking and theory and practice which have made the male experience normative.

What I have called "the problem of the good guy" is an example of both the perduring, noncontextual mindset and the difficulty in changing older, dominant ways of practicing and theorizing. "The problem of the good guy" is the difficulty posed by those who think they are good guys and who fail to be aware of the gap between their professed ideology, their internalized cultural assumptions, and the way in which these shape their actual behavior.

One may have and be able to articulate the most liberal and politically correct views and still behave in ways that are at variance with one's professed beliefs. I have experienced this blind spot among many liberal white men, including myself, as a large impediment to overcoming sexism and racism. For as long as one thinks of oneself as having transcended such prejudices, one is impervious to the continuing, behavior-shaping effects of internalized cultural attitudes. Cultural values and attitudes can be brought into awareness and named, and the undesirable ones more productively dealt with and to some degree with hard work overcome, but they can never be fully erased. "The problem of the good guy" goes beyond psychological denial or admission of normal human frailty and limitation. Indeed, "good guys" are often pastoral psychotherapists with a great deal of insight into their own dynamics and that of their families of origin. What is missing is a sufficient awareness of the extent to which their individual development has been shaped by class, economics, gender, culture, and ethnicity. What is missing is a

critique of self-in-culture and culture-in-self, mainly due to the individualistic paradigm that has for so long informed our thinking and so
thoroughly shaped our perceptions of reality.

In times of social stability and physical health, or in situations where
a person or a group is in a position of privilege, it is easy to ignore context,
to assume its general benevolence, or to overestimate a person's ability
to control what is going on. This attitude has also marked the pastoral
psychotherapy profession despite its own struggle as a minority movement in church and society. When combined with the strong partiality
toward individualism that has characterized Western European and
North American societies for hundreds of years, a milieu in which most
of us have been steeped since birth, it is not surprising that it is difficult
for us to think contextually.

The combination of this individualistic bias of our culture and the
privileged position held by most of those who are white middle-class
people, and in particular white middle-class men, has led to some very
strange ways of thinking, such as confining etiological investigation to
intrapsychic dynamics of persons or to the interpersonal dynamics of
couples and families. Psychotherapeutic theories and training methodologies have until recently been characterized by a virtual neglect of
extrapersonal or extrafamilial context.

In our culture contextual thinking comes more easily to those who
are oppressed. When one is subjugated, in whatever way or to whatever
degree, being able to think contextually becomes a matter of survival, a
skill one learns to acquire out of self-defense. When the environment is
unstable or inimical, one simply has to pay attention to what is going on.
The connection between context and the voice of the oppressed leads
to a second important trend in the crisis which is confronting pastoral
psychotherapy.

Acknowledging Systemic Injustice

The liberation movements of women, people of color, and gays and
lesbians, as well as the social critiques to which these movements have
given rise, have made the pastoral counseling movement aware of the
debilitating effects of sexism, racism, and classism (Boyd-Franklin, 1989;
Glaz and Moessner, 1991; Luepnitz, 1988; McGoldrick, Anderson, and
Walsh, 1989), of the ways psychotherapeutic theories and technologies
of all kinds can be used to maintain the status quo (McGoldrick, 1988),
of the general failure of the pastoral psychotherapy profession to reach

the poor and disadvantaged (Couture, 1991a), of the glaring deficiency of psychotherapeutic theories and theological perspectives to take into account unjust social conditions, which are the breeding ground of so much individual and group suffering and dysfunction. To cite these wrongs has become a familiar litany by now but one that has generally occasioned more denial, irritation, and resistance than efforts at amelioration, as anyone who has tried to change the structure and behavior of seminary faculties and counseling center staffs toward inclusivity and parity has soon found out.

Learning to Cope with Changes in Church and Society

Finally, the third trend in the present crisis results from the multiplicity of societal and ecclesial changes that are taking place and having a profound, disequilibrating effect on pastoral counselors and their profession. Persons in helping professions, including psychiatrists, have diminished their enthusiasm for interdisciplinary work and have retreated toward the safety of original identities and specializations. Furthermore, churches have enforced stricter standards for ordination, raising the prospect of a new clericalism, a concomitant burgeoning of the lay ministry movement, and increasing demands from persons such as gays and lesbians, who must deny who they are to obtain required ecclesial endorsement to be eligible for membership in the American Association of Pastoral Counselors. Moreover, pastoral psychotherapists face financial and legal concerns, which increase their anxieties over legal liability, eligibility for fee reimbursement, participation in managed care companies and malpractice insurance, and the nationwide trend toward making all mental health providers more publicly accountable through state licensing.

CRUCIAL ISSUES

With all these difficult problems facing the pastoral psychotherapy profession, is it possible to identify the more fundamental issues? Certainly, the American Association of Pastoral Counselors must come to terms with the pluralistic society into which the United States is rapidly evolving by being more inclusive on issues of gender, race, ethnicity, religious orientation, and sexual preference. Without a satisfactory solution to the issues of insurance, managed care, legal liability, and state licensing, the profession of pastoral psychotherapy as presently constituted may well cease to exist. The same may happen if the pastoral psychotherapy profession is not able to eliminate sexual exploitation of clients by its practitioners.

Certain issues, however, stand out as particularly pressing, which affect the very identity of pastoral psychotherapy. First, pastoral psychotherapy needs a change in perspective, a paradigmatic shift if you will, toward a more consistent contextual way of thinking and acting. Second, pastoral psychotherapy could be revisioned as a ministry not dependent on ordination and able to go beyond the office model of mental health-care delivery. Third, pastoral psychotherapy needs to recover spirituality as an indispensable element in therapeutic practice.

CONTEXTUAL THINKING

At present the contextual perspective is only beginning to make itself felt in the pastoral psychotherapy profession. The preponderance of theory and practice is still intrapsychically based. This approach has been congruent with a culture which values autonomy and which cherishes the myth of the heroic individual who is able to overcome great obstacles through initiative and self-reliance. But reality is always larger than what our minds construe it to be. Individual human beings are not able to determine the course of their internal and external behavior solely through their own insight, motivation, self-differentiation, ability to define their needs, or skill to connote positively what is going on. It is not possible to understand people's emotional problems or conflicted behavior exclusively in terms of their inner world of needs, wishes, ideation, introjects, personality types, or deficits.

To hold the view that people are basically the authors of their own destiny is clinically untenable. The scapegoating in marriages and families, the widespread abuse of women and children by their relatives, and the sexual exploitation of clients by their therapists show how absurd such a view can be and how readily it lends itself to blaming the victim. Such a view is also politically naive, to which anyone who has endured societal oppression and war trauma can testify, and as liberation movements among women and minorities and Vietnam veterans have been teaching us for some time. Such a view is also theologically inadequate, as would be an understanding of sin that does not take into account the communal participation in all that goes wrong. Such a view compounds a person's guilt, feelings of helplessness, self-hatred, and alienation while aiding and abetting the self-righteousness and dysfunctional behavior of others.

"This tendency to blame the victim," writes Judith Lewis Herman in her recent illuminating study of trauma and recovery, "has strongly influenced the direction of psychological inquiry. It has led researchers and clinicians to seek an explanation for the perpetrator's crimes in the character of the victim. . . . Instead of conceptualizing the psychopathology of the victim as a response to an abusive situation, mental health professionals have frequently attributed the abusive situation to the victim's presumed underlying psychopathology" (Herman, 1992, 115-16).

Insufficient awareness of context by pastoral psychotherapists can lead to their premature and myopic focusing on transference and counter-transference issues, can result in a dangerous naivete about their own contribution to whatever is going on, can blind them to the existence of power differentials between clients and therapists (Poling, 1991), and can obscure the fact that doing therapy with anyone is an intervention, for good or ill, not only into that person's life but into that person's social system. Therapy, including pastoral psychotherapy, is always a political act. Stronger yet, to empower oppressed people in the process of doing pastoral psychotherapy with them can be a very subversive thing to do. And conversely, to help persons who are subjugated accommodate to an unjust or dysfunctional familial or social system in a way that keeps them victimized has earned pastoral psychotherapists the reputation of being keepers of the status quo.

The kind of contextual thinking I am proposing should not be confused with an equally naive and deleterious, environmental or inter-actional reductionism. Context always includes what goes on in the self. In the present climate of polarization between intrapsychic and interpersonal reductionists, pastoral psychotherapists have the opportunity to make a contribution by bridging this false dichotomy of dealing with either inner pathology or outer dysfunction (Graham, 1992).

REVISIONING PASTORAL PSYCHOTHERAPY

Pastoral psychotherapy has been held back, on the one hand, by its continued preferential option for ordination, and, on the other hand, by the uncritical imitation of the office counseling model of traditional psychotherapies. It may seem strange for me to combine ordination and office counseling together this way, for they are completely different.

They are linked when one accepts as self-evident that ordination is the *sine qua non* for those who wish to be pastoral psychotherapists and one assumes as equally indisputable that pastoral psychotherapists must practice their profession by adopting the method and manner of psychiatric and psychological consultation where patients are referred to a specialist who sees them for a fee in a professional treatment room.

Those who marshal theological arguments for the importance of ordination for a ministry of pastoral psychotherapy frequently appear not to be aware of the way the requirement for ordination has favored men over women and heterosexuals over homosexuals, or of the way in which social policy privileges ordained clergy through such legal protections as tax deductions and the confidentiality of the confessional. Such privileges constitute powerful reasons of self-interest, which are not usually stated, for maintaining the ordination requirement. As more and more men and women feel called to a ministry of pastoral psychotherapy but not to ordained ministry and as many religious groups ordain only to "Word and Sacrament" or do not consider pastoral psychotherapy an ordainable call at all, it is becoming increasingly evident that the requirement for ordination not only is unnecessarily restrictive and unjust but also is contributing to collusion with a denominational clericalism, which currently appears to be on the rise.

James Wyrtzen, Director of the Blanton Peale Graduate Institute in New York City, makes this point eloquently:

> Many of the people who come to talk with me at Blanton-Peale, interested in becoming a Pastoral Counselor, are active laypersons who are making a second career decision. They are not looking . . . to become a pastor and then later deciding to specialize in pastoral counseling. . . . They are looking at pastoral counseling as their goal from the beginning of their theological and clinical training. They do not have the time (at 45-55 years of age) to go through nine years of training (three years seminary, three years parish experience, and two-three years of pastoral counseling training) . . . .
> They are not interested in forming a parish minister identity and then reframing it to pastoral counseling, because unlike us [who went the traditional route], they have a very clear vision of God's call to pastoral counseling. The sad part of this is that most of the major Protestant denominations will not ordain this person. Increasingly the denominations will not ordain anyone who does not have a call to parish ministry! (private correspondence, 1992)

The practice of basing pastoral psychotherapy on the psychiatric consultation model has turned out to be equally limiting. It has encouraged a professional elitism, which considers those who do their work in offices and counseling centers as the "real" pastoral psychotherapists and those with equal training and skill who work, for example, in parishes, institutions, and ministries to the homeless as of a different and lesser status. Clergy, of course, have always done counseling in their studies as part of giving pastoral care to their congregants, but the activity of pastoral counseling in the church has not been limited to the church office; it has been done in many other places as well.

With the spread of family systems therapy and the value it has placed on the home visit, a few pastoral psychotherapists working with families are venturing beyond the confines of their offices and have in doing so rediscovered the value of the pastoral call. Pastoral counseling centers and training programs are pioneering innovative ways of training pastoral psychotherapists in nontraditional settings, such as community centers, shelters for the homeless, and storefront churches. The ones that I am familiar with are the Blanton Peale Graduate Institute of the Institutes of Religion and Mental Health in New York City, the Samaritan Pastoral Counseling Center in Rochester, New York, and the Pittsburgh Pastoral Institute.

In retrospect it is easy to understand how the pastoral counseling movement initially and uncritically adopted theories, methods, style, and the manner of the secular psychotherapies. Through their training in these therapies, pastoral counselors often discovered the kind of help and meaning that had eluded them in their own faith of origin. For many pastoral counselors psychotherapy became a new spirituality which replaced their religious faith with something that they experienced as more relevant. The pastoral psychotherapy movement as a result has numerous practitioners who are for all intents and purposes refugees from their own faith groups and whose link with and appreciation of the church is minimal.

RECOVERING SPIRITUALITY

The pastoral psychotherapy movement, therefore, needs to reconnect with its spiritual roots. We appear to be at a stage in the development of pastoral psychotherapy where its limits are becoming clearer. The initial enchantment with the psychotherapeutic arts and the high hopes for its accomplishments have given way to a more sober assessment of what psychotherapy can and cannot do. Pastoral psychotherapists realize that healing involves more than removing obstacles to personal growth, gaining insight and achieving differentiation, and curing individual and familial dysfunctions. Therefore, some pastoral psychotherapists have become interested in spiritual guidance or direction (G. May, 1982).

From a spiritual and theological perspective the care of people who are troubled, hurting, abused, or oppressed is concerned on the most basic level with forgiveness and renewal, with healing and making whole, and with discovering the possibility and presence of grace in their lives. Whatever their psychotherapeutic perspective may be or whatever techniques they may employ, pastoral psychotherapists are intrinsically about the business of helping to redeem human experience. I would argue, in fact, that this same quiddity holds for all psychotherapeutic processes whether or not they are explicitly religious.

Pastoral counselors potentially and hopefully function as enablers of change and empowerment, as providers of a safe holding environment, as wounded healers to be sure, but also at important and always unexpected moments as channels or mediators of grace. We as pastoral psychotherapists bring the good news of forgiveness, renewal, and hope to whomever we are counseling, and we ourselves can discover in the helping process the power of God. We are, of course, never able to compel the appearance of the Numinous, but we can be instrumental in being open to Presence. At times when we are least aware of it, we are used by God as agents of healing.

The central importance of a genuine spirituality in the work of pastoral psychotherapy therefore cannot be overstated. By spirituality I mean the awareness of the import of our own relationship to God, however we may understand and articulate that theologically and by whatever spiritual discipline we endeavor to enrich that connection. The stakes are high. For failure to ground ourselves spiritually will more than anything else contribute to the demise of the pastoral psychotherapy movement. Lack of authentic spirituality may also be the reason why little relevant theologizing has come out of the pastoral psychotherapy profession.

For that reason alone the quality and depth of Charles Gerkin's work, to which this volume of essays is dedicated, has been a breath of fresh air and an inspiration to many. If we succeed in grounding ourselves in a meaningful spirituality, pastoral psychotherapists will not only discover a congruent identity but will be in a position to make a more significant contribution to the church. This recovery of an authentic spirituality is the core issue confronting pastoral psychotherapists and key to a successful transformation of the pastoral psychotherapy profession.

People come to us seeking meaning, but not, I have come to believe, in the first place for meaning that clarifies, explains, makes connections, normalizes, suggests courses of action, or gives insight. Even helping people find a "connection between [their] present lived experience and the grounding narratives that historically have given that experience meaning" (Gerkin, 1986, 30) is secondary. The first and foremost need of people who are suffering is for a very different kind of meaning, that of being affirmed, of discovering self-worth, of having hope rekindled. I therefore do not see the primary task of pastoral psychotherapy as one of providing a hermeneutics of whatever kind. Providing a ministry of presence, with affirmation and with hope, always needs to come first.

The important contribution that Charles Gerkin has made to my learning is to help me understand the singular way in which pastoral psychotherapy can help people reconnect their own narratives to what he calls the grounding narratives of faith that have given human life meaning in the past and to show me a manner in which this can be done. His approach becomes problematical for me if his hermeneutical method is taken to be the primary way in which pastoral counseling is or should be done, or if the relevance of his perspective is presumed for all those who turn to pastoral psychotherapists for help. The hermeneutical method may neglect the importance of a ministry of presence, which I believe to be the *conditio sine qua non* for all pastoral psychotherapy, and may also restrict what pastoral psychotherapy can be about. It also assumes that the people seen by pastoral psychotherapists all have some meaningful historical connection with the church, be it personally or familially.

Aside from the fact that pastoral counselors see people of faiths other than the Christian one, my impression is that Gerkin's view of society is one in which the church still plays a significant role. Although that may be true in certain parts of this country, my own perception is that society both in the United States and in Western Europe is rather thoroughly secularized and that the religious veneer is very thin. If I am right about this, the hermeneutical task of pastoral counseling goes beyond connecting or reconnecting with one's faith of origin to educating about and modeling moral and religious themes that emerge in the counseling process and to sharing faith perspectives in a way that does not become impositional.

CONSTRUCTIVE PROPOSAL: A PSYCHOSYSTEMS
PERSPECTIVE

Efforts at defining pastoral counseling and pastoral psychotherapy have commonly taken the route of clarifying what it is as an entity in itself. In this essay I have been guided by a different understanding of pastoral psychotherapy, one that has emerged from my understanding of context as a continuing, interactional process between inner and outer environments, between psyches and the systems in which they are embedded. For that reason I call this a psychosystems perspective (van den Blink, 1988; Graham, 1992).

Defining pastoral psychotherapy from this perspective takes into account the person doing the pastoral psychotherapy and the environment in which that pastoral psychotherapist is operating. The emphasis in my definition is not on what pastoral psychotherapy is as a disembodied activity, or what its "essence" is, or what characteristics and credentials make someone a pastoral psychotherapist, but rather on the person of the pastoral psychotherapist in the activity, in the process and context of doing pastoral psychotherapy.

A psychosystems definition assumes that there is no such thing as pastoral psychotherapy without women and men doing it, and that what such men and women do is always influenced by the environment in which they live and work. I have found that defining pastoral psychotherapy this way helps me be clearer as to what pastoral psychotherapists are all about. It also helps me to understand better the ramifications of social change.

From this perspective I see three sets of distinguishing characteristics which delineate pastoral psychotherapy: the communal, the functional, and the intentional. By communal I refer to the faith community of which pastoral psychotherapists are members and through participation in which they are spiritually nurtured and anchored. This community of faith does not have to be an established church or denomination. It may be a religious order, or an intentional group of colleagues, or a house church. But it does have to be a group that has meaning and continuity for those participating in it. Faith and spirituality are never a one-person affair but always require participation in community.

By functional I mean the external factors which define someone as a pastoral psychotherapist. I am thinking of things like ordination or endorsement by one's faith group, seminary education, training in psychotherapy, accreditation, the setting in which one works, and the expectations of those who come for help. Functional defines the professional relationships and accountability structures of pastoral psychotherapy. I assume that we may be more aware of some of these functional characteristics than others.

By intentional I refer to the internal, subjective beliefs and commitments which define someone as a pastoral psychotherapist. For example, theological convictions, faith and spirituality, value commitments, basic assumptions about the human condition, having a sense of identity as a caring person who is linked to the historical traditions of the church, and a determination to take the Christian faith seriously. We are at any given moment only partly conscious of, or aware of, our own beliefs and practices. I call these internal factors intentional because of their purposive quality. They shape our behavior whether or not we are aware of them, they aim us in a certain direction, and they guide our choices. This intentional part has to do with what we believe. We are always dealing with belief systems. We therefore need to know that we believe and what we believe. We need to know our own basic assumptions about the human condition and the nature of reality.

The communal, the functional, and the intentional are a cluster of connected but separate processes. For someone to claim the designation of pastoral psychotherapist, all three of these emphases have to be present. This definition of pastoral psychotherapy is one that describes its distinctive process features while retaining a needed flexibility and at the same time pointing to the significance of an often overlooked communal and interior dimension, namely that of the community of faith and the spirituality of the pastoral psychotherapist. Flexibility of definition is of special importance in this time of rapid social change when the whole profession of pastoral psychotherapy is in flux in terms of its identity, its theory, and the focus of its practice; when more and more pastoral counselors receive their training in and continue to affiliate with secular psychiatric or mental health institutions; and when many engage in part-time or full-time private practice.

The usefulness of this definition is that these three characteristics do not have to be equally weighted. Either the functional or the communal or the intentional aspect can be diminished without the pastoral psychotherapist's ceasing to do pastoral psychotherapy. At the same time it helps us to see that we can no longer speak of pastoral psychotherapy when any one of these three is absent altogether. This definition should also prove to be practical in devising ways to integrate lay pastoral counselors into the wider ministry of the church. Experience has shown over and over again that ordination by itself does not guarantee committed faith, responsible behavior, or meaningful accountability to colleagues and superiors.

It exceeds the purposes of this essay to explore the ramifications of accepting lay pastoral counselors into the church's ministry. I submit, however, that examining a lay or ordained person's call to the ministry of pastoral counseling in order to discern whether that person meets the requirements of the functional, is meaningfully engaged in the communal, and is able to articulate the importance of the intentional in his or her life and work as a pastoral psychotherapist, would help to ensure accountability and would make possible a more substantive and contributory relationship of pastoral counselors to their various faith groups.

CHAPTER 15

"If One of Your Number Has a Dispute with Another": A New/Ancient Pastoral Paradigm and Praxis for Dealing with Conflict

Carl D. Schneider

T he current crisis of pastoral care is reflected in the increasingly shared recognition that the old model is no longer adequate. It has not encompassed the needs and concerns of minorities, African Americans, women, gays and lesbians, victims of abuse and violence. It has not transcended the individualism at the core of its model or dealt with the institutional and social determinants that create and perpetuate the structures of oppression and injustice that cripple, deprive, and exclude so many persons—and yet few alternatives have appeared to take its place. Though we keep railing about the inadequacy and idolatry of individualism, reminding of the importance of social justice, and urging the need for a social consciousness and context for pastoral care, until recently social theory has by and large failed to make available a framework and technology equally compelling and usable to organize pastoral care.

True, social theory has enabled us to identify and analyze the impact of many social issues. Witness this volume: It is organized around a long list of issues with which we wrestle—political and economic concerns, race, sex, abortion, gender, aging. But, as the sociologists Thomas Scheff and Suzanne Retzinger have noted (1991), classical social theory—Marx, Durkheim, Weber—is highly abstract. Its horizon is the macrostructure, with little guidance as to how to deal with all this in microprocess. The result is that most of us have little sense of what a technology of social change would look like. When we try to tackle social issues, we often sound ideological and rhetorical, with little sense of direction or concrete means of implementation to guide us in any practical way.

The psychological model, on the other hand, which has so dominated the modern pastoral care movement in the United States, provided precisely that: a practical guide to how to help people individually. Although the therapeutic model has been roundly criticized and frequently lamented, rarely has the reason for its dominance been noted: modern psychotherapy supplied a theory and practice that could readily be appropriated by the church. Few images and technologies have been available as an alternative. The role of Sigmund Freud and Carl Rogers in the pastoral care movement has many critics, but the metaphor of individual psychology (and more recently, its complement, systems theory) has shaped pastoral care for two generations because it has had few viable competitors. Pastoral counseling centers embody the technology of therapy, offering training programs that impart the skills necessary to help people concretely. Seminary courses in pastoral counseling are also standard fare in training even pastors not specializing in pastoral care.

A NEW MODEL

I want to propose, however, that a new model, with an accompanying technology, is now available. That model offers an alternative approach to handling conflict, the concern of this volume and the problem of which our American church, with its culture of politeness and "niceness," is so afraid. The new model, conflict mediation, has significant continuities with therapeutic care and counseling, but also significant differences. It stands as a distinct professional and theoretical model that can be appropriated by the churches to supplement pastoral care and counseling in important ways, giving ministry a competence in working with social conflict that it has not had in the therapeutic pastoral tradition.

In the last two decades alternative dispute resolution (ADR) has become a movement in the United States. It is reshaping the way we handle disputes in many arenas, especially with respect to our legal system. It is called "alternative" dispute resolution because it has appeared as a viable alternative to the adversary system, which is the formal name of the American legal system, which has been the normative forum for dealing with disputes in our society.

Alternative dispute resolution encompasses many mechanisms, including arbitration, mediation, multi-door courthouses, and early neutral evaluation. In this essay, I want to focus on just one component of ADR, mediation, and talk about its usefulness to the church.

Mediation is a method of helping people and disputes through the use of a neutral third party, who assists them in reaching a voluntary agreement. Mediation is a method of handling conflict that has been used by many cultures throughout the ages (cf. Augsburger, 1992). For many, it has been the primary method employed to resolve disputes. However, American society has made very limited use of mediation.

I personally practice divorce mediation. Normally I have to explain to people what I do, because most people have never heard of divorce mediation. It arose only within the last two decades, after an attorney named O. J. Coogler himself went through a difficult divorce and felt that "there had to be a better way." He devised the idea of mediation—of a neutral third party working directly with a divorcing couple to arrive at the agreements they need in order to divorce—as an alternative to the adversary system where someone else, lawyers or a judge, makes decisions for the divorcing couple.

Divorce mediation is the best known use of mediation in a family conflict, but mediators work with a broad range of family conflicts — family-elder care, parent-child disputes, family-school conflicts such as special education disputes, and so forth.

Mediation also can and has been used in other areas of our society; for example, the United States has had a Federal Mediation and Conciliation Service since 1945. Many of us, however, know of mediation only when we hear on a newscast that mediators have now been called in to resolve some kind of deadlocked labor, school, or international dispute.

Few lay people have had much direct experience with mediation. Yet in the last two decades, mediation has appeared in a wide variety of contexts in the United States, from the development of a network of Neighborhood Justice Centers and Community Mediation Centers, which largely handle interpersonal and local disputes (landlord and tenant, barking dog complaints, and the like), on through large-scale public policy mediation of important environmental disputes.

211

Unfortunately, to date this development seems to have made little inroad with the church. This is regrettable since mediation holds the promise of offering a model for the church every bit as powerful as the psychotherapy model which fueled the growth of an entire profession— that of pastoral counselors (membership in the American Association of Pastoral Counselors now numbers approximately three thousand).

THE PROBLEM

There are probably many reasons why the church has not handled conflict well and why so many calls for advocacy and social justice go unheeded. To respond would mean changing the power balance and, for many, losing privilege. There are financial implications: Conflict threatens funding. To deal with social conflict is hard work; it is complex, confusing, and so on. But one particular reason is that many people don't know *how* to deal with such conflicts. We have lacked a praxis, if you will, for conflict. And this is precisely the promise of mediation: It offers a technology for dealing with conflict that avoids both the limitations and the deformations of the adversary system. The adversary system is limited because it is time-consuming, expensive, and cumbersome. Its deformations are that it is organized in a way that pits people against one another in a contest the outcome of which is usually a win/lose solution.

The reader may wonder what all this has to do with pastoral care. Is this not the domain of the legal system? Yes, except that our legal system colors for us how we handle disputes throughout our society. It is a peculiar characteristic of American society that we typically frame disputes in terms of individual rights, a product of our viewing disputes in terms of legal rights and entitlements. Most Americans fail to recognize how distinctive and singular our system for resolving disputes is. With a lawyer for approximately every 350 citizens, we have developed what Jerold Auerbach calls "the most legalistic and litigious society in the world" (Auerbach, 1983, 3).

A PARABLE

It may be helpful to step back for a moment and look at a simple dispute and how we go about solving it. My wife and I have been disagreeing about where to go for vacation this year. I think we should go to the mountains, preferably Vermont, a beautiful state. But she has just built a canoe and wants to go to the Okefenokee swamp. To me, that is hot, sticky, and there are no mountains. We have been arguing over this for weeks. We cannot agree. What do we do? What does anyone with a conflict do?

Sometimes compromise works. Except I feel I have compromised too much already. Sometimes taking separate vacations works. But I feel we have been apart too much. That is not acceptable to me. Sometimes flipping a coin works, but this is too important for me to settle in so arbitrary a manner.

When people are stuck in disputes, they argue, often for a long time. Eventually, however, if they are unable to resolve the dispute themselves, they usually begin to *involve third parties*. My wife talks with her family, telling her mother how insensitive I am. I go out with some of my buddies, and complain about how difficult it is to understand women. Neither of these strategies is likely to resolve the dispute.

But, still stuck, we may have to turn to other third parties. We start near at hand, perhaps asking help from our pastor, or a therapist. If finally that does not work, at an impasse, we may have to turn to attorneys and the courts.

We often have disputes we ourselves are unable to resolve, but which, with the help of third parties, we can work out. There is, moreover, a continuum of third parties to whom we can turn, a continuum that runs the gamut from the *private* to the *public*, from the *voluntary* to the *coercive*, and from the *informal* to the *formal*.

PRIVATE		PUBLIC
VOLUNTARY	family, friends, clergy, therapists, attorneys, courts	COERCIVE
INFORMAL		FORMAL

The people to whom we turn first are at the informal, private end of the continuum, that is, family and friends. When we turn to clergy, the context is more public since we are involving a professional, yet it is still fairly informal since we often simply drop in to talk and the advice we are given is free. By the time we see a therapist, it is becoming even more public, since we have never seen this person before in our life until we had this problem for which we needed help. But it is still relatively voluntary; the therapist, one of those people who try to "help" us make the decision, has no decision-making power himself or herself. Nevertheless, seeing a therapist is more formal: We now need to schedule an appointment and pay money to this person.

If we end up seeing attorneys and going to court, this is at the far end of the continuum of the formal and coercive: Unable to make a decision ourselves, we find that the courts will impose one on us. Should we not like the decision and fail to comply, the courts have the formal police powers of the state behind them and can hold us in contempt.

If all this seems like an extreme way to deal with a family impasse over vacations, we might pause to consider how frequently we find both the church and our society resorting to exactly such drastic measures to deal with differences and disagreements that may be difficult to resolve, may need communal involvement to get unstuck, but are hardly irresolvable. Perhaps it is a mark of sin that we so quickly capitulate to the powers of alienation and fail to bear witness to the reality of reconciliation to overcome separation.

AN ALTERNATIVE REMEDY

In all this, mediation has not been mentioned. Yet there has been much recent interest in mediation, which stems, I believe, from the recognition of what I call "the missing middle" in dispute resolution. Far too often we veer between being stuck ourselves, unable to resolve a dispute, and capitulating to the far end of the continuum, deciding to "Sue the S.O.B.!" without first looking at the available intermediate alternatives.

Mediation supplies what has been the missing middle in dispute resolution, offering a third party's assistance, often essential to resolving the dispute, while avoiding the time-consuming, cumbersome, expensive machinery of the full adversary system.

What difference does it make to have mediation available as an alternative? A big difference, I believe. A shift to mediation is not just a shift in locus or forum but a fundamental paradigm shift from the adversarial system's focus on rights to the focus within mediation on needs and interests (cf. Fisher and Ury, 1991; Glendon, 1991; Ury, Brett, and Goldberg, 1989). That shift means, more fundamentally than anything else, that it is possible to engage in a cooperative, constructive form of conflict resulting in mutually acceptable solutions, rather than in the competitive, ultimately destructive, form of conflict (cf. Deutsch, 1973). It means that we need not fear conflict but can embrace its creative potential. We can engage in conflict and discover a different outcome:

Instead of polarization, we can explore mutual interests and build collaborative skills.

When, instead, conflicts are framed in terms of individual rights, all too frequently the result is polarization and impasse. A number of the "social conflicts" enumerated earlier in this volume are ones that regularly end up in the adversary system, and rarely find a satisfactory solution. For example, Christie Neuger identifies many items which could form the basis of a profitable discourse between pro-life advocates and pro-choice people. But such a dialogue rarely occurs, since much of the current playing field of the abortion controversy is the courts. Restraining orders, conflicts over whether various cases will be heard by the courts, conflicts defined in terms of contradictory individual rights— this is the (insoluble) stuff of the current abortion controversy. Indeed, we speak of this conflict as the "abortion *rights*" controversy.

Again, Don Browning laments the loss of the two-parent family, the inadequacy of economic support for mother-headed single-parent families, and so forth. He finds that an ethic of mutual regard would help. Equally important, however, would be to move this conflict to a forum other than the adversary system, a poor setting indeed to attempt the family reorganization that needs to be worked out in divorce. Divorce mediation offers an alternative, which takes the issue of divorce out of a win/lose struggle, and enables divorcing parents to plan a future that will meet the needs of each parent as well as their children. Studies suggest that when such planning occurs, the results are likely to be both greater involvement of fathers in their children's lives and more consistent child support for the family (cf. Pearson, 1986; Wallerstein and Huntington, 1983).

Maxine Glaz writes about the hard dilemmas that families and hospitals are faced with when they confront contemporary "life-sustaining" medical technology. Again, we are all familiar with how such choices, painful as they are, are made excruciating when put into the vortex of the adversary system: The cases of Karen Ann Quinlan and Nancy Curzon were such epic dramas that they have become a common part of our shared experience.

James Poling speaks of the need to confront the new world of sexual harassment and alludes to the wrenching public hearings of Anita Hill's charges of sexual harassment against Clarence Thomas. The hearings unquestionably raised the consciousness of our society about sexual harassment, and that was a significant step. At the same time, those

215

involved acknowledged the inappropriateness of the forum as a mechanism for dealing adequately and fairly with such issues. In contrast, as several persons have described (cf. Cloke, 1988, 1992), it is possible to deal much more effectively with such cases in mediation.

When made available, mediation has great appeal because it offers us an alternative to having strangers make decisions that may fundamentally alter our lives—whether these are hospital decisions about life and death or abortion, or legal decisions about who will have custody of children after a divorce. It returns these decisions to the people involved and lets them make the decisions the consequences of which they will get to live with.

But I find the significance of mediation goes beyond the element of self-determination.

As Robert Baruch Bush and Joseph Folger have proposed in their new work *Empowerment and Recognition* (1994), ethically mediation has an intrinsic dynamic that offers people the challenge of moving beyond individualism and realizing "the opportunities that conflict presents for moral growth" through the two dimensions of empowerment and recognition—strength of self and the ability to relate to others. Mediation offers an occasion for transformation, for becoming a fully grown moral person, integrating concern and respect for self and respect for other" (Barr, 1993).

Theologically, I believe that to truly embrace mediation is to experience, beyond our penultimate struggles with aggression, competition, and estrangement, the interconnectedness of being and the foundational reality of cooperation and relationship. Such an experience, affirming the diversity of creation, connecting us to a larger whole, is both healing and hopeful.

WHY NOW?

If mediation is such a helpful instrument, why has it been so long in appearing? One answer is that it has in fact been around for centuries in many cultures, including our own (cf. Abel, 1982; Auerbach, 1983). But it has found limited use in our society until recently because we have so overwhelmingly embraced a framework of individual rights as the way to resolve disputes. Increasingly we are now discovering what insoluble nightmares such a relentless stress on legal and individual rights creates and have turned to look for alternatives.

Even the people responsible for implementing the adversary system recognize that it is overwhelmed and incapable of dealing adequately with the conflicts brought before it. The courts themselves are increasingly implementing ADR programs throughout the country. It would be ironic, then, if the church, in spite of its biblical mandate regarding conflict resolution, were to continue to handle its conflicts in an outmoded, legalistic way when the courts themselves are looking for alternatives. Yet many of our churches are indeed involved in an unreflective use of a system that is theologically questionable and practically clogged. As Speed Leas, one of our most experienced church mediators, observes:

> Most congregations have no rules or structure for helping people negotiate or collaborate, only procedures for voting or appealing to denominational authorities. . . . I have not yet been in a church that has a decent set of understandings of how to deal with differences when they arise. Constitutions, Books of Order, and Disciplines are notorious for their vague or missing guidelines about appropriate ways to deal with differences. What is usually offered is warmed-over *Robert's Rules* or directions for what to do after the conflict has become virtually unmanageable. *Robert's Rules* can be helpful when decision-making by voting is appropriate, but it is not helpful for developing consensus or negotiating. (1985, 56, 12)

There are hopeful signs of change: In 1992, The Lutheran Church Missouri-Synod made a denominational decision to embrace a version of mediation-arbitration as a more biblically congruent form of dispute resolution than its traditional highly legalistic system. But all too many current church conflicts—conservative-liberal controversies, disagreements between individual churches and denominations, sexual impropriety by church professionals—end up in court.

IMPLICATIONS

I have had a vision for at least a decade now that one day we will have a Pastoral Mediators Network that will be as significant and vital to the life of the church as AAPC has been over the last three decades and CPE over the last fifty years. Persons in such a network would be trained to help us deal more constructively with conflict. Just as the pastoral counseling movement has taken Jesus' words that he came that we might have life and that more abundantly as a warrant for its work, so too, pastoral mediators would see the biblical warrant for placing dispute resolution at the heart of the church's function (Kraybill, 1981, 13).

Mediation would be seen as a more authentically biblical form of conflict resolution than the adversary system—again, following Jesus' words about how his disciples were to deal with conflicts (Matthew 18; 1 Cor. 6:1-7).

Courses in conflict management would be as common and standard in seminaries as courses in pastoral counseling are today. Without practical skills in conflict management the church's stance in relation to conflict will continue to alternate between avoidance and pious pleas to pray over situations. Prayer is important. If it is all we have to say in the face of conflict, however, it becomes a sop, a confession of our helplessness, a counsel of despair rather than hope.

We have had a dearth of practical skill training in conflict management in theological education. In the sixties, as part of a significant attempt by the church to involve itself in urban ministry, we had technologies such as Saul Alinsky's to guide us in social conflict. Strategies such as Alinsky employed, however, really mirrored the problems of the adversary system and focused on confrontation. We may finally be at a place where we could have a more flexible and responsive technology for addressing social conflict, which could use confrontation where appropriate and collaboration when it is called for. And we could be equally comfortable with either—afflicting the comfortable, empowering the afflicted, and helping both form coalitions for change and transformation.

There have been church pioneers in the mediation area over the years. John P. Adams, a Methodist clergyperson, was a mediator in such disputes as Kent State and Wounded Knee (Adams, 1976). Ron Kraybill, Speed Leas, Sam Leonard, Will Neville, the Mennonite Conciliation Service, and the Alban Institute are among the church leaders and organizations which have been involved in initiating mediation on behalf of and within the religious community.

If we return to the title and theme of this book—dealing with conflict—we can set a clearer vision of the future of pastoral care for the next generation. The prominence of counseling in the pastoral care field is, we have argued, partly an artifact of a ready-to-hand set of skills (e.g., active listening) that could be imparted to caregivers. But if we return to the continuum of third-party intervenors laid out earlier in this essay, we see that there are many kinds of third parties (not just pastoral psychotherapists) to which people turn for a variety of help. We will be able to provide a "full-service ministry," as it were, when we train a variety of professionals *and lay persons* to enable the full ministry of the saints. Dealing effectively with the social and structural context of the problems we encounter would mean not just, as Couture rightly notes, that we add on to the work of pastoral counselors additional social justice committee work. It would involve an understanding of ministry as empowerment and community formation, not just ministry as presence: We would train people in the skills of problem-solving, of administration, of community organizing, of group work, of goal setting, public policy, and negotiating as well as active listening and counseling skills. We need a more adequately incarnational theology. Until we have a level of skill development that matches the passion of our concern, our efforts will remain largely hortatory and ineffectual.

Is this a large agenda? Yes. Why is it necessary? Because early in Christendom the church not only cared for persons but also shaped the laws and institutions of Christendom. With the breakdown of Christendom and the emergence of secular culture, we have been trying to bridge a bifurcation between private and public life by falsely thinking that we could effectively minister to individuals, while being cut out of the loop of shaping the larger context within which those individuals live and function. We are increasingly confronted with the impossibility of adequately ministering to individuals without attending to the shape of the society and public policy within which those individuals live and work. I have endeavored here to identify one specific new "praxis" that would deepen and sharpen our ministry. It is no panacea. But it would be equally an error to get stuck yet once more in a false dichotomy between social advocacy and mediation as the route to the shalom we envision. Both are essential to the concerns outlined in this book—gender, race, diversity, aging, abuse, sexual harassment, economic marginality—and to our ministry of empowerment.

CHAPTER 16

From Relational Humanness to Relational Justice: Reconceiving Pastoral Care and Counseling

Larry Kent Graham

SHIFTING PARADIGMS

T he principal writings in pastoral care and counseling of the last decade reflect a perceptible shift in the field's theory and practice. The field has been awakened in a new way to the world composed of diverse communities, to neglected populations, to systems of injustice, and to its white male middle-class liberal Protestant assumptions and technologies. This awakening is challenging the field to rethink its fundamental identity.

All of the essays in this volume to some degree reflect a restlessness with the inheritance of the pastoral care tradition as well as a desire to build upon and expand its central contributions. In one way or another, the call forward in these writings—and in those of the past decade—is to relativize the individualistic bias in the field, to regain more explicit connection to the ecclesiastical, theological, and ethical dimensions of our work, to elevate justice and mutuality to a central place in our theory and praxis, and to become more open to the challenge and transformative power of neglected populations such as persons of color, marginalized women and children, senior citizens, the homeless and unemployed, gay men and lesbian women, persons with HIV/AIDS, and the survivors of a variety of kinds of violence and sexual abuse.

In addition, the social landscape in which pastoral care and counseling has grown and thrived has radically changed. Issues of ordination, licensing, health-care reform, litigation, and denominational retrenchment from specialized ministries raise serious questions about the identity and social location of the field. Economic factors are constricting the delivery of pastoral care and counseling in specialized settings, while in-depth care in the local congregation is increasingly questioned by both pastoral and secular psychotherapeutic specialists. Contemporary theological writers seem less interested in psychological perspectives and therapeutic thinking for their normative work than once was the case. At the same time there is a growing interest in pastoral care and counseling, Christian counseling, and spiritual direction among large numbers of lay persons. Such interest raises important considerations for degree and training programs as well as for the social context in which care and service will be carried out.

In short, the field of pastoral care and counseling is in the process of "widening its horizons" (Gerkin, 1986) conceptually, methodologically, sociologically, culturally, and functionally. Conceptually, this ferment requires a more comprehensive view of the relationship between persons and the larger world shaping them. Methodologically, it incorporates political, cultural, and sociological disciplines into psychological-therapeutic perspectives, with theology, ethics, and pastoral practice reasserting their centrality as the grounding standpoints for theoretical construction and concrete practice (see esp. chapters 5, 6, 8, and 12 in this volume). Sociologically and culturally, a new paradigm will have to take into account the care needs of a pluralistic world that is fundamentally structured by unjust power differentials and fragmented by contending value orientations between groups (see chapters 5, 9, and 13). Ethically, it calls for the development of criteria which guide practice with respect to just and liberated relationality at all levels of the social order. Further, a new paradigm must attend to the limits and possibilities inherent in the social locations in which care is mediated and in the variety of lay, clergy, and secular providers of religiously based care. Persons practicing with a new paradigm in mind will need to create structures for accountability, economic viability, and accessible and diverse services in the light of conceptual, methodological, sociological, and cultural factors (see chapters 3, 11, 14, and 15).

All of these factors press the field of pastoral care and counseling to reexamine its theory and practice and to construct new paradigms that might more adequately order our teaching. The central purpose of this chapter is to venture one possible paradigm for moving beyond our traditional focus upon the "living human document," toward concern for "the living human web" (see Miller-McLemore, 1993, 366-69, for this juxtaposition of metaphors). My discussion will draw upon the fuller model I developed in *Care of Persons, Care of Worlds: A Psychosystems Approach to Pastoral Care and Counseling* (1992). The theoretical and functional elements of the paradigm will be illustrated by reference to the concrete experience of care received by a late-middle-age lesbian woman whose name is Connie. Finally, I shall briefly discuss how other writers in this volume contribute to this psychosystemic paradigm.

The Creation of a Paradigm

What is a paradigm? A paradigm is a way of organizing one's symbolic and conceptual interpretative schematic in a manner that guides the practice of care. A paradigm is a humanly constructed set of concepts which reflects the self-understanding of a group of caregivers and guides their personal and social interventions. It must be coherent, operational, and accountable in light of the changes it makes possible as well as those it inhibits or prohibits.

The paradigm which follows is especially indebted to the contributions of three colleagues. Howard Clinebell has long combined commitment to personal growth and social change, most recently turning his attention to pastoral care and ecological responsibility (Clinebell, 1984; 1983, 180-94). Archie Smith, Jr., has connected pastoral care with the "emancipatory struggle" of victims to overcome oppression. His book, *The Relational Self* (1982), offers an early model for how concern for individual fulfillment and social transformation co-inhere at the conceptual, social, and functional levels (A. Smith, 1982). Charles Gerkin, in whose honor these essays are written, has built upon ego psychology and hermeneutical theology, including among his concerns communal responsiveness and prophetic pastoral caregiving (cf. Gerkin, 1984, 1986, 1991*b*). I have built on these efforts, and others, in developing the psychosystems paradigm which is profiled in the remainder of this chapter. The main differences between the aforementioned paradigms and mine lie in emphasis and the resources selected to build my theoretical and symbolic schematic framework and the functional technologies upon which I draw to implement the personal and social dimensions of care (Graham, 1992, 36-38).

AN ILLUSTRATION FROM PASTORAL CARE

Any paradigm in pastoral care is valid only to the degree that it reflects the concrete situation of persons who are facing crises and provides resources for positively responding to such crises. Connie, a lesbian Christian, has experienced care that embodies some of the elements of a psychosystemic paradigm and also points toward directions this paradigm might profitably take. After describing Connie, I will discuss the main conceptual features of a psychosystemic paradigm of care in relation both to Connie's story and briefly to some of the other chapters in this volume.*

Connie grew up in a large extended family in the West. Her family was a Presbyterian minority in the dominant Mormon culture of her community. Her family roots, on both sides of her family, "supported us to be who we were and to be in service to others." Her family encouraged Connie to "read and to explore my imagination." She became very literate in the Christian tradition and drew upon it as a foundation for her life. "My church encouraged me to explore my faith."

In spite of these positive experiences, her status as a member of a religious and cultural minority and her unrecognized lesbianism meant that she "grew up with a sense of being a square peg in a round hole—but not able to name the squareness." She had a maiden aunt who because of her lesbianism had been expelled from the WAVES during the witch hunts of the McCarthy era. Yet, the "word lesbian was not in the lectionary [dictionary] in my family and milieu." She found out at her aunt's funeral that her aunt was lesbian. Her memories of the aunt are very positive: "She cared for me as a person; she treated me as an individual, while other aunts treated me like a kid. Every family has a maiden aunt. She let me be a tomboy."

Connie married and had three children. She had a comfortable home in the suburbs. Her husband was a successful English professor and writer. But she was restless and unhappy in the marriage. "I had the

*The description that follows is based upon an interview with Connie under the auspices of a grant from the Association of Theological Schools in the United States and Canada, for a research project on caregiving to and among gay men and lesbian women and their families. This material is used with Connie's permission. Her identity is disguised and her real name has been changed.

American dream, but I was not happy. I was a good mother; I loved my kids and did a great job with them." During this period she found her way to a United Church of Christ congregation. It was a turning point for her. Her minister helped her face her marital unhappiness and supported her through her husband's extramarital affairs and the termination of the marriage. "He helped me to own my [own share of the] responsibility but to see that it wasn't [entirely] my fault." Further, the minister helped Connie to "express my own behavior[s] in terms of my own value system." Concretely, she became involved in the social action ministry of the congregation and led a delegation to the March on Washington in 1963. "That pastor cared for me by showing how I could use my energies positively without fighting the church."

This began a long period of lay involvement in Christian activities. She worked with ecumenical groups which believed in God's activity in the world. "God is good and involved. My life is received. This was a very affirming theology. It was based upon Paul Tillich's [belief in his] sermon, 'You are Accepted' [that grace is found in accepting that one is accepted] and Bonhoeffer's [idea of] freedom in community [in *Life Together*]." Aware of the patriarchal traditions of Christianity from a feminist standpoint, she pulled back from Christianity while still believing that Christianity was centrally affirming. "The church is about acceptance, not about dividing people up. Religion doesn't end after church; my neighbor is my neighbor, not [only the person] who sits next to me in the pew." These groups "provided a climate of struggle to work through issues in the world: alcoholism, homosexuality, etc." She came "to accept responsibility for my life and freedom. I can put that into service."

Currently, Connie is a member of a small urban Methodist congregation, which openly accepts gays and lesbians. The pastor is a married straight white female. Connie said, "The time was right when I came out. I chose a church that would not reject me. I would have come out myself, without my faith community, but that would have been painful and dangerous. They provided a safeguard, security, and encouragement. In coming out, I feel like I've come home." Connie said that when she came out two or three years ago, two friends from her church came to her house to have "a coming out party." "A lot of pieces have fallen into place. I know who I am created to be. My church has been very affirming and inclusive." She is very grateful to the "Bishop, Board, Pastor, Conference, and Board of Ministry for creating that kind of a climate: fertile soil where people can grow."

Connie sought secular psychotherapy for help with her life. Her therapist has affirmed her religious commitments and has helped her to discover and affirm herself as a lesbian. Her therapist is a feminist lesbian, but she did not disclose her lesbianism until late in the therapy process. Of her therapist, Connie says, "Joyce never tells me what is so about myself. She listens to me and encourages me to express myself, my feelings through writing. She helped me sort out what was real and unreal." For Connie, Joyce was like a safety net, or like "a safety string in the labyrinth which helped me go places I've never been and not lose touch, realizing there is a way back." It was through this process, including that of active listening, mirroring, and journaling homework, that Connie came to the point where she said to herself, "I am a lesbian."

She believes that her church is "deeply in ministry. It provides wrap-around care: food and shelter for the homeless, household goods to people with AIDS, tutoring, and other programs." Her church is sexually inclusive, with gay and lesbian persons composing about twenty percent of the membership. She understands why people go to the predominantly gay and lesbian Metropolitan Community Church, but values her inclusive church because "God created us to be many people—gay and lesbian, young and old, straight, and so on—and that variety makes any community strong."

Her church has provided a place for her to advocate gay and lesbian-affirming public policies. She has written poetry and essays on this topic and has preached before the congregation. "My congregation affirmed my sermon on 'nothing shall separate us from the love of God: not the church, not anti-gay amendments, not homophobia.' . . . I read a letter I had written to the newspaper on gay rights and the congregation applauded. This floored me. My husband had denigrated my writing, so it is something I have to work on to feel good about." She and others are working to bring the church "closer to true Christianity" and to remind the church with Peter and the New Testament that "what God declares clean don't [you] say is unclean."

Out of this journey, Connie began to date and to learn to become socially identified and active as a lesbian. Her therapy support group helped her with this, along with friends from the church. She found lovers with whom she could explore both physical and spiritual dimensions of her sexuality. Reflecting upon how her lovers have been a source of positive care for her, she says, "Lovers have confirmed who I am. It left a feeling of 'wow! this is what I have been missing!' Wonderful healing and wholeness. My lovers have allowed me to have a real grace experience; like a total affirmation of loving and being loved. I have been very fortunate."

At the present time, Connie must seek other employment because her company is closing. At age sixty-two she feels anxious about meaningful work opportunities and about finding a hospitable social milieu as a lesbian. "I am not sure how to go about this, especially at my age. It is hard to meet other lesbian women my age, and to meet people within my [life]style. I don't go to bars; I might like to go, but not by myself. I am part of a book group and I attend classes for lesbians at a local Lavender University." She has not yet told her children she is lesbian, though she wonders if they might not know.

A PSYCHOSYSTEMIC MATRIX

Connie's rich familial, social, and cultural embeddedness illustrates the complex relational matrix which necessitates care and shapes the possibilities for the actual care received. I will draw upon her experience, my earlier work, and the insights from others in this volume to reconceive pastoral care and counseling.

Connie's narrative reveals how communal experiences accounted for her distress. She grew up in a family and religious tradition which affirmed her, on the one hand, and neglected a core element of her sexuality on the other. She was marginalized by the dominant Mormon culture surrounding her. Her marriage was injurious and unfulfilling. She has "come out" as a lesbian to a society which is generally hateful and cruel to her. She is devalued as an aging female in a patriarchal, youth-oriented culture. There are few opportunities for her to learn to be who she is without severe penalties, or even danger, or for her to meet people like herself.

Yet, community experience also offered her care and healing. Her church and family provided sure foundations for her to accept herself in spite of rejection and denigration by others. She found pastoral and ecclesiastical support during the dissolution of her marriage and was able to discover opportunities for a ministry of social action and advocacy for a new social order.* The ecumenical organization for which she worked deepened her knowledge of Christianity and enabled her to apply its

---

*For more on "conscientization" and "advocacy" as principles of pastoral care in a psychosystemic framework, see Graham, 1992, 64ff.

gospel of acceptance to gay and lesbian persons. When it became time for her to examine her life more deeply, she benefited from a secular therapist and a United Methodist congregation, both of whom accepted her sexual orientation. Through these caregiving overtures, she was able to envision the organic wholeness of her life and to deal with the interlocking sources of her pain while reaching out to others through her church's mission. The care she has received has set her on a new adventure in the larger world, as she herself seeks to respond to the challenges of her interpersonal, vocational, spiritual, and personal future.

We can account for Connie's suffering and healing only within a paradigm which recognizes that life is inherently relational and interconnected. To empathize with Connie as an individual requires that we open our eyes to the systems of which she is a part. Our humanization takes place in our participation with the multitextured world, not in our isolation and individuation (chapter 14, and van den Blink, 1972). To conceptualize care for persons is to recognize the network of connections in the "living human web" which influences persons for good and ill, and to help persons relate in more loving and just configurations. To practice the ministry of care, at least within the framework of this paradigm, is to increase the love of God, self, and neighbor, to promote justice, and to work for ecological harmony and partnership (Graham, 1992, 44-48). Thus, given the social nature of human experience, any paradigm of care must be centrally concerned with the communal rather than the narrowly clinical dimensions of care (see chapters 1, 12, and 14 for further developments of these points).

The Living Human Web

When the relational and communal dimensions of psychosystemic caregiving are analyzed, several other factors emerge that must be considered in constructing an alternative paradigm of care. First, there must be identification of the multidimensional structures of relatedness within the human situation. And second, there must be some conceptual way of accounting for the links between these relational structures.

How are these contextual-communal structures linked? What makes them a living human web? In the psychosystemic paradigm that I am developing, several concepts account, at least formally, for the links. First, if there is to be an exchange of influence between entities, there must be bipolar power. Bipolar power is understood as the capacity to influence and to be influenced. In itself, bipolar power is neutral; it draws its value from the quality of the relationships brought into being. One of the reasons persons become symptomatic is that they are the recipients of negative or overwhelming influences from their multiple environments and are unable to muster personal and social power adequate to buffer, neutralize, or overcome the power of the world. Connie's religious and therapeutic milieu is presently for her a truly empowering one—combining receptivity to the power of her experience, as well as offering resources for its creative employment. Not all contexts in her life have been this positive, and she struggles to find the kind of power that can create acceptance for gays and lesbians in the larger culture. Similarly, the chapters in this volume by Couture and Steinhoff Smith are directed at advocating greater social power for children, single mothers, and for the homeless poor, including those with HIV/AIDS (see chapters 4 and 10).

Second, links between the systems and subsystems composing the psychosystemic matrix are accounted for by the presence of reciprocal transactions. The concept of reciprocal transactions recognizes that actions interlock and that power is socially efficacious for good or ill. For example, Lyon points out that the increased longevity and financial security of our aging population has a direct correlation with the increase of childhood poverty (see chapter 6). However, on a positive note, the reciprocal transactions between Connie and her lovers were for her a means of understanding God's transactions of grace with human beings. As a consequence of the care she has received as a member of her congregation, she has become empowered to reciprocate by offering care to others. Transactional reciprocity undercuts the myths of individualism, self-sufficiency, and autonomy, and it reconfigures the meaning of self-realization in communal and ecological terms.

Third, the world interconnects through the collision of values. A mosquito's valuation of me as a source of nourishment and my desire to avoid pain and disease causes certain reciprocal transactions and power struggles between us. Likewise, the mutual desire for survival, cooperation, and fulfillment makes it possible for contending groups to harmonize or at least neutralize the harshest differences between them. In the pluralistic contemporary world in which pastoral caregiving occurs, it will be essential for the field to develop theories of value and functional approaches to handling concrete differences. As Hunter and Patton point out, pastoral care and counseling can no longer operate on the assumption of human commonalities, except perhaps at the largest level of generality (see chapter 2). Rather, it is incumbent upon us to promote the integrity of the structures of life by recognizing inherent differences, including the contending values by which they are organized and inter-relate, and find positive ways of harmonizing disparate values. Carl Schneider ably introduces one promising model of mediation into pastoral care by which constructively to negotiate contending values without resorting to the domination-subordination and adversarial patterns which are so pervasive (see chapter 15).

In the face of the challenge of contending values, the concepts of synchronicity and Beauty describe the goals of pastoral care. Synchronicity refers to "the harmonious coming together of contending values to create new patterns of positive experience" for all parties (see Graham, 1992, 263). Beauty is a term from process theology which designates the most positive expression of relationships. When relationships are deep, significant, and challenging, and are combined with harmony, peacefulness, and gratification, they are characterized by Beauty, and are good. Beauty contrasts with evil, which is viewed as shallow, destructive, and acutely disharmonious experience. Synchronicity and Beauty are analogous with the concept of shalom, or well-being at all levels of experience, which is central in the Jewish and Christian traditions (see Graham, 1992, 159-62).

Taylor's assessment of pastoral care and racial conflict underscores the importance of recognizing the differences in cultural and racial experience without making one group inferior or subordinate to another. Difference of experience and the values which contend between groups must be re-worked into a new harmony, without losing the integrity of each group. This is easier said than done but will be increasingly required in our models and practice of caregiving that seek to be responsive to social conflict. Connie's reconciling United Methodist congregation has appeal, precisely because it is a context in which differences enrich the whole community and provide a climate of care and mission to the surrounding neighborhood.

RELATIONAL JUSTICE AS THE CRITERION OF CARE

The centrality of the values of love, justice, and ecological partnership in this paradigm constitutes a fundamental shift from the individual to the communal. The dominant paradigm in pastoral care and counseling, identified elsewhere in this volume by Hunter as the "therapeutic tradition," is essentially based upon an existential-anthropological individualism, whose chief goal is the growth and self-realization of individuals, couples, and families (see chapter 1, and Graham, 1992, 32-37). In the new paradigm I am suggesting, individual experience and fulfillment is affirmed and promoted, but it is taken up into a moral context greater than the horizons of selfhood. The consequences of conditions such as gender, class, race, and sexual orientation help to shape pastoral diagnosis and intervention. "Unconditional positive regard," "unqualified acceptance," and "relational humanness" (see Patton, 1983) are not only interpersonal but also social, cultural concepts. The paradigm suggests that social and cultural realities work against the kind of acceptance by self and others which leads to full participation by citizens and believers. Therefore pastoral care and counseling aims toward *relational justice,* which affirms the individuality of the careseeker and brings the caregiver to advocate for the careseeker in society and culture.

With this framework in place, we can return again to Connie's experience. We can see that she grew up largely marginalized with respect to certain core elements of her being. She was part of a religious and social minority in her community. She was a tomboy and lesbian in a family which did not know how to recognize and affirm her sexual orientation. And while her church taught her to use her mind, it did not have a way to help her with "unconditional positive regard" for her sexuality. She did have an affirming aunt, but that affirmation was muted by the family secrecy about her aunt's sexuality. Her religious community awakened her to a sense of relational justice in racial matters and taught her advocacy skills. Later, her congregation and therapist helped her combine radical self-acceptance with conscientization and public advocacy about gay and lesbian rights. One simply cannot comprehend the full dimensions of the care provided to her without appropriating a foundational concept of relational justice or emancipatory liberation.

Relational justice has been emerging in a variety of liberation, feminist, womanist, and gay rights literature. Rather than perpetuating the domination and subordination which seem so pervasive in our political and moral economy, relational justice seeks to correct power imbalances. A caregiver seeks relational justice in the paradigm I am developing by working to replace domination and subordination with cooperation. The caregiver promotes conditions in which power is accountable and flexible, rather than exclusive, hidden, or inaccessible.

These conditions promote self-determination and fulfillment, full participation in the social order, and nurture of individuals and cultural groups. Relational justice calls for a thoroughgoing revision of our value systems, transactional patterns, and the way we organize the institutions of our world (Graham, 1992, chaps. 6–9).

Relational Justice in the Articles in This Volume

Beyond my own description and Connie's experience of relational justice, most of the writers in this volume also either assume or claim the need for the field of pastoral care and counseling to incorporate relational justice more fully into its thinking and practice. The chapter by Anderson and Miller-McLemore argues for greater awareness of relational justice in the area of gender. They contend that "women and men are equal but different . . . acknowledging differences between men and women serves the greater cause of justice, fairness, and mutuality" (see chapter 7, p. 105). This will require that we "listen with new eyes" for "the subtle and not-so-subtle injustices that are inherent in the world as each person experiences it" (ibid., pp. 109-10). Pastoral care and pastoral theology in this new paradigm of relational justice will require us to "advocate because of what we hear," and to recover "aspects of the prior meaning of reconciling as a communal way of living" as necessary for the modes of care in our time (ibid., p. 111).

Poling realizes that current sexual ethics in pastoral counseling must do more than protest sexual moralisms in a value-neutral manner; they must also identify and protest the organization of power as this is reflected in racism, sexism, classism, and heterosexism (see chapter 8). Neuger adds a much needed and complex historical-economic analysis to questions of justice in the area of pastoral care for women seeking abortion. Her analysis profoundly demonstrates that the abortion question is essentially political, and that the discussion often obscures that "the abortion question is as much about women's value as it is about the value of fetuses. Women, especially women of color and of working and poor classes continue to be devalued and harmed" (see chapter 9, p. 133).

Other authors also emphasize the importance of the theme of relational justice. It is evident, for instance, in Browning's analysis of mutuality as the norm for relational ethics. Browning seems to regard mutuality more as a corrective to an overemphasis upon sacrificial love than as a foundation for justice (as most writers seem to have it), and he tends to be over positive about the degree of mutuality promoted by an essentially patriarchal Christian tradition. Nonetheless, he clearly affirms that an ethic of mutuality is essential for constructing a normative ethic of the family and its care (see chapter 5, pp. 81ff.). Likewise Couture supports a social policy which makes it easier for women and children to leave "unjust or abusive" families without undue strain for them (see chapter 4, p. 67). SteinhoffSmith advocates that those on the margins of society—such as the homeless poor and sufferers from HIV/AIDS—be recognized for the care they can offer. Instead of the hierarchical models of care, which reinforce the exclusion of those who are caregivers from the act of caregiving itself, SteinhoffSmith views care as "the activity of a person or a community that supports the full and powerful participation in communities and societies of those who are suffering, excluded, objectified, or oppressed" (chapter 10, p. 148). Lyon deftly links issues of justice for the aging in the moral and political economy of our society with issues of justice in the arenas of gender and race (chapter 6). Charles Taylor likewise argues that we need a theory and practice in the field of care which challenges the exploitation of blacks by whites and helps identify and practically overcome the barriers to an inclusive church and society. His concern is clearly to replace relational injustice with relational justice between the races (and in other arenas as well) (chapter 11, p. 163).

There are many implications to be derived from making relational justice central in pastoral care. It will mean that all symptomatic behavior occurs, overtly or covertly, for the benefit of someone else, or some other group, that has power over the carrier of the symptoms. This is true whether that carrier is an individual, couple, family, or a group within a larger group. In other words, an individual's symptoms (or those of a family or group) always have a social and even *political* dimension: They stem (in part) from unjust power relationships. Whatever other origins and meanings they have, symptoms also serve the interests of somebody or something else. They perpetuate power relations of dominance and subservience. A victim position is an unjust position. Caregiving in a mode of relational justice challenges the social system that tolerates or even requires victimization; it beckons for the moral agency of victims and perpetrators alike. Pastoral caregiving, rooted in the emerging paradigm, cannot settle for the pretensions of a pseudo-objectivity and "value free" neutrality as its ultimate *modus operandi*. Neither can it settle for liberating persons only from moralistic oppression of the ego by the superego and ego ideal. Rather, it must provide moral assessment of every aspect impinging upon the pastoral situation and help to fashion ethically accountable responses to it. In this model, then, the roles of pastor and prophet combine (Gerkin, 1991 *b;* and Graham, 1992, 18-20).

Theological education and training in pastoral care and counseling will require new educational competencies, including working, practical knowledge of social ethics and public policy. We will also need greater emphasis upon ecclesiology and interfaith engagement. Contextual therapies, social work, and knowledge of culture and personality also will be required for expanding and fulfilling the challenge of relational justice.

CAN PASTORAL CARE AND COUNSELING EMBODY "CONTEXTUAL CREATIVITY"?

The essays in this volume, illustrated in part by Connie's experience, point up the need to recognize not only that the *context* of caregiving and careseeking is changing, but that it *needs* to change if fuller embodiments of relational justice and relational humanness are to emerge. But can pastoral care and counseling itself change?

The concept which most helps me understand the dynamics of personal and systemic change is that of contextual creativity. By contextual creativity I mean "the pervasive capacity for change which is built into every level of reality, however limited it may be in particular cases" (see D. Brown, 1981, 21; and Graham, 1992, 63). Because of the reality of bipolar power, reciprocal transactions, and contending values, there is a capacity for change inherent in the nature of things. This reality constitutes a basis for hope, even if the outcomes are often ambiguous and ambivalent. There are no guarantees concerning the moral value of outcomes; the openness of reality to change can evoke despair as well as hope.

Theologically, this psychosystemic paradigm is founded on a view of God as a radically affirming and transforming power, in whose being diversity and contextual creativity are made possible. Through love, God values the world in all its particularity and instability and is pledged to its fulfillment. Through justice, God seeks to bring harmony out of discord, richness of experience out of triviality. God is the secret "Ally" or "ceaseless working partner" in the caregiving enterprise who brings into focus new possibilities for individual enhancement and creative communality (Jackson, 1983). To celebrate and join this God requires that the pastoral caregiver and caregiving community be one of prayer, worship, and discernment, as well as one of study, training, and service. As Marshall's chapter and Connie's story make so clear, the community is the foundation for care, and the recipient and celebrant of the gifts and graces of those who are transformed by this care.

Conclusion

"New occasions teach new duties," as the great hymn has it. The therapeutic tradition of pastoral care and counseling can take pride in its contribution to bringing about a fuller and richer world of individuality. It can with confidence build upon its commitment to listening in solidarity with suffering persons, by building paradigms for caregiving which promote relational humanness and social justice in the midst of the complexities and particularities of today's contentious, pluralistic, and promising world.

BIBLIOGRAPHY

Abel, R. L., ed.
    1982 *The Politics of Informal Justice.* New York: Academic Press.
Achenbaum, Andrew
    1978 *Old Age in the New Land.* Baltimore: Johns Hopkins Press.
Adams, James Luther, and Seward Hiltner, eds.
    1970 *Pastoral Care in the Liberal Churches.* Nashville: Abingdon Press.
Adams, John P.
    1976 *At the Heart of the Whirlwind.* New York: Harper & Row.
Adler, Nancy, et al.
    1990 "Psychological Responses After Abortion." *Science* 248 (April): 41-44.
Andolsen, Barbara H., Christine E. Gudorf, and Mary D. Pellauer, eds.
    1985 *Women's Conscience, Women's Consciousness: A Reader in Feminist Ethics.*
        San Francisco, New York: Harper & Row.
Aquinas, Thomas
    1917 *Summa Theologica.* II, 2, Q. London: R. & T. Washbourne.
    1948 *Summa Theologica Supplement.* III, Q41. New York: Benziger Brothers.
Aristotle
    1941 *The Basic Works of Aristotle. Politics.* Bk. II. New York: Random House.
Armsworth, Mary
    1991 "Psychological Responses to Abortion." *Journal of Personality and Social
        Psychology* 69 (March-April): 377-79.
Ashbrook, James B.
    1992 "Different Voices, Different Genes: Male and Female Created God
        Them." *Journal of Pastoral Care* 46 (Summer): 174-83.
Auerbach, Jerold S.
    1983 *Justice Without Law?: Resolving Disputes Without Lawyers.* New York: Ox-
        ford University Press.

Augsburger, David W.
    1986 *Pastoral Counseling Across Cultures*. Philadelphia: Westminster Press.
    1992 *Conflict Mediation Across Cultures: Pathways and Patterns*. Louisville:
        Westminster/John Knox Press.

Baehr, Nina
    1990 *Abortion Without Apology: A Radical History for the 1990's*. Boston: South
        End Press.

Balch, David
    1981 *Let Wives Be Submissive*. Chico, Calif.: Scholars Press.

Barr, Suzanne
    1993 "Transformative Theory: Giving Meaning to Mediation." *Mediation
        News*. Vol. 12, no. 1 (spring): 15-16.

Baruch Bush, Robert A., and Joseph P. Folger
    1994 *The Promise of Mediation: Responding to Conflict Through Empowerment
        and Recognition*. San Francisco: Jossey-Bass.

Beck, Ulrich
    1992 *Risk Society: Towards a New Modernity*. Trans. Mark Ritter. London:
        Sage Publications.

Belenky, Mary Field, et al.
    1986 *Women's Ways of Knowing: The Development of Self, Voice, and Mind*. New
        York: Basic Books.

Bellah, Robert, et al.
    1985 *Habits of the Heart: Individualism and Commitment in American Life*.
        Berkeley: University of California Press.

Benson, Peter L., and Eugene C. Roehlkepartain
    1993 "Single Parent Families." *Source* 9:2 (June): 3.

Berger, Peter
    1967 *The Sacred Canopy: Elements of a Sociology and Theory of Religion*. New
        York: Doubleday & Co.

Bly, Robert
    1990 *Iron John*. New York: Addison-Wesley.

Boisen, Anton T.
    1955 *Religion in Crisis and Custom: A Sociological and Psychological Study*. New
        York: Harper.
    1971 *The Exploration of the Inner World: A Study of Mental Disorder and Relig-
        ious Experience*. Philadelphia: University of Pennsylvania Press.

Bondi, Roberta C.
    1987 *To Love as God Loves*. Minneapolis: Augsburg Fortress.

Boyd-Franklin, Nancy
    1989 *Black Families in Therapy: A Multisystems Approach*. New York: Guilford
        Press.

Brister, C.W.
1992 *Pastoral Care in the Church.* San Francisco: Harper.

Brock, Rita Nakashima
1988 *Journeys By Heart: A Christology of Erotic Power.* New York: Crossroad Publishing Co.

Brody, Elaine
1990 *Women in the Middle: Their Parent Care Years.* New York: Springer.

Brown, Delwin
1981 *To Set at Liberty: Christian Faith and Human Freedom.* New York: Maryknoll.

Brown, Joanne Carlson, and Carole Bohn, eds.
1989 *Christianity, Patriarchy, and Abuse: A Feminist Critique.* New York: Pilgrim Press.

Browning, Don S.
1973 *Generative Man.* Philadelphia: Westminster Press.
1976 *The Moral Context of Pastoral Care.* Philadelphia: Westminster Press.
1983 *Religious Ethics and Pastoral Care.* Philadelphia: Fortress Press.
1987 *Religious Thought and the Modern Psychologies: A Critical Conversation in the Theology of Culture.* Philadelphia: Fortress Press.
1991 *A Fundamental Practical Theology: Descriptive and Strategic Proposals.* Minneapolis: Augsburg Fortress Press.

Brueggemann, Walter
1977 "The Covenanted Family: A Zone for Humanness." *Journal of Current Social Issues* 14 (Winter): 19.

Buber, Martin
1962 *The Knowledge of Man.* New York: Harper & Row.

Cabot, Richard C.
1913 *The Christian Approach to Social Morality.* New York: YWCA.

Cabot, Richard C., and Russell L. Dicks
1936 *The Art of Ministering to the Sick.* New York: Macmillan.

Cahill, Lisa Sowle
1985 *Between the Sexes: Foundations for Christian Ethics of Sexuality.* Philadelphia: Fortress Press.

Callahan, Daniel
1987 *Setting Limits.* New York: Simon and Schuster.

Campbell, Alastair
1985 *Professionalism and Pastoral Care.* Philadelphia: Fortress Press.

Cannon, Katie
1988 *Black Womanist Ethics.* Atlanta: Scholars Press.

Capps, Donald
1984 *Pastoral Care and Hermeneutics.* Philadelphia: Fortress Press.
1993 *The Depleted Self: Sin in a Narcissistic Age.* Minneapolis: Fortress Press.

Carmen, Arlene, and Howard Moody
  1973 *Abortion Counseling and Social Change: From Illegal Acts to Medical Practice*. Valley Forge, Pa.: Judson Press.

Carroll, Jackson, Carl S. Dudley, and William McKinney, eds.
  1986 *Handbook for Congregational Studies*. Nashville: Abingdon Press.

Chodorow, Nancy
  1978 *The Reproduction of Mothering: Psychoanalysis and the Sociology of Gender*. Berkeley: University of California Press.

Chopp, Rebecca S., and Duane F. Parker
  1990 *Liberation Theology and Pastoral Theology*. JPCP Monograph No. 2. Decatur, Ga.: Journal of Pastoral Care Publications.

Clebsch, William A., and Charles Jaekle
  1975 *Pastoral Care in Historical Perspective*. New York: Jason Aronson.

Clinebell, Howard J.
  1977 "Creative Fathering: The Problems and Potentialities of Changing Sex Roles." In *Fathering: Fact or Fable*. Ed. E. V. Stein. Nashville: Abingdon.
  1983 "Toward Envisioning the Future of Pastoral Counseling and AAPC," *The Journal of Pastoral Care* 37 (3): 180-94.
  1984 *Basic Types of Pastoral Care and Counseling*. Rev. and enlarged ed. Nashville: Abingdon Press.
  1992 *Well Being*. San Francisco: Harper and Row.

Cloke, Kenneth
  1988 "Date Rape and the Limits of Mediation." *Mediation Quarterly* (Fall): 77-83.
  1992 "Mediating Sexual Harassment Cases." *Mediation News* 11 (Fall): 20-21.

Cole, Thomas
  1991 *The Journey of Life: A Cultural History of Aging in America*. New York: Oxford University Press.

Colston, Lowelle G.
  1969 *Judgment in Pastoral Counseling*. Nashville: Abingdon Press.

Coontz, Stephanie
  1992 *The Way We Never Were: American Families and the Nostalgia Trap*. New York: Basic Books.

Couture, Pamela D.
  1991*a* *Blessed Are the Poor? Women's Poverty, Family Policy, and Practical Theology*. Nashville: Abingdon Press.
  1991*b* "Teaching, Preaching, and Caring in Time of War." *Circuit Rider* 15:3 (April).

Culbertson, Philip
  1992 *Near Adam: The Future of Male Spirituality*. Minneapolis: Fortress Press.

Curtin, Leah L.
  1992 "For Sale to the Highest Bidder?" *Nursing Management* (June).

Damon, William
 1988 *The Moral Child.* New York: Free Press.

Daniels, Norman
 1988 *Am I My Parents' Keeper: An Essay on Justice Between the Young and the Old.* New York: Oxford.

D'Antonio, William
 1983 "Family Life, Religion, and Societal Values." In *Families and Religions.* Ed. William D'Antonio and Joan Aldous. Beverly Hills: Sage Publications.

DeMarinis, Valerie M.
 1993 *Critical Caring: A Feminist Model for Pastoral Psychology.* Louisville: Westminster/John Knox.

Denver Post. September 21, 1992.

Deutsch, Morton
 1973 *The Resolution of Conflict: Constructive and Destructive Processes.* New Haven: Yale University Press.

Dicks, Russell
 1944 *Pastoral Work and Personal Counseling.* New York: Macmillan.

Dinnerstein, Dorothy
 1976 *The Mermaid and the Minotaur: Sexual Arrangements and Human Malaise.* New York: Harper & Row.

Dittes, James E.
 1967 *The Church in the Way.* New York: Scribner.
 1985 *The Male Predicament: On Being a Man Today.* San Francisco: Harper & Row.
 1987 *When Work Goes Sour.* Philadelphia: Westminster Press.

Doehring, Carrie
 1992 "Developing Models of Feminist Pastoral Counseling." *Journal of Pastoral Care* 46 (Spring): 23-31.

Dombeck, Mary-Therese
 1991 "The Contexts of Caring: Conscience and Consciousness." In *Caring: The Compassionate Healer.* Ed. D. Gaut and M. Leininger. New York: National League of Nursing.

Doniger, Simon, ed.
 1953 *Sex and Religion Today.* New York: Association Press.

Dudley, Carl S., Jackson W. Carroll, and James P. Wind, eds.
 1991 *Carriers of Faith: Lessons from Congregational Studies.* Louisville: Westminster/John Knox Press.

Edelman, Marian Wright
 1987 *Families in Peril: An Agenda for Social Change.* Cambridge: Harvard University Press.

Ehrenreich, Barbara
    1983 *The Heart of Men*. Garden City, N.Y.: Doubleday & Co.
    1992 "Making Sense of la Difference." *Time* (January 20).

Ellingsen, Mark
    1990 "The Church and Abortion: Signs of Consensus." *Christian Century*
        (January 3-10).

Ellis, David
    1992 "L.A. Lawless." *Time* (May 11).

Ellwood, David
    1988 *Poor Support: Poverty in the American Family*. New York: Basic Books.

Engels, Frederick
    1985 *The Origin of the Family, Private Property, and the State*. New York: Inter-
        national Publishers.

Enquist, Roy
    1985 "The Churches' Response to Abortion." *Word and World* 5:414.

Eugene, Toinette M.
    1985 "While Love Is Unfashionable: An Exploration of Black Spirituality
        and Sexuality." In *Women's Conscience, Women's Consciousness: A Reader
        in Feminist Ethics*. Ed. Barbara H. Andolsen, Christine E. Gudorf, and
        Mary D. Pellauer. San Francisco, New York: Harper & Row, 121-42.
    1988 "Moral Values and Black Womanists." *The Journal of Religious Thought*
        (Spring).

Farley, Margaret
    1991 "Love, Justice, and Discernment: An Interview." *Second Opinion* (Octo-
        ber): 85-88.

Feilding, Charles Rudolph, et al.
    1966 *Education for Ministry*. Dayton, Ohio: American Association of Theo-
        logical Schools.

Fischer, David Hackett
    1978 *Growing Old in America*. Rev. ed. New York: Oxford.

Fishburn, Janet
    1991 *Confronting the Idolatry of Family*. Nashville: Abingdon Press.

Fisher, Roger, William Ury, with Bruce Patton, ed.
    1991 *Getting to Yes*. New York: Penguin Books.

Fortune, Marie
    1983 *Sexual Violence: The Unmentionable Sin: An Ethical and Pastoral Perspec-
        tive*. New York: Pilgrim Press.
    1989 *Is Nothing Sacred? When Sex Invades the Pastoral Relationship*. New York:
        Harper & Row.

Fowler, James W.
    1986 *Faith Development and Pastoral Care*. Philadelphia: Fortress Press.

Frank, Jerome
  1974 *Persuasion and Healing.* Rev. ed. New York: Schocken Books.
Friedman, Edwin
  1985 *Generation to Generation.* New York: Guilford Press.
Fuchs, Victor, and Diane Reklis
  1992 "American Children and Economic Perspectives and Policy Options."
    Science 255 (January 3): 41.
Furnish, Victor
  1982 "Neighbor Love in the New Testament." *The Journal of Religious Studies*
    10 (Fall): 332.
Furniss, George M.
  1992 "The Forest and the Trees: The Value of Sociology for Pastoral Care."
    The Journal of Pastoral Care 46 (Winter): 349-59.

Gadamer, Hans-Georg
  1982 *Truth and Method.* New York: Crossroad Publishing Co.
Gazzaniga, Michael S.
  1985 *The Social Brain: Discovering the Networks of Mind.* New York: Basic
    Books.
Genne, William H.
  1976 "A Synoptic of Recent Denominational Statements on Sexuality, Sec-
    ond Edition." The National Council of Churches.
  n.d. "A Synoptic of Recent Denominational Statements on Sexuality." The
    National Council of Churches.
Gergin, Kenneth
  1992 "Social Constructionism and Psychotherapy." Unpublished lecture
    given at the American Association of Marriage and Family Therapy
    Annual Meeting.
Gerkin, Charles V.
  1979 *Crisis Experience in Modern Life: Theory and Theology for Pastoral Care.*
    Nashville: Abingdon.
  1984 *The Living Human Document: Re-Visioning Pastoral Counseling in a Herme-
    neutical Mode.* Nashville: Abingdon Press.
  1986 *Widening the Horizons: Pastoral Responses to a Fragmented Society.* Philadel-
    phia: Westminster Press.
  1991*a* "On the Art of Caring." *Journal of Pastoral Care* 45 (Winter): 399-408.
  1991*b Prophetic Pastoral Practice: A Christian Vision of Life Together.* Nashville:
    Abingdon Press.
Gilligan, Carol
  1981 *In a Different Voice.* Cambridge: Harvard University Press.
Glaz, Maxine
  1991 "Reconstructing the Pastoral Care of Women." *Second Opinion* 17 (Oc-
    tober): 94-107.

Glaz, Maxine, and Jeanne Stevenson Moessner, eds.
1991 *Women in Travail and Transition: A New Pastoral Care.* Minneapolis: For-tress Press.

Glendon, Mary Ann
1991 *Rights Talk: The Impoverishment of Political Discourse.* New York: Free Press.

Graham, Larry Kent
1992 *Care of Persons, Care of Worlds: A Psychosystems Approach to Pastoral Care and Counseling.* Nashville: Abingdon Press.

Grant, Jacquelyn
1989 *White Women's Christ and Black Women's Jesus: Feminist Christology and Womanist Response.* Atlanta: Scholars Press.

Griffin, Susan
1978 *Woman and Nature.* New York: Harper & Row.

Griscom, Joan L.
1985 "On Healing the Nature/History Split in Feminist Thought." In *Women's Consciousness, Women's Conscience: A Reader in Feminist Ethics.* Ed. Barbara H. Andolsen, Christine E. Gudorf, and Mary D. Pellauer. San Francisco, New York: Harper & Row, 85-98.

Gudorf, Christine
1985 "Parenting, Mutual Love, and Sacrifice." In *Women's Consciousness, Women's Conscience: A Reader in Feminist Ethics.* Ed. Barbara H. Andol-sen, Christine E. Gudorf, and Mary D. Pellauer. San Francisco, New York: Harper & Row.

Habermas, Jürgen
1987 *The Theory of Communicative Action.* Boston: Beacon Press.

Hall, Douglas John
1989 *Thinking the Faith: Christian Theology in a North American Context.* Min-neapolis: Augsburg.

Hallett, Garth
1989 *Christian Neighbor-Love.* Washington, D.C.: Georgetown University Press.

Hare-Mustin, Rachel T.
1989 "The Problem of Gender in Family Therapy Theory." In *Women in Families.* Ed. Monica McGoldrick, Carol Anderson, and Froma Walsh. New York: W. W. Norton & Co.

Hargrove, Barbara
1983 "Family in the White Protestant Experience." *Families and Religion.* Beverly Hills: Sage Publications.

Harrison, Beverly Wildung
1983 *Our Right to Choose.* Boston: Beacon Press.
1985 "Our Right to Choose: The Morality of Procreative Choice." In

Women's Conscience, Women's Consciousness: A Reader in Feminist Ethics.
Ed. Barbara H. Andolsen, Christine E. Gudorf, and Mary D. Pellauer.
San Francisco, New York: Harper & Row, 101-20.

Herman, Judith Lewis
1992 *Trauma and Recovery.* New York: Basic Books, a Division of HarperCollins Publishers.

Heyward, Carter
1989 *Touching Our Strength: The Erotic as Power and the Love of God.* San Francisco: Harper & Row.

Hiltner, Seward
1949 *Pastoral Counseling.* Nashville/New York: Abingdon-Cokesbury Press.
1953 *Sex Ethics and the Kinsey Reports.* New York: Association Press.
1956 "Freud, Psychoanalysis, and Religion." *Pastoral Psychology* 7 (November): 9-21.
1958 *Preface to Pastoral Theology.* Nashville/New York: Abingdon Press.
1972 *Theological Dynamics.* Nashville/New York: Abingdon Press.

Hodgson, Peter
1988 *Revisioning the Church: Ecclesial Freedom in the New Paradigm.* Philadelphia: Fortress Press.

Hoffman, John C.
1979 *Ethical Confrontation in Counseling.* Chicago: University of Chicago Press.

Holifield, E. Brooks
1980 "Ethical Assumptions of Clinical Pastoral Education." *The Journal of Pastoral Care* 34 (March): 39-53.
1983 *A History of Pastoral Care in America.* Nashville: Abingdon Press.

Homans, Peter, ed.
1968 *The Dialogue Between Theology and Psychology.* Chicago: University of Chicago Press.

Homer, Paul, and Martha Holstein
1990 *A Good Old Age? The Paradox of Setting Limits.* New York: Simon and Schuster.

Hopewell, James
1987 *Congregations: Stories and Structures.* Philadelphia: Fortress Press.

Howe, Reuel L.
1963 *The Miracle of Dialogue.* Greenwich, Conn.: Seabury Press.

Hunt, Mary
1991 *Fierce Tenderness.* New York: Crossroad Publishing Co.

Hunter, James Davison
1991 *Culture Wars: The Struggle to Define America.* New York: Basic Books.

Hunter, Rodney J., gen. ed.
1990 *Dictionary of Pastoral Care and Counseling.* Nashville: Abingdon Press.

243

Ignatius of Antioch
　　1953 "Letter to Polycarp." In Cyril C. Richardson, ed., *Early Christian Fathers*. The Library of Christian Classics. Vol. 1.

In Health
　　1991 (July/August). Informational item from *In Health* cited by author from *Second Opinion* (October 1991): 141.

Jackson, Gordon E.
　　1983 *Pastoral Care and Process Theology*. Washington, D.C.: University Press of America.

Jacob, Herbert
　　1988 *The Silent Revolution*. Chicago: University of Chicago Press.

Janssens, Louis
　　1977 "Norms and Priorities in a Love Ethic." *Louvain Studies* 6 (Spring): 220.

Johnson, Paul Emanuel
　　1953 *Psychology of Pastoral Care*. Nashville/New York: Abingdon-Cokesbury Press.

Jung, C. G.
　　1933 *Modern Man in Search of a Soul*. New York: Harcourt, Brace & World.

Justes, Emma J.
　　1985 "Women." In *Clinical Handbook of Pastoral Counseling*. Ed. Robert J. Wicks, Richard D. Parsons, and Donald E. Capps. New York: Paulist Press, 279-99.

Kahn, Alfred J., and Kamerman, Sheila B.
　　1975 *Not for the Poor Alone: European Social Services*. Philadelphia: Temple University Press.

Kamarck, Elaine Ciulla, and William Gallston
　　1990 *Putting Children First: A Progressive Family Policy for the 1990s*. Progressive Policy Institute (September 27).

Keen, Sam
　　1992 *Fire in the Belly: On Being a Man*. New York: Bantam.

Kegan, Robert
　　1982 *The Evolving Self*. Cambridge: Harvard University Press.

Kelsey, Morton T.
　　1986 *Prophetic Ministry: The Psychology and Spirituality of Pastoral Care*. New York: Crossroad Publishing Co.

Kemp, Charles F.
　　1947 *Physicians of the Soul: A History of Pastoral Counseling*. New York: Macmillan.

Keniston, Kenneth
　　1965 *The Uncommitted*. New York: Harcourt, Brace, & World.

Kinast, Robert L.
1993 *If Only You Recognized God's Gift*. Grand Rapids, Mich.: Wm. B. Eerdmans Publishing Co.

Klein, Joe
1992 "Whose Values?" *Newsweek* (June 8).

Kleinman, Arthur
1988 *The Illness Narratives*. New York: Basic Books.

Klink, Thomas W.
1965 *Depth Perspectives in Pastoral Work*. Successful Pastoral Counseling Series. Englewood Cliffs, N.J.: Prentice-Hall.

Kraybill, Ronald S.
1981 *Repairing the Breach: Ministering in Community Conflict*. Scottdale, Pa.: Herald Press.

Lapsley, James N.
1972 *Salvation and Health: The Interlocking Processes of Life*. Philadelphia: Westminster Press.
1990 "Moral Dilemmas in Pastoral Perspective." In *Dictionary of Pastoral Care*, Rodney J. Hunter, gen. ed. Nashville: Abingdon Press, 752-55.

Lasch, Christopher
1977 *Haven in a Heartless World: The Family Besieged*. New York: Basic Books.

Lear, Martha Weinman
1968 "The Second Feminist Wave." *New York Times Magazine* (March 10).

Leas, Speed B.
1985 *Moving Your Church Through Conflict*. New York: Alban Institute.

Lebacqz, Karen, and Ronald G. Barton
1991 *Sex in the Parish*. Louisville: Westminster/John Knox Press.

Leeuwen, Mary Stewart Van
1990 *Gender and Grace: Love, Work, and Parenting in a Changing World*. Downers Grove, Ill.: InterVarsity Press.

Lemkau, Jeanne Parr
1988 "Emotional Sequelae of Abortion." *Psychology of Women Quarterly* 12:461-72.
1991 "Post-Abortion Adjustment of Health Care Professionals in Training." *American Journal of Orthopsychiatry* 61 (January): 92-102.

Luepnitz, Deborah Anna
1988 *The Family Interpreted: Feminist Theory in Clinical Practice*. New York: Basic Books.

Luker, Kristin
1984 *Abortion and the Politics of Motherhood*. Berkeley: University of California Press.

Lyon, K. Brynolf
1985 *Toward a Practical Theology of Aging*. Philadelphia: Fortress Press.

1988 "Aging in Theological Perspective." *Educational Gerontology* 4:243-54.

McGoldrick, Monica
1988 "Women and the Family Life Cycle." In *The Changing Family Life Cycle: A Framework for Family Therapy.* Ed. Betty Carter and Monica McGoldrick. New York: Gardner Press.

McGoldrick, Monica, Carol Anderson, and Froma Walsh, eds.
1989 *Women in Families: A Framework for Family Therapy.* New York: W. W. Norton & Co.

McNeill, John
1988 *The Church and the Homosexual.* Boston: Beacon Press.

Major, Brenda, et al.
1990 "Perceiver Social Support, Self-Efficacy, and Adjustment to Abortion." *Journal of Personality and Social Psychology* 59:452-63.

Mather, Cotton
1690 *The Old Man's Honour, or, the Hoary Head Found in the Way of Righteousness.* Boston.
1726 *A Good Old Age: An Essay on the Glory of Aged Piety.* Boston.

May, Gerald G.
1982 *Care of Mind/Care of Spirit: Psychiatric Dimensions of Spiritual Direction.* San Francisco: Harper.

May, William F.
1983 *The Physician's Covenant.* Philadelphia: Westminster Press.

Mayer, Karl Ulrich, and Urs Schoepflin
1989 "The State and the Life Course." *Annual Review of Sociology* 15:187-209.

Meeks, Douglas
1989 *God the Economist: The Doctrine of God and Political Economy.* Minneapolis: Fortress Press.

Melnyk, Janet L. R.
1993 "When Israel Was a Child: Ancient Near Eastern Adoption Formulas and the Relationship Between God and Israel." In *History and Interpretation: Essays in Honor of John H. Hayes.* Ed. M. P. Graham, W. P. Brown, and J. K. Kuan, 245-59. *Journal for the Study of the Old Testament,* Supplement Series, no. 173. Sheffield, England: JSOT Press.

Mermann, Alan C.
1992 "Faith at the End of Life." *The Journal of Pastoral Care* 46 (Winter): 337.

Miller, Janet B.
1976 *Towards a New Psychology of Women.* Boston: Beacon Press.

Miller-McLemore, Bonnie J.
1989 "Produce or Perish: A Feminist Critique of Generativity." *Union Seminary Quarterly Review* 43:201-21.
1992 "Epistemology or Bust: A Feminist Maternal Knowledge of Knowing." *Journal of Religion* 72 (April): 229-47.

1993 "The Human Web: Reflections on the State of Pastoral Theology."
    Christian Century (April 7): 366-69.
1994 *Also a Mother: Work and Family as Theological Dilemma.* Nashville: Abing-
    don Press.

Minkler, Meredith
1990 "Gold in Gray: Reflections on Business' Discovery of the Elderly Mar-
    ket." In *Critical Perspectives on Aging: The Political and Moral Economy of
    Growing Old.* Ed. Meredith Minkler and Carroll Estes. New York: Bay-
    wood Publishing.

Mitchell, Stephen A.
1988 "The Problem of the Will." In *Relational Concepts in Psychoanalysis: An
    Integration.* Cambridge: Harvard University Press.

Mollenkott, Virginia Ramey
1987 "Reproductive Choice: Basic to Justice for Women." *Christian Scholar's
    Review* 17:290.

Moore, Robert, and Douglas Gillette
1990 *King, Warrior, Magician, Lover.* San Francisco: Harper.

Mowrer, O. Hobart
1961 *The Crisis in Psychiatry and Religion.* Princeton, N.J.: Van Nostrand
    Press.

Mueller, Pallas, and Brenda Major
1989 "Self-blame, Self-efficiency, and Adjustment to Abortion." *Journal of
    Personality and Social Psychology* 57:1059-68.

Myers, Gary E.
1989 *A Critical Study of Modern Pastoral Counseling's Identity Crisis.* Doctoral
    Dissertation, Emory University.

Myles, John F.
1989 *Old Age in the Welfare State: The Political Economy of Public Pensions.*
    Lawrence: University of Kansas Press.

Nelson, James
1978 *Embodiment.* Minneapolis: Augsburg Press.

Neuger, Christie Cozad
1992 "Feminist Pastoral Theology and Pastoral Counseling: A Work in Pro-
    gress." *Journal of Pastoral Theology* 2 (Summer): 35-57.

Niebuhr, Reinhold
1941 *The Nature and Destiny of Man.* New York: Scribner's Sons.

Niebuhr, H. Richard
1978 *The Responsible Self.* San Francisco: Harper.

Nygren, Anders
1953 *Agape and Eros.* Philadelphia: Westminster Press.

Oates, Wayne E.
  1953 *The Bible in Pastoral Care*. Philadelphia: Westminster Press.
  1962 *Protestant Pastoral Counseling*. Philadelphia: Westminster Press.

Oden, Thomas C.
  1967 *Contemporary Theology and Psychotherapy*. Philadelphia: Westminster Press.

Patrick, Mary W.
  1984 *The Love Commandment: How to Find Its Meaning for Today*. St. Louis: CBP Press.

Patton, John
  1983 *Pastoral Counseling: A Ministry of the Church*. Nashville: Abingdon Press.
  1985 *Is Human Forgiveness Possible? A Pastoral Care Perspective*. Nashville: Abingdon Press.
  1993 *Pastoral Care in Context*. Louisville: Westminster/John Knox Press.

Pearson, Jessica, and Nancy Thoennes
  1986 "Will This Divorced Woman Receive Child Support?" *The Judges Journal* (Winter): 40-46.

Plato
  1968 *The Republic of Plato*, Alan Bloom, ed. New York: Basic Books.

Poling, James N.
  1984 "Ethical Reflections and Pastoral Care," Part I. *Pastoral Psychology* 32 (Winter): 106-14.
  1988 "A Critical Appraisal of Charles Gerkin's Pastoral Theology." *Pastoral Psychology* 37 (Winter): 85-96.
  1991 *The Abuse of Power: A Theological Problem*. Nashville: Abingdon Press.

Poling, James N., and Donald Eugene Miller
  1985 *Foundations for a Practical Theology of Ministry*. Nashville: Abingdon Press.

Popenoe, David
  1988 *Disturbing the Nest: Family Change and Decline in Modern Societies*. New York: A. de Gruyter.
  1989 "The Family Transformed." *Family Affairs* 2 (Summer-Fall): 1-5.

Posner, Richard
  1992 *Sex and Reason*. Cambridge: Harvard University Press.

Presbyterian Church (USA)
  1991*a* *Keeping Body and Soul Together: Sexuality, Spirituality, and Social Justice*. The General Assembly Special Committee on Human Sexuality.
  1991*b* Minority Report of the Special Committee on Human Sexuality.

Pruyser, Paul W.
  1976 *The Minister as Diagnostician: Personal Problems in Pastoral Perspective*. Philadelphia: Westminster Press.

Quadagno, Jill, and Madonna Harrington Meyer
  1990 "Gender and Public Policy." *Generations* (Summer): 64-66.

Rediger, G. Lloyd
  1990 *Ministry and Sexuality: Cases, Counseling, and Care.* Minneapolis: Fortress Press.

Relman, Arnold
  1992 "What Market Values Are Doing to Medicine." *The Atlantic Monthly* (March).

Rieff, Philip
  1968 [1966] *The Triumph of the Therapeutic: The Uses of Faith After Freud.* Harper Torchbooks. New York: Harper & Row.

Roberts, David E.
  1950 *Psychotherapy and a Christian View of Man.* New York: Scribner.

Rogers, Carl R.
  1951 *Client-Centered Therapy: Its Current Practice, Implications, and Theory.* Boston: Houghton Mifflin.
  1961 *On Becoming a Person: A Therapeutic View of Psychotherapy.* Boston: Houghton Mifflin.

Rossi, Alice
  1977 "A Biosocial Perspective on Parenting." *Daedalus: Journal of the American Academy of Arts and Sciences* 106:1-31.

Ruddick, Sara
  1983 "Maternal Thinking." In *Mothering in Feminist Theory.* Ed. Joyce Treblicot. Totowa, N.J.: Rowman and Allanheld, 213-30.

Ruether, Rosemary Radford
  1975 *New Woman, New Earth.* Nashville/New York: Abingdon Press.
  1985 *Women-Church: Theology and Practice of Feminist Liturgical Communities.* San Francisco: Harper & Row.

Rzepka, Jane Ranney
  1980 "Counseling the Abortion Patient: A Pastoral Perspective." *Pastoral Psychology* 28 (Spring): 168.

Saussy, Carroll
  1991 *God Images and Self-Esteem: Empowering Women in a Patriarchal Society.* Louisville: Westminster/John Knox Press.

Scheff, Thomas J., and Suzanne M. Retzinger
  1991 *Emotions and Violence: Shame and Rage in Destructive Conflicts.* Lexington, Mass.: Lexington Books.

Schottroff, Luise
  1975 "Non-Violence and the Love of One's Enemies." In *Essays on the Love Commandment.* Ed. Reginald Fuller. Philadelphia: Fortress Press.

Schrieter, Robert J.
    1992 *Reconciliation*. Maryknoll, N.Y.: Orbis Books.

Schüssler Fiorenza, Elisabeth
    1983 *In Memory of Her*. New York: Crossroad Publishing Co.

Shannon, Thomas A., and Allan B. Wolter
    1990 "Reflections on the Moral Status of the Pre-Embryo." *Theological Studies* 51 (December): 603-26.

Shapiro, David
    1965 *Neurotic Styles*. New York: Basic Books.
    1981 *Autonomy and Rigid Character*. New York: Basic Books.

Shelp, Earl E.
    1986 *AIDS: Personal Stories in Pastoral Perspective*. New York: Pilgrim Press.

Sidel, Ruth
    1990 *On Her Own: Living in the Shadow of the American Dream*. New York: Basic Books.

Smeeding, Timothy
    1990 "Economic Status of the Elderly." In *Handbook of Aging and the Social Sciences*. Ed. Robert Binstock and Linda George. 3rd ed. San Diego: Academic Press.

Smith, Archie, Jr.
    1982 *The Relational Self: Ethics and Therapy from a Black Church Perspective*. Nashville: Abingdon.

Smith, David H.
    1990 "Called to Profess: Religious and Secular Theories of Vocation." *The Centennial Review* 34 (Spring): 275-94.

Speckhard, Anne
    1987 *The Psycho-social Aspects of Stress Following Abortion*. Kansas City: Sheed and Ward.

Stacey, Judith
    1987 "Sexism by a Subtler Name: Postindustrial Conditions and Postfeminist Consciousness in the Silicon Valley." *Socialist Review* (November-December): 7-11.
    1990 *Brave New Families: Stories of Domestic Upheaval in Late Twentieth-Century America*. New York: Basic Books.

Stamato, Linda
    1992 "Sexual Harassment in the Workplace: Is Mediation an Appropriate Forum?" *Mediation Quarterly* 10 (Winter): 167-72.

Steere, David A.
    1989 *The Supervision of Pastoral Care*. Louisville: Westminster/John Knox Press.

Stokes, Allison
    1985 *Ministry After Freud*. New York: Pilgrim Press.

Strunk, Orlo, Jr., ed.
1973 *Dynamic Interpersonalism for Ministry. Essays in Honor of Paul E. Johnson.* Nashville/New York: Abingdon Press.

Sullivan, Louis
1992 "Fatherless Families." *Television and Families* (Summer): 34-36.

Taylor, Paul
1992 "Life without Father." *Washington Post* (June 7).

Thistlethwaite, S., and M. Engel, eds.
1990 *Lift Every Voice.* New York: Harper & Row.

Thornton, Edward
1964 *Theology and Pastoral Counseling.* Englewood Cliffs, N.J.: Prentice Hall.

Tillich, Paul
1984 *The Meaning of Health: Essays in Existentialism, Psychoanalysis, and Religion.* Ed. Perry LeFevre. Chicago: Exploration Press.

Time "Sizing Up the Sexes." (January 20, 1992): 42-51.

Tribe, Lawrence
1990 *Abortion: The Clash of Absolutes.* New York: W. W. Norton & Co.

Underwood, Ralph L.
1993 *Pastoral Care and the Means of Grace.* Minneapolis: Fortress Press.

United Church of Christ
1977 *Human Sexuality: A Preliminary Study.* New York: United Church Press.

Ury, William L., Jean M. Brett, and Steve B. Goldberg
1989 *Getting Disputes Resolved: Designing Systems to Cut the Costs of Conflict.* San Francisco: Jossey-Bass.

Van den Blink, A. J.
1972 "The Helping Response: A Study and Critique of Family Therapy with Suggested Implications for Theological Anthropology." Ph.D. Dissertation, Princeton Theological Seminary.
1988 "Thinking About Values in Psychotherapy." *New Jersey Psychologist* 38 (Summer): 7-12.
1989 "Pastoral Counseling: A Psychosystems Perspective." Lecture at the Annual Meeting of the Rocky Mountain-Plains Region of the American Association of Pastoral Counselors, Denver, October 6.

Wallerstein, Judith S., and Dorothy S. Huntington
1983 "Bread and Roses: Nonfinancial Issues Related to Fathers' Economic Support of Their Children Following Divorce." In *The Parental Child Support Obligation: Research, Practice, and Social Policy.* Ed. J. Cassetty. Lexington, Mass.: D.C. Heath and Co.

Wallwork, Ernest
1991 *Psychoanalysis and Ethics.* New Haven: Yale University Press.

Weber, Max
  1964 [1922] *Sociology of Religion*. Boston: Beacon Press.

Weitzman, Lenore
  1985 *The Divorce Revolution: The Unexpected Social and Economic Consequences for Women and Children in America*. New York: Free Press.

Whitehead, Barbara Defoe
  1993 "Dan Quayle Was Right." *The Atlantic Monthly* 271/4 (April): 47-84.

Whitehead, James D., and Evelyn E. Whitehead
  1980 *Method In Ministry*. New York: Seabury Press.

Whitney, Catherine
  1991 *Whose Life?* New York: William Morrow and Co.

Williams, Daniel Day
  1961 *The Minister and the Care of Souls*. New York: Harper.

Wilson, William Julius
  1987 *The Truly Disadvantaged: The Inner City, the Underclass, and Public Policy*. Chicago: University of Chicago Press.

Wimberly, Edward
  1979 *Pastoral Care in the Black Church*. Nashville: Abingdon.
  1991 *African American Pastoral Care*. Nashville: Abingdon Press.

Winquist, Charles
  1981 *Practical Hermeneutics: A Revised Agenda for the Ministry*. Chico, Calif.: Scholars Press.

Wise, Carroll A.
  1951 *Pastoral Counseling: Its Theory and Practice*. New York: Harper and Brothers.
  1989 [1966] *The Meaning of Pastoral Care*. Bloomington, Ind.: Meyer-Stone Books.

Witte, John
  1988 "The Transformation of Marriage Law in the Lutheran Reformation." *The Weightier Matters of the Law*. Atlanta: Scholars Press.

Wolfe, Alan
  1989 *Whose Keeper: Social Science and Moral Obligation*. Berkeley: University of California Press.

Wolfe, Barbara
  1991 "Treating Children Fairly." *Transaction* 6:23-28.

Woodruff, Roy
  1975 "Pastoral Considerations on Abortion and Sterilization." *Pastoral Psychology* 24 (Fall).

Wynn, J. C.
  1970 *Sexual Ethics and Christian Responsibility: Some Divergent Views*. New York: Association Press.

Wynn, J. C., ed.
   1966 *Sex, Family, and Society in Theological Focus.* New York: Association Press.
Wyrtzen, James
   1992 Private Correspondence with A. J. van den Blink.

Yee, Barbara W. K.
   1990 "Gender and Family Issues in Minority Groups." *Generations* (Summer): 39-42.

Zill, N., and C. A. Schoenborn
   1990 "Developmental, Learning, and Emotional Problems: Health of Our Nation's Children, United States, 1988." *Advance Data* (U.S. Department of Health and Human Services), 190.
Zohar, Danah
   1990 *The Quantum Self: Human Nature and Consciousness Defined by the New Physics.* New York: Quill/William Morrow.

SELECTED BIBLIOGRAPHY OF WORKS BY CHARLES V. GERKIN

BOOKS

Crisis Experience in Modern Life: Theory and Theology for Pastoral Care. Nashville: Abingdon, 1979.

The Living Human Document: Revisioning Pastoral Counseling in a Hermeneutical Mode. Nashville: Abingdon Press, 1984.

Widening the Horizons: Pastoral Responses to a Fragmented Society. Philadelphia: Westminster Press, 1986.

Prophetic Pastoral Practice: A Christian Vision of Life Together. Nashville: Abingdon Press, 1991.

ARTICLES AND CHAPTERS IN BOOKS

"Crisis Ministry." In Rodney J. Hunter, gen. ed., *Dictionary of Pastoral Care and Counseling.* Nashville: Abingdon Press, 1990.

"Pastoral Care and Models of Aging." In Barbara Brown Taylor, ed., *Ministry and Mission.* Atlanta: Post Horn Press, 1985.

"Practical Theology, Pastoral Theology, and Pastoral Care Practice." In Adrian Visscher, ed., *Pastoral Studies in the University Setting.* Ottawa, Can.: University of Ottawa Press, 1990.

"Psychoanalysis and Pastoral Care." In Rodney J. Hunter, gen. ed., *Dictionary of Pastoral Care and Counseling.* Nashville: Abingdon Press, 1990.

JOURNAL ARTICLES AND PAPERS

"A Religious Story Test: Some Findings with Delinquent Boys," with George H. Weber. *Journal of Pastoral Care,* vol. 7, no. 2 (Summer 1953).

"On Becoming a Pastor." *Pastoral Psychology,* vol. 16, no. 151 (February 1965).

"Interprofessional Healing and Pastoral Identity." *The St. Luke's Journal of Theology,* The School of Theology, University of the South, vol. 11, no. 1 (October 1969).

"Clinical Pastoral Education and Social Change." *The Journal of Pastoral Care,* vol. 25, no. 3 (September 1971).

"Pastoral Ministry Between the Times." *Journal of Pastoral Care*, vol. 30, no. 3 (Fall 1976).

"Faith and Praxis: Pastoral Counseling's Hermeneutical Problem" *Pastoral Psychology*, vol. 35, no. 1 (Fall 1986).

"Thomas W. Klink's Theory of Supervision: Memories and Reflections." *Journal of Supervision and Training in Ministry*, vol. 11 (1989).

"On the Art of Caring: A Meditative Address" (Inaugural Address for Franklin N. Parker Chair in Pastoral Theology), *The Journal of Pastoral Care*, vol. 45, no. 4 (Winter 1991).

CONTRIBUTORS

Herbert Anderson teaches at Catholic Theological Union, Chicago, Illinois.

Don Browning teaches at The Divinity School, University of Chicago, Chicago, Illinois.

Pamela D. Couture teaches at Candler School of Theology, Emory University, Atlanta, Georgia.

Maxine Glaz is a Chaplain at Presbyterian-St. Luke's Regional Medical Center, Denver, Colorado.

Larry Kent Graham teaches at Iliff School of Theology, Denver, Colorado.

Richard Hester is Executive Director of the Georgia Association for Pastoral Care.

Rodney J. Hunter teaches at Candler School of Theology, Emory University, Atlanta, Georgia.

K. Brynolf Lyon teaches at Christian Theological Seminary, Indianapolis, Indiana.

Joretta L. Marshall teaches at Iliff School of Theology, Denver, Colorado.

Bonnie J. Miller-McLemore teaches at Chicago Theological Seminary, Chicago, Illinois.

Christie Cozad Neuger teaches at United Theological Seminary of the Twin Cities, New Brighton, Minnesota.

John Patton teaches at Columbia Theological Seminary, Decatur, Georgia.

James N. Poling teaches at Colgate Rochester Divinity School/Bexley Hall/Crozer Theological Seminary, Rochester, New York.

Carl D. Schneider is the Mediation Director of Woodbury Institute and the Director of the Mediation Program at Woodbury College, Montpelier, Vermont.

Roy SteinhoffSmith teaches at Phillips Graduate Seminary, Enid, Oklahoma.

Charles W. Taylor teaches at Church Divinity School of the Pacific, Berkeley, California.

A. J. van den Blink teaches at Colgate Rochester Divinity School/Bexley Hall/Crozer Theological Seminary, Rochester, New York.